PETER TAYLOR

A Descriptive Bibliography

1934–87

PETER TAYLOR

A Descriptive Bibliography

1934-87

STUART WRIGHT

Published for the Bibliographical Society of
the University of Virginia
by the University Press of Virginia
Charlottesville

A Linton R. Massey Descriptive Bibliography
THE UNIVERSITY PRESS OF VIRGINIA
Copyright © 1988 by the Rector and Visitors
of the University of Virginia

First published 1988

LIBRARY OF CONGRESS
Library of Congress Cataloging-in-Publication Data
Wright, Stuart T.
    Peter Taylor : a descriptive bibliography, 1934–1987 / Stuart
Wright.
        p.   cm.
    "A Linton R. Massey descriptive bibliography"—T.p. verso.
    Includes index.
    ISBN 0–8139–1168–0
    1. Taylor, Peter Hillsman, 1917–   —Bibliography.   I. Title.
Z8862.7.W75 1988
[PS3539.A9633]
016.813′54—dc19   87–32044
                                                                                          CIP

Printed in the United States of America

Jacket and frontispiece photographs by John Moran, The New York Times

For Peter and Eleanor

Contents

Acknowledgments

My greatest debt in the preparation of this bibliography is to Peter Taylor. Without his encouragement, invaluable assistance, and friendship, my task would have been much greater.

The staffs of Peter Taylor's publishers were very helpful in supplying information about his books. I am especially indebted to Robert Giroux, of Farrar, Straus, and Giroux. Robie Macauley and Lisa Jacobsen of Houghton Mifflin Company deserve my deepest thanks for information generously supplied. At Doubleday, I extend sincere thanks to Sally Arteseros, senior editor, who located all the information I needed for Doubleday publications containing stories by Peter Taylor, as well as for publication information for The Old Forest. *I also extend my warm thanks to the following individuals: Frederic C. Beil, publisher; Kent Carroll of Carroll & Graf; Jonathan Galassi of Random House; David O'Connor of Routledge & Kegan Paul; Judith Jones, Howard Reeves, and Dianne Wachtel, all of Alfred A. Knopf; Stephen Rogers of Chatto & Windus; and Jean Kennedy of Macmillan.*

Finally, while it is impossible for me to acknowledge everyone who has offered assistance and encouragement, I would especially like to thank the following individuals, in turn accepting responsibility for any omissions. First, special thanks go to Aleta Edwards Schroeder; then to Bertie Babcock; Carter Burden; Fred Chappell; George Core; Don Keck DuPree; Laney Evans; George Garrett; Patricia Giles; Lynn Hartman; Hamilton C. Horton, Jr.; G. William Joyner; Hubert McAlexander; Joseph O. Milner; William Moss; John Radziewicz; Eleanor Ross Taylor; Henry Turlington; Robert Penn Warren; Dr. Tom White; Edwin G. Wilson; Virginia Woltz; and, as always, the members of The Wednesday Club. Special thanks to Gerald W. Esch, Dean of the Graduate School, Wake Forest University, for a grant from the Research and Publication Fund in support of this project.

Bibliographical Method

This bibliography lists and describes the known publications of American writer Peter Taylor, November 1934 through August 1987. It uses as a starting point the selected bibliography of primary sources included by Albert Griffith in his *Peter Taylor* (New York: Twayne, 1970), pp. 168–71. Secondary sources are not included here, but the reader and student of Taylor's work is referred to *Andrew Lytle, Walker Percy, Peter Taylor: A Reference Guide*, comp. Victor A. Kramer et al. (Boston: G. K. Hall, 1983).

Section A, which contains separate publications (books and pamphlets) by Peter Taylor, lists titles chronologically by editions and by country, American editions followed by English editions. For each of Taylor's books there is a detailed description of the first American and first English edition. Subsequent editions are described in such detail as distinguishes them from earlier editions. A simple numbering system has been employed for A-section entries. **A7c**, for example, signifies the Noonday paperback issue (photo-offset from **A7a**) of *The Collected Stories of Peter Taylor*. **A** refers to the section, 7 indicates that this is Taylor's seventh separate publication, and **c** designates the proper chronological position within the sequence of published editions of this title. Advance proof copies issued for review purposes are described in the *Notes* paragraph.

The descriptive formularies are taken from Fredson Bowers, *Principles of Bibliographical Description* (Princeton, N.J.: Princeton Univ. Press, 1949), with modifications by G. Thomas Tanselle, and further modifications by James L. W. West III. Descriptions for each book contain paragraphs for collation, contents, running titles (when present), typography, paper and binding, dust jacket, text contents, publication information, locations, and first appearance of new material (republication information about first-appearance material is regularly noted in this paragraph). Leaf, board, and dust jacket measurements in descriptions of first printings are given in inches and millimeters; all other measurements are given in millimeters only.

Title Page: Title pages of first and subsequent reset editions have been photographically reproduced from the originals; unless otherwise indicated, all printing is in black ink.

Copyright Page: This page is also reproduced from the original, in compressed format, for first and subsequent reset editions.

Collation: The standard Bowers formulary is used with two changes: there is no indication of format (8°, 16°), and dimensions of the leaves are given in the description of the paper (below).

Contents: Standard Bowers formularies are again used.

Running Titles: The location of the running title (at head or foot) is first given. Then the printing is quasi-facsimiled from the left margin of the verso page across the gutter (indicated by a single vertical rule) to the right margin of the recto page.

Typography: Here the method is adapted from Tanselle's "The Identification of Type Faces in Bibliographical Description," *PBSA*, 60 (1966), 185–202.

Paper and Binding: Tanselle's "The Bibliographical Description of Paper," *SB*, 24 (1971), 26–67, serves as the guide here. Sheet size and bulking measurement are not given. Binding descriptions are based on Tanselle's "The Bibliographical Description of Patterns," *SB*, 23 (1970), 71–102. Cloth patterns are described verbally; stamping is quasi-facsimiled; edges, endpapers, and bands (when present) are also described.

Dust Jacket: Descriptions here are patterned after those in Tanselle's "Book-Jackets, Blurbs, and Bibliographers," *Library*, 5th ser., 26 (June 1971), 91–134.

Text Contents: This paragraph lists the items included.

Publication: The date of publication and price are given first, followed by the number of copies printed (if known). Library of Congress registration and renewal information follows. The dates and size of subsequent printings complete this paragraph.

Locations: Although no fewer than fifteen copies of each book were examined, only copies in the following private collections or institutional libraries have been noted:

DLC	Library of Congress
GU	University of Georgia, Athens
NcGU	University of North Carolina at Greensboro
NcU	University of North Carolina, Chapel Hill
NcWsW	Wake Forest University, Winston-Salem, N.C.

NN   New York Public Library
PT   Peter Taylor Collection, Charlottesville, Va.
STW   Stuart Wright Collection, Winston-Salem, N.C.
TxU   University of Texas, Austin
ViU   University of Virginia, Charlottesville

First Appearance: This paragraph identifies material by Peter Taylor that appears in print for the first time; reprinted appearances of this material are regularly noted within this paragraph as well.

Notes: These paragraphs contain descriptions of advance proof copies, oddities of manufacture, and miscellaneous supplemental information pertaining to the book described.

Section B lists chronologically first book appearances of material contributed by Peter Taylor, and one book that he coedited (**B15**) as well as contributed to.

Section C lists chronologically first periodical appearances of works by Peter Taylor, including juvenilia, poems, stories, essays, and plays. Reprinted appearances of this material in books and periodicals, as well as textual collations, are also included with the first appearance entry.

Section D contains an annotated chronological listing of interviews with Peter Taylor, as well as published quotes or comments by him.

Section E contains three dust jacket blurbs by Taylor.

Section F contains a list of sound recordings, tape and disc, of Taylor reading from his work. Copies of the tape recordings prepared at the Recording Laboratory of the Library of Congress are identified by the numbering system used in *Literary Recordings: A Checklist of the Archive of Recorded Poetry and Literature in the Library of Congress*, comp. Jennifer Whittington, rev. and enl. ed. (Washington, D.C.: Poetry Office, Manuscript Division, Research Services, Library of Congress, 1981).

Section G contains a listing of translations of Taylor's stories, alphabetically arranged by country.

Section H contains a drawing (self-portrait) by Taylor.

Abbreviations

CS	*The Collected Stories of Peter Taylor* (1969)
HF	*Happy Families Are All Alike* (1959)
LF	*A Long Fourth and Other Stories* (1948)
MD	*In the Miro District* (1977)
ML	*Miss Leonora When Last Seen* (1963)
OF	*The Old Forest* (1985)
Pr	*Presences* (1973)
PT	Peter Taylor
SM	*A Summons to Memphis* (1986)
WM	*A Woman of Means* (1950)
WT	*The Widows of Thornton* (1954)

A

Separate Publications

A1 *A LONG FOURTH*

A1a *First Edition (1948)*

PETER TAYLOR

A

LONG FOURTH

and Other Stories

New York

HARCOURT, BRACE AND COMPANY

Title Page: 8 × 5 ¼ in. (203 × 133 mm.).

Collation: [unsigned 1–4¹⁶ 5⁸ 6¹⁶]; 88 leaves; [i–vi] vii–x, [1–2] 3–166.

Contents: p. i: half title; p. ii: blank; p. iii: title page; p. iv: copyright page; p. v: 'contents'; p. vi: acknowledgments, 4 lines, prin. in roman; pp. vii–x: 'INTRODUCTION' by Robert Penn Warren; p. 1: dedication, '*To Eleanor*'; p. 2: blank; pp. 3–166, text.

Running Titles: head, '[page number in roman numerals] *Introduction* | *Introduction* [page number in roman numerals]' or '[page number in arabic numerals] *A Long Fourth and Other Stories* | [indiv. story title in all ital.; page number in arabic numerals]'.

Typography: text, 10/11 Caledonia; 40 lines; 158 (163) × 97 mm.; 20 lines = 89 mm.

Paper and Binding: leaf measures 8 × 5¼ in. (203 × 134 mm.); yWhite (Centroid 92) wove, unwatermarked paper; uncoated smooth. Black calico-cloth (302) boards measure 8⅜ × 5½ in. (208 × 145 mm.); spine stamped in gold, '[horiz.] *Peter* | *Taylor* | [fancy rule, 16 mm.] | A | LONG FOURTH | *and* | *Other* | *Stories* | [fancy rule, 16 mm.] | [two lines at base, vert., from top to bottom] [right] *Harcourt, Brace* [left] *and Company*'; yWhite (Centroid 92) wove, unwatermarked endpapers; uncoated smooth; all edges cut, unstained.

Dust Jacket: total measurement, 8⅜ × 19 in. (208 × 483 mm.); wove, unwatermarked paper; inner side coated smooth, outer side coated glossy; inner side, flaps, and back are white; front and spine are v. O (Centroid 48), with d. Gy (Centroid 266) panels; printed in dark gray and vivid orange; front: '[in vivid orange, against a white panel in upper two-thirds, surrounded by a heavy gray frame, the two vert. sides of which are connected top and bottom by dark gray rules; in dark gray open-face type] A

LONG | [frame of vivid orange single rules, broken at top by 'FOURTH']
FOURTH | [within frame, in vivid orange; roman] and other | stories | [in
dark gray] *With an Introduction by* | ROBERT PENN WARREN | [rev. out
in white, against a dark gray panel] by [open-face type] PETER TAY-
LOR'; spine: '[rev. out in white, against an elongated dark gray panel, in
open-face type] A | LONG | FOURTH | [roman] and other | stories |
[against a second dark gray panel] by | PETER | TAYLOR | [at base,
against a third dark gray panel, in vivid orange] *Harcourt, Brace | and Com-
pany*'; back: in dark gray, 'OTHER COLLECTIONS OF | Distin-
guished Short Stories | [ornamental rule, 106 mm.] | [list of six authors
and six titles, in roman and ital.] | [ornamental rule, 106 mm.] | *Harcourt,
Brace and Company* | 383 MADISON AVENUE, NEW YORK 17, N.Y.';
front flap: in dark gray, '$3.00 | *A Long Fourth and* | *Other Stories* | By
PETER TAYLOR | *Introduction by Robert Penn Warren* | [37 lines, prin. in
roman, about the author and the book] | *Harcourt, Brace and Company* |
383 MADISON AVENUE, NEW YORK 17, N.Y.'; back flap: in dark
gray, '[31 lines, prin. in roman, about the author] | *Harcourt, Brace and
Company* | 383 MADISON AVENUE, NEW YORK 17, N.Y.'

Text Contents: "The Scoutmaster" (**C50**); "The Fancy Woman" (**C46**);
"Allegiance" (**C52**); "Rain in the Heart" (**C49**); "Sky Line" (**C45**); "A
Spinster's Tale" (**C44**); "A Long Fourth" (**C51**).

Publication: published 4 March 1948 at $3.00; 1,500 copies printed. Reg-
istered in the name of Harcourt, Brace and Co., Inc., under A 16501;
introduction renewed under R 607033, 9 June 1975, by Robert Penn
Warren.

Locations: DLC, GU, NcGU, NN, PT, STW (8), TxU, ViU.

A1b *First English Edition (1948, i.e., 1949)*

PETER TAYLOR

———————

A

LONG FOURTH

and Other Stories

LONDON
ROUTLEDGE & KEGAN PAUL LTD.

Title Page: 7½ × 4¹³⁄₁₆ in. (190 × 122 mm.).

> *First published in England*
> by ROUTLEDGE & KEGAN PAUL LTD.,
> Broadway House, 68–74 Carter Lane,
> London, E.C.4
> 1948
> Printed in Great Britain by Butler & Tanner Ltd., Frome and London

Collation: [unsigned A^{16}] B–D^{16}; E–G^8; 88 leaves; [i–vi] vii–x, [1–2] 3–166.

Contents: identical to **A1a**.

Running Titles: identical to **A1a**.

Typography: text, 9/10 Caledonia; 40 lines per page; 145 (150) × 90 mm.; 20 lines = 73 mm.

Paper and Binding: leaf measures 7½ × 4$^{15}/_{16}$ in. (190 × 125 mm.); yWhite (Centroid 92) wove, unwatermarked paper; uncoated smooth. Black bead-cloth (202) boards measure 7$^{11}/_{16}$ × 5⅛ in. (195 × 131 mm.); spine: stamped in gold, 'A | LONG | FOURTH | *Peter* | *Taylor* | ROUTLEDGE | & | KEGAN PAUL'; all edges cut, unstained; yWhite (Centroid 92) wove, unwatermarked endpapers; uncoated smooth.

Dust Jacket: total measurement, 7¾ × 20¼ in. (197 × 515 mm.); wove, unwatermarked paper; inner side, flaps, and back are yellowish white; front and spine are yellowish green (no Centroid equiv); printed in m. rBr (Centroid 43); front: in moderate reddish brown, '[open-face type] A LONG | FOURTH | [roman] AND OTHER STORIES | PETER TAY-LOR'; spine: in moderate reddish brown, 'PETER | TAYLOR | ★ | A | LONG | FOURTH | [at base] ROUTLEDGE | & | KEGAN | PAUL'; back: in moderate reddish brown, 'ROUTLEDGE & KEGAN PAUL | *Novels : Spring 1949* | [swelled rule, 100 mm.] | [47 lines, prin. in roman, including advertisements for novels by Alex Comfort, Jean Giono, and Georges Simenon (two titles)]'; front flap: in moderate reddish brown, '[29 lines in roman, about the book and author] | 8*s.* 6*d. net*'; back flap: unprinted.

Text Contents: identical to **A1a**.

Publication: published in January 1949 at 8s. 6d.; 1,500 copies printed.

Locations: DLC, PT, STW (3), TxU.

> *Note:* All copies examined contain a publisher's leaf tipped in on p. v, printed on white wove paper, 63 × 25mm., that reads: '*Owing to production delays* | *this book was not published* | *until 1949*'. Routledge and Kegan Paul records indicate that *A Long Fourth* was to have been published in September 1948.

A2 *A WOMAN OF MEANS*

A2a *First Edition, First Printing (1950)*

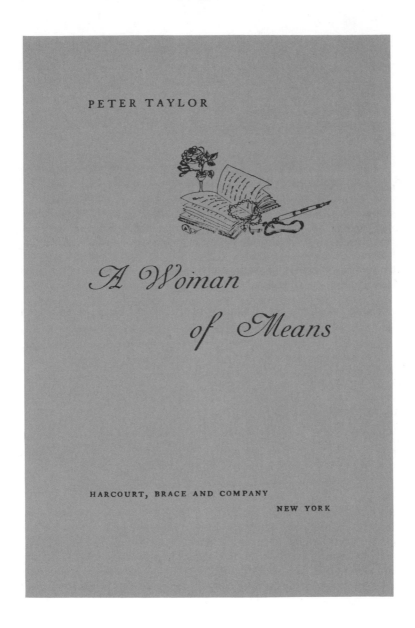

Title Page: 8 × 5¼ in. (203 × 131 mm.).

Collation: [unisgned 1–10⁸]; 80 leaves; [1–8] 9–160.

Contents: p. 1: half title; p. 2: list of books by PT; p. 3: title page; p. 4: copyright page; p. 5: dedication: '*For | Katherine Baird Taylor*'; p. 6: blank; p. 7: second half title; p. 8: blank; pp. 9–160: text.

Running Titles: head, '[in semiscript] *A Woman of Means | A Woman of Means*'.

Typography: text, 12/15 Caslon Old Face; 27 lines per page; 142 (149.5) × 90 mm.; 20 lines = 105 mm.

Paper and Binding: leaf measures 8 × 5⅜ in. (203 × 131 mm.); yWhite (Centroid 92) wove, unwatermarked paper; uncoated smooth. Full-cloth boards measure 8⅜ × 5½ in. (209 × 140 mm.); spine and 49 mm. of front and back are black calico (302), remainder in m. rO (approx. Centroid 37) linen cloth (304); front: stamped in black and contains the billiards rack and accoutrements from p. 9 of the text; spine: stamped in gold, '[vert., from top to bottom, in two lines] [right] PETER [left] TAY-LOR [in semiscript] *A Woman of Means* [in two lines, right] HARCOURT, BRACE [left] AND COMPANY'; yWhite (Centroid 92) wove, unwatermarked endpapers; uncoated smooth; all edges cut, unstained.

Dust Jacket: total measurement, 8⅜ × 18⅞ in. (207 × 479 mm.); wove, unwatermarked paper; both sides coated smooth; inner sides, back, and flaps are white; front and spine are black; printed in black and s. rO (Centroid 35); front: '[left, in strong reddish orange fancy type] *A* [right, illustration from title page, rev. out in white, of flower, open book, and fountain pen] | [in strong reddish orange fancy type] *W* [rev. out in white semiscript] *oman | of* | [in strong reddish orange fancy type] *M* [rev. out in white semiscript] *eans* | [in strong reddish orange, roman] PETER TAYLOR'; spine: '[vert., from top to bottom, in strong reddish orange] PETER TAY-LOR ['*A*', '*W*', '*M*' in strong reddish orange fancy type, like front; remainder rev. out in white semiscript] *A Woman of Means* [in strong reddish orange, two lines] [right] Harcourt, Brace [left] and Company'; back: in black, '[semiscript] *Also by Peter Taylor* | [roman] A LONG FOURTH | [semiscript] *And Other Stories* | [ital.] *Introduction by Robert Penn Warren* | [24 lines, prin. in roman, including excerpts from reviews from the *New Yorker, Commonweal* (J. F. Powers), *New York Herald Tribune, Partisan Review* (Elizabeth Hardwick), *New York Times,* and *Saturday Review of Literature*; each of the six excerpts is preceded by a floral ornament] | [in semiscript] *Harcourt, Brace and Company* | 383 Madison Avenue, New York 17, N.Y.'; front flap: in black, '$2.75 | PETER TAYLOR | [in semiscript] *A Woman* | *of Means* | [25 lines, prin. in roman, about the book] | *Illustrated by* | *Margaret Bloy Graham* | *Harcourt, Brace and Company* | 383 MADISON AVENUE, NEW YORK 17, N.Y.'

Text Contents: A Woman of Means.

Publication: published 4 May 1950 at $2.75; 2,500 copies printed. Registered in the name of Peter Taylor, under A 43777; renewed under R 673855, 11 October 1977. A second printing was issued, although the publisher could not locate any evidence of it (John Radziewicz of Harcourt, Brace, Jovanovich to SW, 26 July 1985). Copies are identical to **A2a** except the words *'first edition'* have been deleted from the copyright page.

Locations: 1st printing: DLC, GU, NcGU, NcWsW, NN, PT, STW (5), TxU, ViU; 2d printing: PT, STW (3).

> *Note:* Advance review copies consisting of unbound signatures laid in a trial dust jacket (flaps and back are unprinted; remainder identical to **A2a**) were issued before publication to selected reviewers.

A2b *Second Edition (1984)*

Peter Taylor

A Woman of Means

Frederic C. Beil, Publisher

New York

Title Page: 8⅛ × 5 in. (206 × 127 mm.).

Collation: [unsigned 1–9⁸]; 72 leaves; [1–6] 7–140 [141–144].

Contents: p. 1: 'Peter Taylor A Woman of Means'; p. 2: blank; p. 3: title page; p. 4: copyright; p. 5: dedication; p. 6: blank; pp. 7–140: text; p. 141: blank; p. 142: colophon: 'Set in the Diotima typeface of | Gudrum Zapf-von Hesse. | Design by Jerry Kelly. | New York, 1983.'

Typography: text, 12/15 Gudrum Zapf-von Hesse Diotima; 30 lines; 157 (164) × 93 mm.; 20 lines = 104 mm.

Paper and Binding: leaf measures 8⅛ × 5⅛ in. (206 × 130 mm.); yWhite (Centroid 92) wove, unwatermarked paper; uncoated smooth; v. R (Centroid 11) linen-cloth boards measure 8⅜ × 5⅜ in. (213 × 136 mm.); front: stamped in gold and d. B (Centroid 183): '[in gold, all on right side] A | Woman | of | Means | [heavy dark blue rule, 59 mm.] | PETER TAY-LOR'; spine: '[in gold, against a dark blue panel, 95 × 8 mm.; vert., from bottom to top] Peter Taylor \ A Woman of Means'; tan wove, unwater-marked endpapers; uncoated rough; all edges cut, unstained; dark blue cloth head and tail bands.

Dust Jacket: clear unprinted plastic protective jacket measures 8⁷⁄₁₆ × 14⅜ in. (214 × 437 mm.).

Text Contents: identical to **A2a**.

Publication: published August 1984 at $13.95; 2,000 copies printed.

Locations: PT (2), STW (2).

A2c   *Third Edition (1986)*

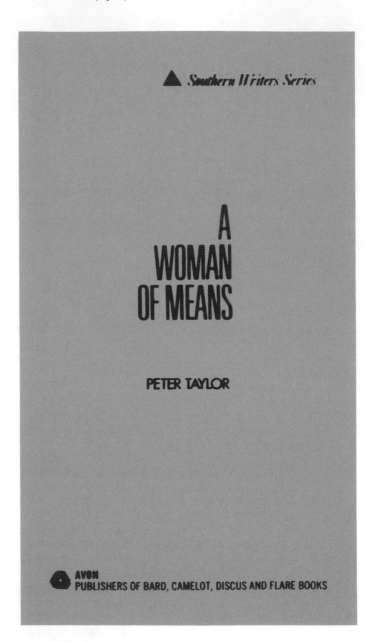

▲ *Southern Writers Series*

A
WOMAN
OF MEANS

PETER TAYLOR

▲ **AVON**
PUBLISHERS OF BARD, CAMELOT, DISCUS AND FLARE BOOKS

Title Page: 6⅞ × 4 in. (176 × 100 mm.).

Collation: 63 leaves perfect bound; [i–viii], 1–118 [119–120].

Contents: p. i: 'THE SOUTHERN WRITERS SERIES | [5 lines in roman, about the series] | [rule] | [list of 9 authors and titles; *WM* is listed fourth]'; p. ii: another advertisement for series, with list of forthcoming titles; p. iii: title page; p. iv: copyright page; p. v: dedication; p. vi: blank; p. vii: second half title; p. viii: blank; pp. 1–118: text; p. 119: blank; p. 120: third advertisement for Southern Writers series.

Running Titles: head, 'A W O M A N O F M E A N S | P E T E R T A Y L O R'.

Typography: text, 10/12 Optima Medium Condensed; 30 lines; 136 (147) × 84 mm.; 20 lines = 84 mm.

Paper and Binding: leaf measures 6⅞ × 4 in. (176 × 100 mm.); yWhite (Centroid 92) wove, unwatermarked paper; uncoated rough; perfect bound in stiff white wove, unwatermarked wrapper, 6⅞ × 4¼ in. (175 × 107 mm.); printed in m. pB (Centroid 200), l. gB (Centroid 172), brO (Centroid 54), v.l. B (Centroid 180), d. Pk (Centroid 6), with cover illus. prin. in shades of brown, green, yellow, tan, and blue; front: '[against moderate purplish blue vert. panel; lettered vert. from top to bottom; 'P' and 'T' in very light blue, remainder in brownish orange] PETER TAY-LOR | [brownish vert. rule along separating panel and right side, which is white; in black, vert. from bottom to top] [publisher's device] AVON BOOKS • 0–380–7099–9 • (CANADA $4.95) • U.S. $3.95 | [right, in brownish orange] A | WOMAN | OF MEANS | [illus. within 3-sided dark pink frame, with brownish orange panel beneath, also within 3-sided dark pink frame]'; spine: '[rev. out in white against moderate purplish blue] [publisher's device] | AVON | [rule] | FICTION | [vert. from top to bottom] A WOMAN OF MEANS PETER TAYLOR [in two lines separated by a vert. rule; right] 0–380–70099–9–$4.95 (CAN.) [left] $3.95 (U.S.)'; back: '[right side contains author's name, ident. to front] | [in dark pink] *CRIES OF THE HEART* | [brownish orange rule] | [10 lines in roman, about the book] | [6 lines in roman caps, about the book] | —Robert Penn Warren, *The New York Times* | [all with moderate purplish blue single-rules frame, against light blue panel; '*Peter Taylor*' in moderate purplish blue, remainder in black; 14 lines about PT] | [framed at left side and bottom by moderate purplish blue thin rules and brownish orange thick rules] | [bar code in black] | [in fancy type] ISBN 0–380–70099–9 | [at right side, vert. from bottom to top] Printed in U.S.A.'.

Text Contents: identical to **A2a**.

Publication: published in April 1986 at $3.95; 25,000 copies printed.

Locations: PT, STW (5).

A2d *First English Edition (photo-offset from **A2a**) (1950)*

All identical to **A2a** except for:

Title Page: 7½ × 4⅞ in. (190 × 124 mm.); '[at base] ROUTLEDGE & KEGAN PAUL LTD | LONDON'.

Copyright Page: 'First published in England by | ROUTLEDGE & KEGAN PAUL LTD | *Broadway House, 68–74 Carter Lane* | *London, E.C.4* | 1950'.

Collation: [unsigned A⁸] B–K⁸.

Contents: all identical to **A2a** except for copyright page.

Paper and Binding: leaf measures 7½ × 5 in. (190 × 127 mm.); yWhite (Centroid 92) wove, unwatermarked paper; semicoated smooth. Full l. Br

(Centroid 57) linen-cloth (304) boards measure 7¾ × 5 in. (197 × 127 mm.); front: printed in black with title-page illustration at bottom, right; spine: stamped in gold, '[vert., from bottom to top] [two lines, top] *Routledge &* [bottom] *Kegan Paul* [one line, in semiscript] A Woman of Means [in two lines; top] *Peter* [bottom] *Taylor*'; yWhite (Centroid 92) wove, unwatermarked endpapers; uncoated smooth; all edges cut, unstained.

Dust Jacket: total measurement, 7¾ × 18 in. (197 × 457 mm.); wove, unwatermarked paper; front and spine are black, inner side, back, and flaps are p. Y (Centroid 89); both sides coated smooth; front; in pale yellow, '[in semiscript] A | Woman | of | Means | [corkscrewlike rule, 80 mm.] | [corkscrewlike rule, 60 mm.] | [in roman] PETER TAYLOR | *author of A Long Fourth*'; spine: in pale yellow, '[in fancy type] A | Woman | of | Means | [corkscrewlike rule, 29 mm.] | [in roman] PETER | TAYLOR | [publisher's device] | Routledge | and | Kegan | Paul'; back: in black, 'A LONG FOURTH AND OTHER | STORIES | *by Peter Taylor* | 8s. 6d. net | [9 lines prin. in roman, including excerpts from reviews in the *Observer, Times Literary Supplement, Yorkshire Post*, and *Times and Tide*] | THE CIRCLE OF THE MINOTAUR | *by Stuart C. Hood* | 8s. 6d. net | [14 lines prin. in roman, about the book] | [rule, 97 mm.] | ROUTLEDGE AND KEGAN PAUL'; front flap: '[20 lines prin. in roman, about this book, *A Long Fourth*, and PT] | 7'6 | NET'; back flap: '[photograph of the author, 80 × 63 mm.] | [9 lines prin. in roman, about the author] | [in lower left corner] APT/T106'.

Publication: published in October 1950 at 7s. 6d.; 2,000 copies printed.

Locations: PT, STW.

A3 *THE WIDOWS OF THORNTON*

First Edition (1954)

Peter Taylor

THE WIDOWS OF THORNTON

Harcourt, Brace and Company

New York

Title Page: 8 × 5¼ in. (203 × 130 mm.).

Collation: [unsigned 1–10¹⁶]; 160 leaves; [i–viii], [1–2] 3–310 [311–312].

Contents: p. i: half title; p. ii: list of books by PT; p. iii: title page; p. iv:
copyright page; p. v: dedication: 'TO ALLEN AND CAROLINE'
[Tate]; p. vi: blank; p. vii: contents; p. viii: blank; p. 1: second half title; p.
2: blank; pp. 3–310: text; pp. 311–312: blank.

Running Titles: head, 'THE WIDOWS OF THORNTON | [indiv. story
title or play title in all caps]'.

Typography: text, 11/13 Baskerville; 30 or 31 lines per page; pages with 30
lines measure 142 (147) × 90 mm., and pages with 31 lines, 143
(148) × 90 mm.; 20 lines = 91 mm.

Paper and Binding: leaf measures 8 × 5⅜ in. (201 × 131 mm.); yWhite
(Centroid 92) wove, unwatermarked paper; uncoated smooth. Cloth- and
paper-covered boards measure 8¼ × 5½ in. (210 × 140 mm.); spine

and 43 mm. of front and back are v.d. bG (Centroid 166) linen cloth (304) and mottled paper prin. in m. B (Centroid 182) and m. G (Centroid 145); spine: stamped in silver, '[horiz., in semiscript] *Peter Taylor* [vert., from top to bottom] THE WIDOWS OF THORNTON [horiz., in semiscript] *Harcourt, Brace | and Company*'; yWhite (Centroid 92) wove, unwatermarked endpapers; all edges cut, unstained.

Dust Jacket: total measurement, 8⅜ × 19¾ in. (207 × 502 mm.); wove, unwatermarked paper; inner side coated smooth, outer side coated glossy; inner side, flaps, and back are white; front and spine are black; front contains an illustration of a gingerbread-decorated mansion against an irregular panel, prin. in light grayish blue (no Centroid equiv.), brill. Y (approx. Centroid 83), gray, and white, with a bust of a woman facing right, in m. R (approx. Centroid 15); spine contains an illustration of a decayed tree in brilliant yellow and gray; printed in black, white, brilliant yellow, and moderate red; front: '[in moderate red semiscript] *The Widows of | Thornton* | [illustrations, with remainder to right of bust of woman] | [rev. out in white semiscript] *Peter Taylor* [in brilliant yellow] AUTHOR OF "A WOMAN OF MEANS"'; spine: '[rev. out in white semiscript] *Peter | Taylor | The | Widows of | Thornton* | [illustration] | [in roman, at base] HARCOURT, BRACE | AND COMPANY'; back: '[left, black-and-white photograph of PT, 72 × 59 mm.] | *Wilfred Desen* [right of photograph, in moderate red semiscript] *Peter Taylor* | [in black, 11 lines prin. in roman, about the author] | [against a brilliant yellow panel, 110 × 65 mm., each corner of which is broken by a fancy ornament; blurb by Randall Jarrell, 9 lines in roman]'; front flap: '[in black] $3.95 | [in moderate red semiscript] *The Widows of Thornton | Peter Taylor* | [remainder in black, 32 lines prin. in roman, about the book, including a long statement about PT's idea for the book]'; back flap: '[in black] Comments on Peter Taylor's | [in moderate red] A WOMAN OF MEANS | [in black, 30 lines in roman and ital., including blurbs by or from J. F. Powers, *Time*, John K. Hutchens (*New York Herald Tribune*), Herbert Lyons (*Memphis Commercial Appeal*), Paul Engle (*Chicago Tribune*), Coleman Rosenberger (*New York Herald Tribune Book Review*), Frances Cheney (*Nashville Banner*), and the *New Yorker*] | [in moderate red] HARCOURT, BRACE AND COMPANY | *383 Madison Avenue, New York 17, N.Y.*'

Text Contents: "Their Losses" (**C59**); "What You Hear from 'Em?" (**C60**); "Porte-Cochere" (**C56**); "A Wife of Nashville" (**C57**); "The Death of a Kinsman" (**C54**); "Cookie" (**C36**); "Two Ladies in Retirement" (**C61**); "Bad Dreams" (**C62**); "The Dark Walk" (**C63**).

Publication: published 29 April 1954 at $3.75; 2,000 copies printed. Registered in the name of Peter Taylor, under A 135733. Renewed under RE 147–410, on 30 December 1982, by Peter Taylor as author.

Locations: DLC, GU, NcGU, NcU, NcWsW, NN, PT, STW (4), TxU, ViU.

A4   *TENNESSEE DAY IN ST. LOUIS*

First Edition (1957)

Peter Taylor

TENNESSEE
DAY
IN ST. LOUIS

A COMEDY

RANDOM HOUSE

NEW YORK

Title Page: 7¹⁵/₁₆ × 5³/₈ in. (202 × 132 mm.).

Collation: [unsigned 1–6¹⁶]; 96 leaves; [i–x], [1–2] 3–54 [55–56] 57–99 [100–102] 103–128 [129–130] 131–177 [178–182].

Contents: p. i: half title; p. ii: contains a list of books by PT; p. iii: title page; p. iv: copyright page; p. v: dedication: 'FOR | my mother and | father'; p. vi: blank; p. vii: 'CAST OF CHARACTERS'; p. viii: blank; p. ix: 5 lines in roman and ital., listing '*The Time*', '*The Place*', and four act designations; p. x: blank; p. 1: part title; p. 2: blank; pp. 3–177: text; p. 178: blank; p. 179: 'ABOUT THE AUTHOR', including 22 lines prin. in roman (identical to back of dust jacket); pp. 180–182: blank. Contents divided into four acts, separated by part titles.

Running Titles: head, 'TENNESSEE DAY IN ST. LOUIS | TENNESSEE DAY IN ST. LOUIS'.

Typography: text, 11/14 Granjon; 30 lines per page; 149 (156) × 93 mm.; 20 lines = 99 mm.

Paper and Binding: leaf measures 7¹⁵⁄₁₆ × 5¼ in. (202 × 134 mm.); yWhite (Centroid 92) wove, unwatermarked paper; uncoated smooth. Cloth and paper boards measure 8⅜ × 5⅝ in. (208 × 142 mm.); spine and 22 m. of front and back are grayish tan (no Centroid equivalent) linen cloth (304), remainder in light grayish blue (approx. Centroid 186, but lighter) paper boards; stamped in white and black; front contains the Random House device stamped at lower left; spine: '[vert., from top to bottom, in white semiscript] *Peter Taylor* [in black, roman; two lines] [right] TENNESSEE DAY [left] IN ST. LOUIS [in white semiscript] *Random House*'; yWhite (Centroid 92) wove, unwatermarked endpapers; all edges cut; top edges stained black.

Dust Jacket: total measurement, 8⅜ × 19½ in. (208 × 495 mm.); wove, unwatermarked paper; inner side coated smooth, outer side coated glossy; inner side, flaps, and back are white; front and spine are grayish blue (no Centroid equivalent); printed in black and v. O (Centroid 48); front: '[rev. out in white] TENNESSEE DAY | IN ST. LOUIS [in black] *a play by* | PETER TAYLOR | *author of* [rev. out in white] A WOMAN OF MEANS | [in vivid orange, illustration by Kass of 18 heavy, irregular, spattered circles-within-circles, and 3 more broken by bottom edge]'; spine: '[in vivid orange, one spattered circle-within-circle, like front] | [vert., from top to bottom, rev. out in white; two lines] [right] TENNESSEE DAY [left] IN ST. LOUIS [in two lines the height of the left line preceding and continuing it; in black] [right] *by* [left] PETER TAYLOR [horiz., Random House device in vivid orange] | [in black] RANDOM | HOUSE'; back: all in black, 'ABOUT THE AUTHOR | [24 lines prin. in roman; text identical to p. 179]'; front flap: in black, 'TENNESSEE | DAY | IN ST. LOUIS | *by* | Peter Taylor | [16 lines, prin. in roman, about the book and author] | *(Continued on the back flap)* | [20 lines, prin. in roman, continuation from front flap] | *Jacket design by Warren Alan Kass* | RANDOM HOUSE, INC. | 457 Madison Avenue, New York 22, New York | [2-line advertisement, prin. in roman] | Printed in U. S. A.'

Text Contents: Tennessee Day in St. Louis.

Publication: published 20 February 1957 at $2.95; number of copies printed unknown. Registered in the name of Peter Taylor, under Dp 2891.

Locations: DLC, GU, NcU, NN, PT, STW (8), TxU, ViU.

Notes: Tennessee Day in St. Louis was registered in an earlier version, *The Southern Colony*, under Du 39256. Act 1 was previously published (**C65**) and registered under B 570479. Taylor revised *Tennessee Day in St. Louis* for a production at Kenyon College, Gambier, Ohio, in April 1957. The acting version of the comedy consists of 85 leaves, reproduced by ditto process from typescript original, wire-stitched at left, and measures 7³⁄₁₆ × 8½ in. (182 × 216 mm.). Randall Jarrell was very fond of Taylor's dramatic works. In one of the compiler's copies of *Tennessee Day in St. Louis*, Taylor has written: "This was Randall's favorite book of mine. He said: 'Some day you'll be known as a playwright who also wrote some stories.'"

Happy Families Are All Alike

A COLLECTION OF STORIES BY PETER TAYLOR

NEW YORK

McDOWELL OBOLENSKY

Title Pages: each page measures 7¹⁵⁄₁₆ × 5³⁄₁₆ in. (202 × 131 mm.).

A5 *HAPPY FAMILIES ARE ALL ALIKE*

A5a *First Edition (1959)*

Collation: [unsigned 1–10^{16}]; 160 leaves; [i–xii], [1–3] 4–35 [36] 37–69 [70] 71–110 [111–113] 114–141 [142] 143–147 [148] 149–169 [170] 171–206 [207] 208–246 [247] 248–267 [268] 269–305 [306–308].

Contents: p. i: half title; p. ii: blank; p. iii: list of books by PT; pp. iv–v: title pages; p. vi: copyright page; p. vii: dedication: 'for my son | Peter Ross Taylor'; p. viii: blank; p. ix: contents; p. x: blank; p. xi: epigraph from Tolstoy; p. xii: blank; p. 1: section title; p. 2: blank; pp. 3–110: text; p. 111: section title; p. 112: blank; pp. 113–305: text; p. 306: blank; p. 307: 'ABOUT THE AUTHOR | [18 lines, prin. in roman]'; p. 308: blank.

Running Titles: head, '[page number in arabic numerals] HAPPY FAMILIES ARE ALL ALIKE | [indiv. story title in all caps.; page number in arabic numerals]'.

Typography: text, 11/13 Baskerville; 32 lines per page; 147 (155) × 97 mm.; 20 lines = 91 mm.

Paper and Binding: leaf measures 7^{15}⁄₁₆ × 5³⁄₁₆ (202 × 132 mm.); yWhite (Centroid 92) wove, unwatermarked paper; uncoated smooth; m. bG (Centroid 164) fine bead-cloth (202b) boards measure 8¼ × 5½ in. (209 × 140 mm.); spine stamped in silver and dp. pPk (Centroid 248), '[in silver] Happy | Families | Are | All Alike | [rule in deep purplish pink, 31 mm.] | [in silver] PETER | TAYLOR | [publisher's device] | McDOWELL | OBOLENSKY'; greenish-bluish gray (no Centroid equiv.) wove endpapers, uncoated rough; all edges cut; top edges stained brill. Y (Centroid 83).

Dust Jacket: total measurement, 8¼ × 19⅜ in. (210 × 492 mm.); wove, unwatermarked paper; inner side coated smooth, outer side coated glossy; inner side, flaps, and back are white; front and spine are black and contain irregular elongated panels in white, v. Y (Centroid 82), v. O (Centroid 48); printed in black, vivid orange, and vivid yellow; front: letters in black against the colored panels are in mixed display types and are arranged in an irregular, wavy fashion: '[in black, against white, vivid yellow, white, vivid orange, and white panels, respectively] H A P P Y | [against white, vivid orange, white, vivid orange, white, vivid orange, vivid yellow, and white panels, respectively] F A M I L i E S | [against vivid orange, white, and vivid yellow panels, respectively] a R E | [against vivid yellow, vivid orange, and white panels, respectively] A *L* L | [against white, vivid orange, white, white, and vivid yellow panels, respectively] A L I K E | [right of second and third lines, in roman, vivid yellow] by | [in vivid orange] Peter Taylor | [rev. out in white] *Author of* | A WOMAN OF MEANS *and* | THE WIDOWS OF THORNTON'; spine: '[rev. out in white] Peter | Taylor | [in black, against oblong irregular panels in color patterns identical to front] H A P P Y | F A M I L i E S | a R E | A L L | A L *I* K E | [rev. out in white, roman] McDowell | [publisher's device in vivid yellow] | [rev. out in white] OBOLENSKY'; back: in black, 'Some comment on the previous work of Peter Taylor— | [32 lines, prin. in roman, including excerpts from reviews by Orville Prescott (*New York Times*), Dan Wickenden (*New York Herald Tribune Book Review*), John K. Hutchens (*New York Herald Tribune*), Caroline Gordon, Randall Jarrell, the *San Francisco Chronicle*, Frank H. Lyell (*New York Times Book Review*)]'; front flap: all in black, '$3.95 | HAPPY FAMILES | ARE ALL ALIKE | by Peter Taylor | [46 lines prin. in roman, about the author and book]'; back flap: '[black-and-white photograph of the author, 83 × 62 mm.] | ABOUT THE AUTHOR | [25 lines, prin. in roman] | McDOWELL, OBOLENSKY, INC. | New York | N.Y.'

Text Contents: section I, 'CHATHAM': "The Other Times" (**C66**); "Promise of Rain" (**C67**, as "The Unforgivable"); "Venus, Cupid, Folly, and Time" (**C68**); section II, 'OTHER PLACES': "A Friend and Protector" (**C71**, as "Who Was Jesse's Friend and Protector?"); "A Walled Garden" (**C47**, as "Like the Sad Heart of Ruth"); "The Little Cousins" (**C70**, as "Cousins, Family Love, Family Life, All That"); "Guests" (**C73**); "1939" (**C64**, as "A Sentimental Journey"); "*Je Suis Perdu*" (**C69**, as "A Pair of Bright-Blue Eyes"); "Heads of Houses" (**C72**).

Publication: published 25 November 1959 at $3.95; number of copies unknown (publisher's records were destroyed by fire). Registered in the name of Peter Taylor, under A 449562.

Locations: DLC, GU, NcGU, NcU, NcWsW, NN, PT, STW (7), TxU, ViU.

A5b *First Edition, Lippincott Paperback Issue (photo-offset from* **A5a***)*
(1962)

All identical to **A5a**, except for:

*Happy Families
Are All Alike*

A COLLECTION OF STORIES BY

Peter Taylor

J. B. Lippincott Company
Philadelphia   New York
19   62

Title Page: 8 × 5⅛ in. (202 × 128 mm.).

Copyright Page: 'Copyright © 1959 by Peter Taylor | [. . .] | FIRST KEY-STONE EDITION'.

Collation: 160 leaves perfect bound in printed pictorial wrappers.

Contents: p. iii: list of books by PT reset for this edition; *Happy Families Are All Alike* deleted; p. iv: blank; p. v: title page: '[fancy rule, 35 mm.] | A COLLECTION OF STORIES BY | *Peter Taylor* | J. B. Lippincott Company | Philadelphia [publisher's device, height of last two lines, and breaking them] New York | 19 [base of publisher's device] 62'; p. iv: copyright page: '. . . | FIRST KEYSTONE EDITION | Originally published in 1959 by McDowell, Obolensky, Inc. | . . .'; pp. 1 and 111: section title reset in all ital.; pp. 307–308: contains a list of other Keystone Books; 'ABOUT THE AUTHOR' deleted.

Paper and Paper Binding: leaf measures 8 × 5⅛ in. (202 × 128 mm.); yWhite (Centroid 92) wove, unwatermarked paper; uncoated smooth; thick, wove, unwatermarked wrapper; inner side, front, back, and spine are white; front contains an abstract illustration of three standing figures, in s. B (Centroid 178), v. R (Centroid 11), s. OY (approx. Centroid 68), dp. OY (Centroid 69), and m. Ol (Centroid 107); printed in strong blue, black, and vivid red; front: '[in strong blue] KB–41 $1.95 [publisher's device] KEYSTONE BOOKS | [in black] *Happy Families | Are All Alike* | [in vivid red[| *by Peter Taylor* | [color illustration]'; spine: '[in black] KB–41 | $1.95 | [vert., from top to bottom, in vivid red] *Peter Taylor* [in black] *Happy Families Are All Alike* [horiz., publisher's device in strong blue] | LIPPINCOTT'; back: '[rev. out in white against a strong blue panel, 30 × 118 mm.] Keystone Short Stories | Distinguished collections of stories, both originals and re-|prints, by contemporary American and European writers | [below panel, in black] From the reviews of | HAPPY FAMILIES ARE ALL ALIKE | A Collection of Stories | [16 lines, prin. in roman, including excerpts from reviews by F. H. Lyell (*New York Times Book Review*) and Richard Sullivan (*Chicago Sunday Tribune*) | [left, black-and-white photograph of the author, the height of the last 8 lines, 36 × 25 mm.] [right, 8 lines prin. in roman, about the author (whose date of birth is given incorrectly as 1919)] [right edge, vert., from top to bottom] *Cover design by Ben Feder*'.

Publication: published as Keystone KB–41 on 28 March 1962 at $1.95; unknown number of copies.

Locations: PT, STW (2).

A5c *First English Edition (photo-offset from A5a) (1960)*

Title Pages: each page measures 7¾ × 5 in. (197 × 128 mm.); '[at base] LONDON 1960 MACMILLAN & CO LTD'.

Copyright Page: 'Copyright © 1959 by Peter Taylor | [. . .] | PRINTED IN GREAT BRITAIN'.

Collation: [unsigned A⁸] B-U⁸; [i–x], [1–3] 4–35 [36] 37–69 [70] 71–110 [111–113] 114–141 [142] 143–147 [148] 149–169 [170] 171–206 [207] 208–246 [247] 248–267 [268] 269–305 [306–310].

Contents: p. i: 22 lines prin. in roman, about the book; pp. ii–iii: title pages; p. iv: copyright page; p. v.: dedication; p. vi: blank; p. vii: contents; p. viii: blank; p. ix: epigraph from Tolstoy, *Anna Karenina*, 3 lines prin. in roman; p. x: blank; p. 1: section title; p. 2: blank; pp. 3–110: text; p. 111: section title; p. 112: blank; pp. 113–305: text; pp. 306–307: blank; p. 308: 'Printed in Great Britain by Lowe and Brydone (Printers) Ltd., | London, N. W. 10'; pp. 309–310: blank.

Paper and Binding: leaf measures 7¾ × 5 in. (197 × 128 mm.); yWhite (Centroid 92) wove, unwatermarked paper; uncoated smooth. Light bluish green (no Centroid equiv.) coarse linen-cloth (304c) boards measure 8 × 5⅜ in. (202 × 137 mm.); spine: stamped in gold, '[fancy rule] *Happy* | *Families* | *are all* | *alike* | • | *Peter* | *Taylor* | [fancy rule] | [at base] MACMILLAN'; yWhite (Centroid 92) wove, unwatermarked endpapers; top edges cut, fore and bottom edges untrimmed.

Dust Jacket: total measurement, 8 × 18⅝ in. (202 × 473 mm.); wove, unwatermarked paper; both sides coated smooth; inner side, flaps, and back are white; front and spine printed in black, brill. Y (approx. Centroid 83 but slightly orange), and dp. Pk (Centroid 3); flaps and back are printed in black and deep pink; front, spine, and approx. 8 mm. of back contain an illustration of a small town scene with six buildings, trees, telephone poles and wires, and a teenager in a convertible picking up his girlfriend, in black, white, brilliant yellow, and deep pink; front: lettered in black, '[at top, reprod. from hand-lettering] HAPPY FAMILIES ARE ALL | ALIKE | [lower right side, same lettering] BY | PETER | TAY-LOR'; spine: in black lettering identical to front, 'HAPPY | FAMILIES | ARE ALL | ALIKE | BY | PETER | TAYLOR | [at base] MACMIL-LAN'; back: in black and deep pink, advertisement for *Winter's Tales 6*, '[in deep pink] WINTER'S TALES 6 | [within vert. ornamental columns, list of 9 authors and story titles; names in deep pink and story titles in black] | [in deep pink] MACMILLAN AND CO LTD'.; front flap: in black, '[21 lines, prin. in roman, about the book, and a 9-line blurb from the *New York Times*, in roman] | [at lower right, in deep pink] *16s net*'; back flap: '[in deep pink] PETER TAYLOR | [18 lines, prin. in roman, about the author]'.

Publication: published 14 July 1960 at 16s.; number of copies printed unknown.

Locations: PT, STW.

Miss Leonora   When Last Seen

AND FIFTEEN OTHER STORIES BY

PETER TAYLOR

NEW YORK

IVAN OBOLENSKY, INC.

Title Pages: each page meaures 7⅞ × 5³⁄₁₆ in. (201 × 134 mm.).

A6 *MISS LEONORA WHEN LAST SEEN*

A6a *First Edition, First Issue (1963, i.e., 1964)*

Collation: [unsigned 1–13^{16}]; 208 leaves; [i–xii], [1] 2–31 [32] 33–49 [50] 51–81 [82] 83–103 [104] 105–133 [134] 135–164 [165] 166–191 [192] 193–204 [205] 206–245 [246] 247–279 [280] 281–308 [309] 310–327 [328] 329–342 [343] 344–359 [360] 361–388 [389] 390–398 [399–404].

Contents: pp. i–iii: blank; pp. iv–v: title pages; p. vi: copyright page; p. vii: 'EDITOR'S NOTE' | [19 lines, prin. in roman, about the stories included]'; p. viii: blank; p. ix: contents; p. x: blank; p. xi: half title; p. xii: blank; pp. 1–398: text; pp. 399–404: blank.

Running Titles: head, '[page number in arabic numerals] MISS LEONORA WHEN LAST SEEN | [indiv. story title in all caps.; page number in arabic numerals]'.

Typography: text, 11/13 Baskerville; 35 lines per page; 161 (166) × 101 mm.; 20 lines = 92 mm.

Paper and Binding: leaf measures 7⅞ × 5⁵⁄₁₆ in. (201 × 135 mm.); yWhite (Centroid 92) wove, unwatermarked paper; uncoated smooth; light orange yellow (between Centroid 67 and 70) coarse linen-cloth (304c) boards measure 3³⁄₁₆ × 5⁹⁄₁₆ in. (209 × 141 mm.); stamped in d.gy. rBr (Centroid 47); spine: '[vert., from top to bottom] taylor   Miss Leonora   OBOLENSKY [publisher's device]'; yWhite (Centroid 92) wove, unwatermarked endpapers; all edges cut, unstained.

Dust Jacket: total measurement, 8³⁄₁₆ × 20⅞ in. (207 × 531 mm.); wove, unwatermarked paper; both sides uncoated, rough; inner side, back, and flaps are yWhite (Centroid 92); front is printed with a mottled, or sky-with-clouds, pattern, in brill. Y (Centroid 83) and l. OlBr (approx. Centroid 94); spine is light olive brown; printed in brilliant yellow and gy. rBr (Centroid 46); front: '[rev. out in white, with lettering set in wavy fashion, usually alternating high-low] MISS | LEONORA | WHEN LAST SEEN | [in brilliant yellow] AND 15 OTHER STORIES | [rev. out in white] by PETER TAYLOR'; spine: '[rev. out in white; vert., from top to bottom] Miss Leonora   peter taylor   OBOLENSKY [publisher's device in light olive brown and billiant yellow]'; back: all in grayish reddish brown, '*What reviewers have said about | Peter Taylor's short stories:* | [18 lines in roman, including excerpts from the *New York Times*, *Virginia Quarterly Review*, Chicago *Sunday Tribune*, Chicago *Sun Times*, and *New York Herald Tribune*]'; front flap: in grayish reddish brown, '$4.95 | Miss Leoonora When Last Seen | and Fifteen Other Stories | by Peter Taylor | [23 lines, prin. in roman, about the book]'; back flap: in grayish reddish brown, '[21 lines, prin. in roman, about the author] | *Jacket design by Richard Dilley* | Ivan Obolensky, Inc. | New York'.

Text Contents: "Reservations" (**C75**); "An Overwhelming Question" (**C77**); "At the Drugstore" (**C78**); "Sky Line" (**C45**; *LF*); "A Strange Story" (**C79**); "The Fancy Woman" (**C46**; *LF*); "A Spinster's Tale" (**C44**; *LF*); "Allegiance" (**C52**; *LF*); "The Death of a Kinsman" (**C54**; *WT*); "Miss Leonora When Last Seen" (**C74**); "A Wife of Nashville" (**C57**; *WT*); "What You Hear From 'Em?" (*WT*; **C60**); "Two Pilgrims" (**C80**); "Their Losses" (**C59**; *WT*); "Bad Dreams" (**C62**; *WT*); "Cookie" (**C36**; *WT*).

Publication: published 28 February 1964 at $4.95; number of copies unknown (publisher's records were destroyed by fire). There were 1,500 sets of unbound sheets in inventory as of late spring 1967, according to a letter from Ivan Obolensky to Peter Taylor. These unbound sheets apparently were used for a second issue prepared by one of the publisher's distributors; see **A6b**.

Locations: DLC, GU, NcGU, NcU, NcWsW, NN, PT, STW (4), TxU, ViU.

A6b *First Edition, Second Issue (ca. 1967 or 1969)*

All identical to **A6a**, except for:

Title Pages: each page measures 7¹⁵⁄₁₆ × 5⅛ in. (203 × 131 mm.).

Binding: brill. Y (Centroid 83) glossy-coated linen-cloth (304) boards, stamped in gold.

Publication: This second issue was likely done up from 1,500 sets of un-bound sheets by Obolensky's distributor, Grosset and Dunlap, sometime in late 1967, or by a later distributor of Obolensky books, Astor-Honor, Inc., of New York City, in early 1969. Ivan Obolensky went into bank-ruptcy in 1966 or early 1967, and his inventory was taken over by his distributors.

Location: NcWsW.

A7 *THE COLLECTED STORIES OF PETER TAYLOR*

A7a *First edition (1969)*

The Collected Stories of

PETER TAYLOR

Farrar, Straus and Giroux

NEW YORK

Title Page: 8⅜ × 5⁷⁄₁₆ in. (212 × 139 mm.).

Acknowledgment is made to the editors of *The New Yorker* for the following stories that first appeared in their pages: "Reservations," "The Other Times," "Their Losses," "Two Pilgrims," "What You Hear from 'Em?," "A Wife of Nashville," "Cookie" (originally "Middle Age"), "1939" (originally "A Sentimental Journey"), "Guests," "Heads of Houses," "Mrs. Billingsby's Wine," *"Je Suis Perdu"* (originally "A Pair of Bright-Blue Eyes") and "Miss Leonora When Last Seen"; to *McCall's* for "The Elect"; *Shenandoah* for "First Heat"; *Sewanee Review* for "At the Drug Store"; *Southern Review* for "A Spinster's Tale" and "The Fancy Woman"; *Kenyon Review* for "Venus, Cupid, Folly and Time" and "There"; and *Virginia Quarterly Review* for "Dean of Men."

Collation: [unsigned 1–17^{16}]; 272 leaves; [i–vi] vii–viii, [1–2] 3–535 [536].

Contents: p. i: half title; p. ii: list of books by PT; p. iii: title page; p. iv: copyright page; p. v: dedication: 'For my mother | KATHERINE TAYLOR TAYLOR | who was the best teller of tales I know | and from whose lips I first heard many | of the stories in this book.'; p. vi: blank; pp. vii–viii: contents; p. 1: second half title; p. 2: blank; pp. 3–535: text; p. 536: blank.

Running Titles: head, '[page number in arabic numerals, within square brackets] PETER TAYLOR | [indiv. story title in ital.; page number in arabic numerals, within square brackets]'.

Typography: text, 11/13.5 Granjon; 32 lines per page; 154 (161) × 100 mm.; 20 lines = 96 mm.

Paper and Binding: leaf measures 8⅜ × 5⁷⁄₁₆ in. (212 × 139 mm.); yWhite (Centroid 92) wove, unwatermarked paper. Black calico-cloth

(202) boards measure 8%16 × 5⅞ in. (218 × 148 mm.); stamped in gold; front: '[blindstamped in lower right, fancy rule, 38 mm.] | [in gold] '*P T*'; spine: '[fancy rule blindstamped at top, 38 mm.] | *The* | *Collected* | *Stories of* | *PETER* | *TAYLOR* | [blindstamped fancy rule, 38 mm.] | [at base, in gold] *Farrar, Straus* | *&* | *Giroux*'; grayish greenish blue (no Centroid equiv.) wove, unwatermarked endpapers; uncoated rough; top and bottom edges cut, fore edges untrimmed; top edges stained light grayish blue (no Centroid equiv.).

Dust Jacket: total measurement, 8%16 × 20⅜ in. (216 × 518 mm.); wove, unwatermarked paper; both sides uncoated, rough; inner side, front, back, and flaps are white; spine is dark greenish blue (between Centroid 169 and 173); printed in black and dark greenish blue; front: '[in dark greenish blue] *The Collected Stories of* | *PETER TAYLOR* | [black-and-white photograph of the author occupies lower two-thirds of right front]'; spine: '[rev. out in white] *The* | *Collected* | *Stories of* | *PETER TAYLOR* | [at base] *Farrar, Straus* | *&* | *Giroux*'; back: '[in dark greenish blue] BOOKS OF STORIES FROM | FARRAR, STRAUS AND GIROUX | [in black; two columns, roman; left column contains 15 lines (list of 17 authors, the last of whom is PT); right column contains 24 lines (list of 24 titles, the last of which is *The Collected Stories of Peter Taylor*)]'; front flap: '[in black] $10.00 | [in dark greenish blue] *The Collected Stories of* | PETER TAYLOR | [in black, 29 lines, prin. in roman, about the book] | [in dark greenish blue] *(continued on back flap)*'; back flap: '[in dark greenish blue] (continued from front flap) | [in black, 23 lines, prin. in roman, about the book] | *Jacket design by Herb Johnson* | [in dark greenish blue] FARRAR, STRAUS AND GIROUX | 19 UNION SQUARE WEST | NEW YORK'.

Text Contents: "Dean of Men" (**C92**); "First Heat" (**C88**); "Reservations" (**C75**; *ML*); "The Other Times" (**C66**; *HF*); "At the Drugstore" (**C78**; *ML*); "A Spinster's Tale" (**C44**; *LF*); "The Fancy Woman" (**C46**; *LF*); "Their Losses" (**C59**; *WT, ML*); "Two Pilgrims" (**C80**; *ML*); "What You Hear from 'Em?" (**C60**; *WT, ML*); "A Wife of Nashville" (**C57**; *WT, ML*); "Cookie" (**C36**; *WT, ML*); "Venus, Cupid, Folly and Time" (**C68**; *HF*); "1939" (**C64**; *HF*); "There" (**C81**); "The Elect" (**C90**); "Guests" (**C73**; *WT*); "Heads of Houses" (**C72**; *HF*); "Mrs. Billingsby's Wine" (**C87**); "*Je Suis Perdu*" (**C69**; *HF*); "Miss Leonora When Last Seen" (**C74**; *ML*).

Publication: published 28 August 1969 at $10.00; 10,000 copies printed. Registered in the name of Peter Taylor, under A 104637. A second cloth-bound printing of 700 copies was issued simultaneously with **A7c** on 15 October 1979 at $17.50. This issue is identified on the copyright page as '*Third Printing*' because it follows the second (paperback) printing of 1971, **A7b**.

Locations: DLC, GU, NcGU, NcU, NcWsW, NN, PT, STW (4), TxU, ViU.

A7b   *First Edition, Sunburst Paperback Issue (photo-offset from* **A7a** *(1971)*

All identical to **A7a** except for:

Title Page: 8¼ × 5¼ in. (209 × 134 mm.).

Copyright Page: '[. . .] *Second printing, 1971* [. . .]'.

Collation: 272 leaves perfect bound in printed wrappers.

Paper and Paper Binding: leaf measures 8¼ × 5¼ in. (209 × 134 mm.); yWhite (92) wove paper; perfect bound in thick, white, wove paper wrapper, 8¼ × 5⅜ in. (201 × 137 mm.); inner side coated smooth, outer side coated glossy; printed in black, v. R (Centroid 11), and v. YG (Centroid 115); front: '[in vivid yellow green] sunburst 11 | [in black] *PETER TAYLOR* | [decorative design, 61 × 64 mm., in black, vivid red, and vivid yellow green] | *THE* | *COLLECTED* | *STORIES* | [in lower right corner, in vivid green] $3.95'; spine: '[vert. from top to bottom, in two lines; in black] [top] *The Collected Stories of* [bottom] *PETER TAYLOR* [horiz., in vivid green, Sunburst books device] | [in black] S 11'; back: '[in black] SBN 374.6.0927.6 | [6 lines in ital, about the series; '*SUNBURST BOOKS*' in vivid green, remainder in black] | [in black, 23 lines in ital, including a list of Sunburst books] | [in black] *Design by Patricia de Groot* | [in vivid green] SUNBURST BOOKS | [in black] A Division of FARRAR STRAUS & GIROUX | 19 Union Square West | New York 10003'; all edges cut, unstained.

Publication: published 5 March 1971 at $3.95; 5,100 copies printed.

Locations: PT, STW (2).

A7c   *First Edition, Noonday Paperback Issue (photo-offset from* **A7a***) (1979)*

All identical to **A7a** except for:

Title Page: 8³⁄₁₆ × 5⅜ in. (208 × 137 mm.).

Copyright Page: '[. . .] | *Third printing, 1979* | [. . .]'.

Paper and Paper Binding: leaf measures 8³⁄₁₆ × 5⅜ in. (208 × 137 mm.); yWhite (92) wove, unwatermarked paper; perfect bound in thick, white, wove paper wrapper, 8³⁄₁₆ × 5⅜ in. (209 × 137 mm.); spine is printed s. gB (Centroid 169), and front contains a black-and-white photograph of PT and is lettered in strong greenish blue; inner side coated smooth, outer side coated glossy; front: '[in strong greenish blue] *The Collected Stories of* | *PETER TAYLOR* | [remainder of front contains a black-and-white photograph of PT, facing right to left]'; spine: '[rev. out in white; horiz.] *The* | *Collected* | *Stories of* | *PETER* | *TAYLOR* | *Farrar, Straus* | *&* |

Giroux | N625'; back: '[in black] $10.95   374–51542–5/1045 | [in strong greenish blue] *The Collected Stories of* | PETER TAYLOR | [in black, 13 lines prin. in roman, about the book] | *Cover design by Herb Johnson* | [in strong greenish blue] *FARRAR • STRAUS • GIROUX* | *19 Union Square West* | *New York 10003*'.

Publication: published as Noonday N625 on 15 October 1979 at $10.95; 2,058 copies printed and issued simultaneously with a second clothbound printing of 700 copies (see **A7a**). Two additional Noonday printings have been issued: a *'Fourth printing'* of 2,000 copies, on 16 December 1980, and a *'Fifth printing'* of 1,428 copies, on 5 May 1983.

Locations: PT, STW.

A7d   *First Edition, Penguin Paperback Issue (photo-offset from* **A7a** *(1986)*

All identical to **A7a** except for:

Title Page: $7\frac{3}{4} \times 4\frac{7}{8}$ in. (198 × 127 mm.); at base, publisher's device and '*Penguin Books*'.

Copyright Page: '[. . .] | First published in the United States of America by | Farrar, Straus and Giroux 1969 | Published in Penguin Books 1986 | [. . .]'.

Collation: 272 leaves perfect bound.

Contents: p. i: contains a note about PT.

Paper and Binding: leaf measures $7\frac{3}{4} \times 4\frac{7}{8}$ in. (198 × 127 mm.); yWhite (Centroid 92) wove, unwatermarked paper; perfect bound in thick, white, wove paper wrapper, $7\frac{3}{4} \times 4\frac{7}{8}$ in. (198 × 127 mm.); inner side coated smooth, outer side coated glossy; printed in v. pB (Centroid 194), d. rBr (Centroid 44), medium pinkish brown (between Centroid 33 and 45), and black, with cover illus. in shades of brown and gray; front: '[all within fancy frame of vivid purplish blue rules with Penguin devices at top left and right; in vivid purplish blue, with large caps 'C', 'A', and 'F' set below line] CONTEMPORARY AMERICAN FICTION | [rule connecting sides of frame; in dark reddish brown] [rule] THE [rule] | COL-LECTED STORIES | [rule] OF [rule] | [in medium pinkish brown overlapping letters] PETER | TAYLOR | [within dark reddish brown square-U frame, in dark reddish brown] "An American master" | —*Washington Post Book World* | [illustration by Neil Stuart]'; spine: '[vert. from top to bottom, in dark reddish brown] THE COLLECTED STORIES OF PETER TAYLOR | [two lines, in black; right] ISBN o 14 [left] 00.8361 8 | [publisher's device in vivid purplish blue]'; back: '[within frame of vivid purplish blue rules, like front, with identical 'CONTEMPORARY AMERICAN FICTION' at top] | [in dark reddish brown] "ONE OF

THE MAJOR WORKS | OF OUR LITERATURE" —JOYCE CAROL OATES | [in black, rule] | [12 lines in roman, about the author and his work] | "He comes as close as an American writer can to rivaling | Chekhov." —*The New York Times* | "He writes a prose as clear as a fine pane of glass." —*Time* | [rule] | [left] CAN. $12.95 | U.S.A $9.95 [right] Fiction | [within frame of rules, in fancy type] ISBN 0 14 00 . 83618 | [in 2 lines, vert. from bottom to top; left] Cover design by Neil Stuart | Cover photograph by Katherine Stuart'.

Publication: published in February 1986 at $9.95; number of copies printed unknown.

Locations: PT, STW (6).

A8 *LITERATURE, SEWANEE, AND THE WORLD*

First Edition (1972)

Cover Title: 'LITERATURE, | SEWANEE, | AND THE | WORLD | by Peter Taylor | Founders' Day Address 1972'.

Copyright Page: none.

Collation: [unsigned 1⁶]; 6 leaves; [1–12].

Collation: [unsigned 1^6]; 6 leaves; [1–12].

Contents: p. 1: cover title; p. 2: blank; pp. 3–10: text of PT's speech; pp. 11–12: blank.

Typography: text, unidentified offset type; irregular number of lines per page; 165 × 68 mm. (p. 5); 20 lines = 61 mm.

Paper and Paper Wrapper: leaf measures 8⅜ × 4 in. (213 × 102 mm.); yWhite (Centroid 92) wove, unwatermarked paper; uncoated smooth; self-wrapper wire-stitched; front: printed in black, 'LITERATURE, | SEWANEE, | AND THE | WORLD | by Peter Taylor | Founders' Day Address 1972'; back: blank.

Text Contents: text of PT's Founders' Day Address, the University of the South, Sewanee, Tenn., 10 October 1972.

Publicaton: approx. 100 copies printed for distribution in December 1972; not for sale.

Location: PT, STW (3).

> *Notes:* A portion of this address appeared in the *Sewanee News*, December 1972, pp. 3–4. Photocopies of the typescript of this address were prepared for distribution to the press and consist of 9 numbered pages stapled in the upper left corner. No title is given, only 'FOUNDERS DAY SPEECH', typed at the top center, and the date 'October 10, 1972'.

A9 *PRESENCES*

First Edition, Cloth Issue (1973)

PETER TAYLOR

Presences

SEVEN DRAMATIC PIECES

BOSTON
HOUGHTON MIFFLIN COMPANY
1973

Title Page: 8⁵⁄₁₆ × 5³⁄₈ in. (212 × 138 mm.).

Collation: [unsigned 1–7¹⁶]; 112 leaves; [i–viii], [1–2] 3–24 [25–26] 27–52 [53–54] 55–89 [90–92] 93–120 [121–122] 123–156 [157–158] 159–186 [187–188] 189–215 [216].

Contents: p. i: half title; p. ii: list of books by PT; p. iii: title page; p. iv: copyright page; p. v: dedication: 'for | *James E. Michael* | whose encouragement and friendship | and whose productions of my plays at | the Hill Theatre gave me the confidence | to write the seven dramatic pieces | in this book'; p. vi: blank; p. vii: contents; p. viii: blank; p. 1: part title; p. 2: blank; pp. 3–215: text; p. 216: blank.

Typography: text, 12/14 Bodoni; irregular number of lines per page; 145 (150) × 96 mm. (p. 37); 20 lines = 96 mm.

Paper and Binding: leaf measures 8⁵/₁₆ × 5⅜ in. (211 × 137 mm.); yWhite (Centroid 92) wove, unwatermarked paper; uncoated smooth. Black calico-cloth (304) boards measure 8⅝ × 5⅞ in. (218 × 147 mm.); stamped in dp. rO (Centroid 36); front: '[within a blindstamped panel, 95 × 76 mm., containing a reduction of the design from the front of the jacket; in deep reddish orange] *Presences*'; spine: '[vert., from top to bottom, in deep reddish orange] PRESENCES [blindstamped ornament, in deep reddish orange] TAYLOR [blindstamped ornament like first, in deep reddish orange] HMCO'; grayish yellow (between Centroid 90 and 91) laid paper, vert. chainlines 24 mm. apart; unwatermarked; uncoated rough; all edges cut; top edges stained dp. Pk (Centroid 3); bands: cloth head and tail bands have alternating deep pink and black stripes.

Dust Jacket: total measurement, 8%16 × 20½ in. (218 × 520 mm.); wove, unwatermarked paper; inner side coated smooth, outer side coated glossy; inner side, front, spine, and flaps are white; back contains a black-and-white photograph of the author; printed in black and v. R (Centroid 11); front: '[in black] Peter Taylor | [in vivid red] PRESENCES | seven dramatic pieces | [in black, ornamental design, approx. 129 × 126 mm.]'; spine: '[in vivid red, vert., from top to bottom] Taylor [in black, ornamental design like front, approx. 29 × 24 mm.; in vivid red] PRESENCES [horiz., in black] HOUGHTON | MIFFLIN | COMPANY'; back: contains a black-and-white photograph of the author, and '6–96852' rev. out in white in lower right corner; front flap: all in black, '$6.95 | [42 lines, prin. in roman, about the book, including a long statement by PT] | [vert., from top to bottom, the height of the last two lines] 0273 | continued on back flap'; back flap: '[in black] continued from front flap | [28 lines, prin. in roman, about PT's work, including excerpts from comments in the *New York Times*, and from Randall Jarrell, Gene Baro, and Joyce Carol Oates] | [5 lines in roman, about the author; 'PETER TAYLOR' in vivid red, remainder in black] | [in vivid red] Photograph of Peter Taylor | by Jill Krementz | HOUGHTON MIFFLIN COMPANY | 2 Park Street | Boston, Massachusetts 02107'.

First Edition, Paper Issue (1973)

All identical to cloth issue except for:

Title Page: 8⅜ × 5⅜ in. (213 × 137 mm.).

Paper and Paper Binding: leaf measures 8⅜ × 5⅜ in. (213 × 137 mm.); yWhite (Centroid 92) wove, unwatermarked paper; perfect bound in thick, white, wove paper wrapper, 5⅜ × 5⅝ in. (213 × 143 mm.); spine: compressed format but identical to dust jacket of cloth issue; back: contains photograph of PT; rev. out in white in upper right corner, '$3.95'; rev. out in white in lower right corner, '6–96851'; inner side of front wrapper: 44 lines, prin. in roman, identical to flaps of dust jacket of cloth issue, except the 5 lines about PT from the back flap have been omitted; edges are unstained.

Text Contents: "Two Images" (**C95**); "A Father and a Son" (**C96**); "Missing Person" (**C97**); "The Whistler" (**C98**); "Arson" (**C99**); "A Voice through the Door" (**C100**); "The Sweethearts" (**C101**).

Publication: published 14 February 1973 at $6.95 (cloth) and $3.95 (paper); 4,250 copies printed; 1,750 were issued in cloth and 2,500 in paper. Registered in the name of Peter Taylor, under A 410555.

Locations: DLC, GU, NcGU, NcU, NcWsW, NN, PT (5), STW (5), TxU, ViU.

Note: Advance proof copies were issued for review purposes before publication: 118 leaves perfect bound in gy. YG (approx. Centroid 122) paper wrapper, 8⅞₁₆ × 5 in. (214 × 127 mm.); printed in black on front: 'UNCORRECTED PROOFS | *Presences* | SEVEN ONE-ACT PLAYS | PETER TAYLOR | *BOSTON* | HOUGHTON MIFFLIN COMPANY | 1972 [*sic*]'; white wove, unwatermarked paper. The 'Contents' on p. 7 of the proof copy lists an introduction which was not in fact included in either proof or published book. Bound and jacketed copies of *Presences* were available 1 December 1972 (Charles P. Corn, Houghton Mifflin editor, to PT, 1 Dec. 1972). By publication day, 1,732 copies had been sold, 923 in cloth and 809 in paper (Craig Wylie, Houghton Mifflin vice president, to PT, 14 Feb. 1973).

A10 *IN THE MIRO DISTRICT*

A10a *First Edition (1977)*

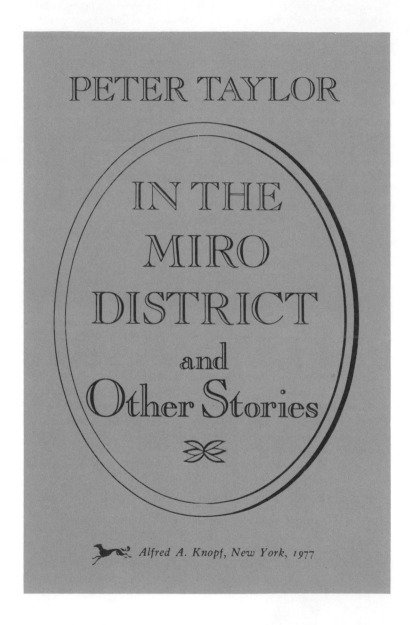

PETER TAYLOR

IN THE

MIRO

DISTRICT

and

Other Stories

Alfred A. Knopf, New York, 1977

Title Page: 8⁵/₁₆ × 5⁷/₁₆ in. (211 × 138 mm.).

THIS IS A BORZOI BOOK
PUBLISHED BY ALFRED A. KNOPF, INC.

Copyright © 1974, 1975, 1976, 1977 by Peter Taylor
All rights reserved under International and Pan-American Copyright
Conventions. Published in the United States by Alfred A. Knopf, Inc.,
New York, and simultaneously in Canada by Random House of Canada
Limited, Toronto. Distributed by Random House, Inc., New York.

LIBRARY OF CONGRESS CATALOGING IN PUBLICATION DATA
Taylor, Peter Hillsman, (Date)
In the Miro District, and other stories.
Contents: The captain's son.—The instruction of a
mistress.—The throughway.—The hand of Emmagene. [etc.]
I. Title
PZ3.T21767In [PS3539.A9633] 813'.5'4 76–28760
ISBN 0–394–41061–0

"In the Miro District" and "The Captain's Son" originally appeared in
The New Yorker. "Three Heroines" was first published in
The Virginia Quarterly Review, "The Instruction of a Mistress" in
The New Review, and "The Hand of Emmagene" and "Her Need"
in *Shenandoah*.

Acknowledgment is made to *The Sewanee Review* for permission
to reprint "The Throughway" and "Daphne's Lover." Copyright © 1964, 1969
by the University of the South.

Manufactured in the United States of America

First Edition

Collation: Smyth-sewn; 112 leaves; [i–xii], [1–4] 5–36 [37–38] 39–78 [79–80] 81–101 [102–104] 105–130 [131–132] 133–139 [140–142] 143–156 [157–158] 159–204 [205–212].

Contents: pp. i–iii: blank; p. iv: list of books by PT; p. v: half title; p. vi: blank; p. vii: title page; p. viii: copyright page; p. ix: dedication: '*to* | *Dick Crampton* | *in appreciation for* | *an extension* | *of time*'; p. x: blank; p. xi: contents; p. xii: blank; p. 1: second half title; p. 2: blank; p. 3: part title; p. 4: blank; pp. 5–204: text; pp. 205–206: blank; p. 207: '*A Note About the Author* | [12 lines, prin. in roman]'; p. 208: blank; p. 209: '*A Note on the Type* | [19 lines, prin. in roman]'; pp. 210–212: blank.

Running Titles: head, 'IN THE MIRO DISTRICT | [indiv. story title in ital.]'.

Typography: text, 11/13 Linotype Janson; 35 lines per normal page; 160 (169) × 103 mm.; 20 lines = 92 mm.

Paper and Binding: leaf measures 8⁵⁄₁₆ × 5⁷⁄₁₆ in. (211 × 142 mm.); white wove, unwatermarked paper; uncoated smooth. Black calico-cloth (304) boards measure 8⁹⁄₁₆ × 5⅞ in. (218 × 148 mm.); stamped in gold; front: blindstamped, '[all within two concentric double ovals, the right sides of which are swelled; in open-face type] IN THE | MIRO | DISTRICT | and | Other Stories | [ornament]'; spine: in gold, '[vert., from top to bottom; in open-face type] Peter Taylor [ornament] IN THE MIRO DISTRICT and Other Stories [roman] *Knopf*'; back: publisher's device blindstamped in lower right corner; white wove, unwatermarked endpapers; uncoated smooth; top and bottom edges cut, fore edges untrimmed; top edges stained s. B (Centroid 178); cloth head and tail bands have alternating blue and yellow stripes.

Dust Jacket: total measurement, 8⁹⁄₁₆ × 20¹¹⁄₁₆ in. (217 × 526 mm.); wove, unwatermarked paper; inner side, back, and flaps are white; front and spine are printed with a marbled-paper design, prin. in yellowish white, l. OlGy (Centroid 112), v.p. B (Centroid 184), and d.gy. Br (Centroid 62); printed in s. pB (Centroid 196), black, and d.gy. G (Centroid 151); front: '[in strong purplish blue fancy type] Peter | Taylor | [in black] In the | Miro | District | [in dark grayish green] & Other | Stories'; spine: '[in two lines, vert., from top to bottom; right, in black fancy type] In the Miro District [left, in strong purplish blue fancy type] Peter Taylor [horiz., at base, in dark grayish green] [publisher's device] | Knopf'; back: '[in black fancy type] In Praise of Peter Taylor | [17 lines, prin. in roman, including excerpts from reviews by Geoffrey Wolff (*Newsweek*), William C. Hamlin (*Saturday Review*), R. V. Cassill (*Book World*), Joyce Carol Oates, Albert J. Griffith (*Commonweal*), and John Thompson (*Harper's*)] | [lower right corner] 394–41061–0 | [at lower left edge, vert. from bottom to top] PRINTED IN U.S.A.'; front flap: '[in black] $7.95 | [8 lines, prin. in roman, blurb signed 'ROBERT PENN WARREN'] | [31 lines, prin. in roman, about the book]'; back flap: '[black-and-white photograph of the author, within a frame of single rules, 116 × 84 mm.; at upper right edge of photograph, vert., from bottom to top, '*John De Vivi*'] | [11 lines, prin. in roman, about the author] | *Jacket design by Muriel Nasser* | [publisher's device] | Alfred A. Knopf, Publisher, New York | 4 / 77'.

Text Contents: "The Captain's Son" (**C110**); "The Instruction of a Mistress" (**C104**); "The Throughway" (**C82**); "The Hand of Emmagene" (**C105**); "Daphne's Lover" (**C93**); "Her Need" (**C111**); "Three Heroines" (**C106**); "In the Miro District" (**C112**).

Publication: published 14 April 1977 at $7.95; 8,000 copies printed and bound by the American Book–Stratford Press, Inc., of Saddle Brook, N.J.. Registered in the name of Peter Taylor, under A 887331.

Locations: DLC, GU, NcGU, NcU, NN, PT, STW (6), TxU, ViU.

Note: Advance proof copies in yellowish orange (no Centroid equiv.) wrappers were sent to selected reviewers before publication. Total measurement, $10^{13}/_{16} \times 5^{3}/_{8}$ in. (274 × 137 mm.); 78 leaves; white wove, unwatermarked paper; front wrapper printed in black: 'THIS IS AN UNCORRECTED PROOF. | It should not be quoted without comparison | with the finally revised text. | IN THE | MIRO | DISTRICT | and | Other Stories | *Alfred A. Knopf* | *New York* | 1977'; text contents identical to **A10a**. The "Note on the Type," found on the recto of l. 77 (p. 145) states that *In the Miro District* was composed by The Book Press, Brattleboro, Vermont, and was printed and bound by the Haddon Craftsmen, of Scranton, Pa.; see *Publication* paragraph above, and p. 209 of the printed text.

A10b   *First Edition, Quality Paperback Book Club Issue (photo-offset from* **A10a***) (1977, i.e., 1978)*

All identical to **A10a** except for:

Title Page: $8^{3}/_{16} \times 5^{3}/_{8}$ in. (208 × 135 mm.).

Copyright Page: 'First Edition' dropped.

Collation: 112 leaves perfect bound in printed wrappers.

Paper and Paper Binding: leaf measures $8^{3}/_{16} \times 5^{3}/_{8}$ in. (208 × 135 mm.); yWhite (Centroid 92) wove, unwatermarked paper; uncoated smooth; wrappers: thick, wove, unwatermarked paper; inner side coated smooth, outer side coated glossy; inner side and spine are white, back is printed yellowish white; featherlike marbled-paper design on front like dust jacket of **A10a**; printed in colors identical to dust jacket of **A10a** except slightly duller hue; spine: '[vert., from top to bottom, in black fancy type] In the Miro District [in strong purplish blue fancy type] Peter Taylor [horiz. at base, in dark grayish green, publisher's logo] | Knopf'; back: all identical to back of dust jacket of **A10a** except at base, in black, '[publisher's logo] *Alfred A. Knopf, Publisher, New York*', and along lower right edge, vert., from bottom to top, *'design by Muriel Nasser'*.

Publication: there is no record of this paperback issue in Knopf files (Howard Reeves to SW, 14 August 1985), and the Quality Paperback Book Club declined to reveal the press run. Copies were available to members by June 1978.

Locations: PT, SW (2)

A10c   *First Edition, Carroll & Graf Paperback Issue (photo-offset from* **A10a***) (1983)*

All identical to **A10a** except for:

Title Page: 8 × 5⅛ in. (204 × 131 mm.); '[at base] [rule, 52 mm.] | CAR-ROLL & GRAF PUBLISHERS, INC. | [rule, 52 mm.] | New York'.

Copyright Page: '[. . .] | Carroll & Graf Publishers, Inc. | 260 Fifth Avenue | New York, N.Y. 10001 | Published by arrangement with Alfred A. Knopf, Inc. | First Carroll & Graf Edition 1983 | First Printing | [. . .]'.

Collation: 104 leaves.

Paper and Paper Binding: grayish yellowish white (no Centroid equiv.) wove, unwatermarked paper; perfect bound in thick, wove wrapper, 8 × 5³⁄₁₆ in. (204 × 133 mm.); inner side white, outer side light blue (between Centroid 180 and 185); inner side coated smooth, outer side coated glossy; lettered in black and white; front contains a reprod. of René Magritte's "The False Mirror" in shades of brown, greenish brown, white, gray, and black; front: [in black] "Taylor is an American master. These are incredibly graceful, witty | and elegant fictions." —Jonathan Yardley, *The Washington Post.* | [rev. out in white] IN THE MIRO | DISTRICT | [in black] AND OTHER STORIES BY | Peter Taylor | [Margritte illus.]'; spine: '[in black] CARROLL | & | GRAF | [vert., rev. out in white] IN THE MIRO DISTRICT [in black] Peter Taylor'; back: '[rev. out in white, 16 lines prin. in roman, about the book, including excerpts from *Harper's* and *New York Times Book Review*, and blurbs by Robert Penn Warren and Walker Percy] | [in black] Cover art: René Magritte, The False Mirror 1928. | ISBN: 0–88184–005–X | $7.95 | [rev. out in white, publisher's logo]'.

Publication: Published in July 1983 at $7.95; 5,000 copies printed.

Locations: PT (5), STW (2).

A10d   *First English Edition (photo-offset from* **A10a***) (1977)*

All identical to **A10a** except for:

Title Page: 7¹¹⁄₁₆ × 4⅞ in. (196 × 123 mm.); '[at base] CHATTO AND WINDUS • LONDON • 1977'.

Copyright Page: 'Published by | Chatto & Windus Ltd | 42 William IV Street | London WC2N 4DF | [. . .] | Printed in Great Britain by | Redwood Burn Limited | Trowbridge & Esher'.

Collation: [unsigned A–E¹⁶ F⁸ G⁴ H¹⁶]; 108 leaves.

Contents: notes on the author and type (pp. 207 and 209 respectively of **A10a**) have been deleted.

Typography: 144 (151) × 92 mm.; 20 lines = 82 mm.

Paper and Binding: leaf measures 7¾ × 5 in. (196 × 126 mm.); white wove, unwatermarked paper; uncoated smooth. Black paper-covered boards (imitation bead cloth, 202) measure 8 × 5³⁄₁₆ in. (203 × 131 mm.); spine stamped in gold, 'IN THE | MIRO | DISTRICT | & | *Other Stories* | PETER TAYLOR | [at base] CHATTO | & WINDUS'; white wove, unwatermarked endpapers; uncoated smooth; all edges cut, unstained.

Dust Jacket: total measurement, 8¹⁄₁₆ × 19⅛ in. (204 × 486 mm.); wove, unwatermarked paper; inner side uncoated, outer side coated glossy; inner side, flaps, and back are white; front and spine are black; printed in black; front: '[rev. out in white] IN THE MIRO DISTRICT | & OTHER STORIES | [within a frame of thick single rules, 134 × 105 mm., black-and-white illustration of a man and two children, a boy and a girl] | [rev. out in white] PETER TAYLOR'; spine: '[rev. out in white] PETER | TAYLOR [vert., from top to bottom] IN THE MIRO DISTRICT & OTHER STORIES [illustration in black and white of a boy's head, from front of dust jacket] [panel, 14 × 17 mm., rev. out in white; horiz., in black] CHATTO | & | WINDUS'; back: '*Some Short Story Collections from* | *Chatto & Windus and The Hogarth Press* | [swelled rule, 24 mm.] | | [15 lines in roman, including 14 authors and titles] | [lower right] ISBN 0 7011 2253 6'; front flap: '[in black, 24 lines, prin. in roman, about the book] | [8 lines, prin. in roman, Robert Penn Warren blurb from front flap of dust jack of **A10a**] | [left] *Jacket design by Stephen Ryan* | [right] £4.50 *net* | *in U.K. only*'; back flap: '[photograph of the author, 52 × 75 mm.] [right of photograph, vert., from bottom to top] Photograph: Wright Langley | [9 lines, prin. in roman, about the author] | Some reviews of Peter Taylor's works: | [8 lines, prin. in roman, including excerpts from the *New York Times Book Review*, Joyce Carol Oates, and Paul Theroux] | CHATTO & WINDUS LTD. | 40 William IV Street London WC2N 4DF'.

Publication: published 22 September 1977 at £4.50; 1,750 copies printed.

Locations: PT, STW (3).

A11 *THE EARLY GUEST*

First Signed and Limited Edition (1982)

PETER TAYLOR

The Early Guest

(a sort of story, a sort of play,
a sort of dream)

PALAEMON PRESS LIMITED

Title Page: $9^{15}/_{16} \times 5^{7}/_{8}$ in. (253 × 150 mm.); 'The Early Guest' in dp. R (Centroid 13).

Collation: [unsigned 1¹⁶]; 16 leaves; [1–4] 5–28 [29–32].

Contents: pp. 1–2: blank; p. 3: title page; p. 4: copyright page; pp. 5–28: text; p. 29: statement of limitation; pp. 30–32: blank.

Typography: 11/13 Baskerville; 39 lines per normal page; 181 × 93 mm., or 181 × 101 mm., with pages containing character names or stage directions; 20 lines = 92 mm.

Paper and Paper Wrapper: leaf measures 9¹⁵⁄₁₆ × 5⅞ in. (253 × 150 mm.); white wove paper, watermarked '[script] *Arches*'; uncoated smooth; hand-sewn with white cord in black wove, unwatermarked wrapper, 10⅛ × 6³⁄₁₆ in. (257 × 157 mm.); uncoated, rough.

Decorative Jacket: total measurement, 10⅛ × 20³⁄₈ in. (257 × 517 mm.); wove, unwatermarked, hand-block–printed Japanese paper; uncoated rough; inner side white, outer side printed with regular design of bright red (no Centroid equiv.) circles, each containing a four-leaf petal design, every other one of which is crossed by a heavy 'X' in d. B (Centroid 183); label: white paper label pasted on front, 38 × 92 mm., printed in black and dp. R (Centroid 13), '[within a frame of black single rules, 27 × 80 mm.] [in deep red] THE EARLY GUEST | [type ornament in black] | *by* PETER TAYLOR'.

Text Contents: "The Early Guest" (**C103**).

Publication: published in February 1982 at $35.00; 145 copies printed.

Locations: PT (4), STW (2).

Statement of Limitation: p. 29: 'This first edition is limited to 140 | copies, of which 100 are for sale. | [arabic number or roman letter (A-Z) supplied in red ink] | [author's signature in black ink]'.

Notes: "The Early Guest" was first published in *Shenandoah* (**C103**). The paper labels on the front of the earliest issued copies were attached approx. 85 mm. from the top of the decorative jacket; between 35 and 40 such copies were distributed. The labels on the remaining copies were soaked off and repasted approx. 55 mm. from the top of the decorative jacket. Five overrun copies were sewn in wrappers thicker than the rest and marked in pencil below the statement of limitations, 'AUTHOR'S COPY', for distribution by PT. No authorial changes in the text have been noted.

A12 *THE OLD FOREST AND OTHER STORIES*

A12a *First Edition (1985)*

Title Page: 8⅛ × 5⁵⁄₁₆ in. (206 × 135 mm.).

Collation: 180 leaves Smyth-sewn; [1–11] 12–30 [31] 32–89 [90] 91–115 [116] 117–141 [142] 143–163 [164] 165–168 [169] 170–180 [181] 182–197 [198] 199–236 [237] 238–255 [256] 257–265 [266] 267–295 [296] 297–321 [322] 323–358 [359–360].

Contents: p. 1: half title; p. 2: blank; p. 3: list of books by PT; p. 4: blank; p. 5: title page; p. 6: copyright page; p. 7: contents; p. 8: blank; p. 9: second half title; p. 10: blank; pp. 11–358: text; pp. 359–360: blank.

Running Titles: head, '[page number in arabic numerals] *The Old Forest and Other Stories* | [individual story title in roman caps.; page number in arabic numerals]'.

Typography: text, 11/13 Electra; 37 lines per normal page; 169 (175) × 101 mm.; 20 lines = 91 mm.

Paper and Binding: leaf measures 8⅛ × 5⅜ in. (201 × 136 mm.); yWhite (Centroid 92) wove, unwatermarked paper; uncoated smooth. Black linen cloth (304) on spine and 30 mm. of front and back boards, with very pale grayish white (no Centroid equivalent) paper with bluish threads covering remainder; boards measure 8½ × 5¾ in. (210 × 143 mm.); spine stamped in silver, in two lines, '[top] THE OLD FOREST *and Other Stories* [bottom] *Peter Taylor* [at base, publisher's device] THE DIAL PRESS'; yWhite (Centroid 92) wove, unwatermarked endpapers, uncoated smooth; top and bottom edges cut, fore edges rough-trimmed.

Dust Jacket: total measurement, 8½ × 20 in. (214 × 508 mm.); wove, unwatermarked paper; inner side coated smooth, outer side coated glossy; both sides are white; front and spine are printed in black, gy. B (Centroid 186), d. Br (approx. Centroid 59), brO (Centroid 54); cover illustration in shades of pale blue, gray, and brown; front: '[illustration at top] [black letters outlined in grayish blue] The Old | Forest | [dark brown rule, 103 mm.] | [in brownish orange semiscript] and Other Stories | [dark brown rule, 103 mm.] | [in dark brown] PETER | TAYLOR'; spine: [horiz., in dark brown] PETER | TAYLOR | [vert., in two lines; top, in black] The Old Forest [bottom] [dark brown rule, 26 mm.] [in brownish orange semiscript] and Other Stories [dark brown rule, 26 mm.] [at base, in black, publisher's device] [horiz.] THE | DIAL | PRESS'; back: all in black, '[photograph of PT, 98 × 117 mm.] [vert., from top to bottom, at lower right border of photograph] PHOTO BY BILL BURKE | [12 lines, prin. in roman, including blurbs and comments from Jonathan Yardley, Geoffrey Wolff (*Newsweek*), Joyce Carol Oates, Albert Griffith (*Commonweal*), and Linda Kuehl (*Saturday Review*)] | ISBN: 0-385-27983-3'; front flap: '[in black] T.O.F.A.O.S. | $16.95 | The Old | Forest | [rule, 65mm.] | [in semiscript] and Other Stories | [rule, 65 mm.] | PETER TAYLOR | [24 lines in roman, about the book] | (*continued on back*)'; back flap, '(*continued from front flap*) | [22 lines in roman, about the book and author] | JACKET BY TERRENCE FEHR | *Printed in the U.S.A.* | 0285'.

Text Contents: "The Gift of the Prodigal" (**C118**); "The Old Forest" (**C114**); "Promise of Rain" (**C67**; *HF*); "Bad Dreams" (**C62**; *WT, ML*); "A Friend and Protector" (**C71**; *HF*); "A Walled Garden" (**C47**; *HF*); "Allegiance" (**C52**; *LF, ML*); "The Little Cousins" (**C70**; *HF*); "A Long Fourth" (**C51**; *LF*); "Rain in the Heart" (**C49**; *LF*); "Porte Cochere" (**C56**; *WT*); "The Scoutmaster" (**C50**; *LF*); "Two Ladies in Retirement" (**C61**; *WT*); "The Death of a Kinsman" (**C54**; *WT, ML*).

Publication: published 8 February 1985 at $16.95; 6,000 copies printed. There have been four additional printings: a second on publication day, 8 February 1985, 2,000 copies; a third printing on 22 February 1985, 3,000 copies; a fourth printing on 19 March 1985, 5,000 copies; and a fifth printing on 25 March 1985, 5,000 copies.

Locations: DLC, GU, NcGU, NcU, PT, STW (4), ViU.

Note: Uncorrected proof copies printed on thin white, wove paper were distributed to selected reviewers before publication. These proof copies are perfect bound in light gray wrappers, printed in black. Text contents are identical to **A12a**. The recto of the first leaf contains publication information and a brief description of the book. The back of the wrapper contains the same blurbs and comments as the back of the dust jacket of **A12a**.

A12b   *Second Edition (1986)*

Title Page: 6⅞ × 4 1/16 in. (175 × 103 mm.).

Collation: 184 leaves perfect bound; [i–viii], 1–359 [360].

Contents: pp. i–iii: excerpts from reviews of *OF*; p. iv: blank; p. v: title page;
p. vi: copyright page; p. vii: contents; p. viii: blank; pp. 1–359: text; p. 360:
about the author.

Running Titles: head, '[page number in arabic numerals] THE OLD
FOREST AND OTHER STORIES | [indiv. story title in ital.; page
number in arabic numerals]'.

Typography: unidentified offset typeface; 41 lines per page; 152 (158) ×
84 mm.; 20 lines = 74 mm.

Paper and Paper Binding: leaf measures 6⅞ × 4¹⁄₁₆ in. (175 × 103 mm.);
yWhite (Centroid 92) wove, unwatermarked paper; uncoated rough; thick
white wove wrapper, 6⅞ × 4¼ in. (175 × 107 mm.); inner side coated
smooth, outer side coated glossy; printed in black, d. Gy (Centroid 266),

v. R (Centroid 11), with cover illus. prin. in shades of orange, yellow, brown, and gray; front: '[in black] THE NATIONAL BESTSELLER | [in dark gray] The | [initial 'O'] Old | [initial 'F'] Forest | *and Other Stories* | [photograph of autumn leaves on a rock] | [in black] PETER | TAYLOR | [rule in vivid red] | [in black] "Quite simply, there is not a better writer of | fiction now at work in the United States." | Jonathan Yardley | "The undisputed master of the | short story form." | Anne Tyler | [publisher's device] Ballantine/Fiction/32778/$4.95'; spine: '[publisher's device in black] | [in dark gray, in 2 lines; vert. from top to bottom; right] THE OLD FOREST [left] and Other Stories | [horiz., illus. from front] | [in black; in 2 lines, vert. from top to bottom; right] PETER [left] TAYLOR | 345–32778–0–495'; back: '[in vivid red] PETER TAYLOR | "ONE OF THE FINEST WRITERS OF FICTION | OF THIS CENTURY . . . | [in black, 8 lines prin. in roman, excerpt from Robb Forman Dew's review in the *Boston Globe*] | [vivid red rule] | [in black, 11 lines prin. in roman, excerpt from review in *San Francisco Chronicle-Examiner*] | [vivid red rule] | [in black, 8 lines prin. in roman, excerpt from review in the *Atlanta Journal*] | [vivid red rule] | [in black, bar code] | [in fancy type, left side] ISBN 0–345–32778–0 [right side, in roman] Cover printed in USA'.

Text Contents: identical to **A12a**.

Publication: Published in February 1986 at $4.95; the publisher declined to reveal the number of copies printed.

Location: PT (3), STW (3).

A12c *First English Edition (photo-offset from **A12a**) (1985)*

All identical to **A12a** except for:

THE OLD FOREST
Peter Taylor

CHATTO & WINDUS
THE HOGARTH PRESS
London

Title Page: 8¾ × 5⅝ in. (222 × 144 mm.).

Copyright Page: 'Published in 1985 by | Chatto & Windus • The Hogarth Press | [. . .]'.

Collation: [unsigned A-L¹⁶ M⁴ N¹⁶]; 180 leaves; [1–11] 12–30 [31] 32–89 [90] 91–115 [116] 117–141 [142] 143–163 [164] 165–168 [169] 170–180 [181] 182–197 [198] 199–236 [237] 238–255 [256] 257–265 [266] 267–295 [296] 297–321 [322] 323–358 [359–360].

Contents: p. 1: half title; p. 2: blank; p. 3: list of books by PT; p. 4: blank; p. 5: title page; p. 6: copyright page; p. 7: contents; p. 8: blank; p. 9: second half title; p. 10: blank; pp. 11–358: text; pp. 359–360: blank.

Paper and Binding: leaf measures 8¾ × 5¹¹⁄₁₆ in. (222 × 147 mm.); yWhite (Centroid 92) wove, unwatermarked paper; uncoated smooth; d.gy. rBr (approx. Centroid 47) paper-covered boards (imitation bead cloth) measure 9¹⁄₁₆ × 6 in. (231 × 155 mm.); spine: stamped in gold, '[vert. from top to bottom] THE OLD FOREST • PETER TAYLOR | [horiz. at base] CHATTO | [rule] | HOGARTH'; yWhite (Centroid 92) wove, unwwatermarked endpapers; all edges cut, unstained.

Dust Jacket: total measurement, 9¹⁄₁₆ × 20¾ in. (231 × 527 mm.); white wove, unwatermarked paper; inner side white, outer side printed d. G (approx. Centroid 146); inner side coated smooth, outer side coated glossy; printed in black and orange yellow (between Centroid 67 and 68); front: '[in orange yellow fancy type] The | Old Forest | [reprod. of John Nash woodcut in black against panel rev. out in white] | [in orange yellow roman] PETER TAYLOR'; spine: '[vert. from top to bottom, in orange yellow] THE OLD FOREST • [rev. out in white] PETER TAYLOR | [horiz. at base, publisher's device in yellowish orange]'; back: '[against a yellowish orange panel within a frame of heavy rules rev. out in white; in black] [22 lines prin. in roman, including excerpts from reviews in the *Washington Post, Newsweek*, by Robert Penn Warren, *Time Magazine, Boston Globe*, and *Chicago Tribune*] | [bar code in dark green against orange yellow panel]'; front flap: '[in black] The Old Forest | [32 lines prin. in roman, about the book and including an excerpt from the *New York Times Books Review* and a comment by Paul Theroux] | [left side] ISBN 0 7011 3967 6 [right side] £9.95 net | in UK only'; back flap: '[black-and-white photograph of PT, 91 × 81 mm.] | Peter Taylor | [13 lines prin. in roman, about the author] | [4 lines in roman, information about the photograph of PT and cover illus.] | Chatto & Windus • The Hogarth Press | 40 William IV Street, London WC2N 4DF'.

Publication: published 15 August 1985 at £9.95; 1,500 copies printed.

Location: PT, STW.

A12d *Second English Edition, King Penguin Issue (photo-offset from* **A12a***)*
(1987)

All identical to **A12a** except for:

PETER TAYLOR

———

THE
OLD FOREST

A KING PENGUIN
PUBLISHED BY PENGUIN BOOKS

Title Page: 7½ × 4⅞ in. (191 × 123 mm.).

Copyright Page: '[. . .] | First published by Chatto & Windus • The Hogarth Press 1985 | Published in Penguin Books 1987 | Copyright © Peter Taylor, 1941, [. . .], 1985 | All rights reserved | [. . .]'.

Collation: 184 leaves perfect bound; foliation begins on p. 3; [3–11] 12–30 [31] 32–89 [90] 91–115 [116] 117–141 [142] 143–163 [164] 165–168 [169] 170–180 [181] 182–197 [198] 199–236 [237] 238–255 [256] 257–265 [266] 267–295 [296] 297–321 [322] 323–358 [359–370].

Contents: p. 3: King Penguin imprint and 12 lines about the book; pp. 359–68: advertisements for other books in the King Penguin series; pp. 369–70: blank.

Paper and Paper Binding: leaf measures 7½ × 4⅞ in. (191 × 123 mm.); yWhite (Centroid 92) wove, unwatermarked paper; uncoated rough; perfect bound in thick white wove paper wrapper, 7½ × 5 in. (191 × 127 mm.); inner side uncoated, outer side coated smooth; printed in black and p. B (approx. 185); front: '[in black] KING PENGUIN | PETER TAYLOR | [illus. based on front of dust jacket of A12a, in black and pale blue] | [in black] THE | OLD FOREST | '*AN AMERICAN MASTERPIECE* | — *WASHINGTON POST BOOK WORLD* | [7 lines prin. in roman caps, excerpt from *The Times* (London)]'; spine: '[publisher's device] | [vert. from top to bottom] PETER TAYLOR • THE OLD FOREST [in two lines; right] ISBN 0 14 [left] 00.8951 9'; back: 'KING PENGUIN | [left, photograph of PT in black and pale blue, bordered by a frame of heavy black rules, all within a single-rule frame, 46 × 35 mm.; 'PETER TAYLOR' within single-rule frame below photograph] | [remainder right or below photograph; 26 lines in roman and ital., including excerpts from reviews in *Washington Post Book World, Listener, Newsweek, New York Times Book Review*, Boston Globe, and another from *Newsweek*] | [left] Cover engraving by Andrew Davidson | Photograph of Peter Taylor by Bill Burke | **Fiction** | **U.K. £4.95** | **Aust. $16.95** | **(recommended)** | **N.Z. $16.99** | **(incl. GST)** | [right, bar code]'.

Publication: Published in July 1987 at £4.95; the publisher declined to reveal the number of copies printed.

Locations: PT, STW.

A13 *A STAND IN THE MOUNTAINS*

(First Edition 1985, i.e, 1986)

A STAND
IN THE MOUNTAINS
by
PETER TAYLOR

FREDERIC C. BEIL
NEW YORK

Title Page: 9⁹⁄₁₆ × 6³⁄₁₆ in. (244 × 156 mm.); title in deep Red (Centroid 13).

Collation: signatures Smythe-sewn; 58 leaves; [1–8] 9–21 [22] 23–112 [113–116].

Contents: pp. 1–3: blank; p. 4: black-and-white photograph of PT at Kenyon College in the late 1930s; p. 5: title page; p. 5: copyright page; p. 6: dedication, '*To | Eleanor Ross Taylor | for many good reasons*'; p. 7: blank; pp. 9–19: preface by PT; pp. 20–21: list of characters; p. 22: blank; pp. 23–113: text; p. 114: blank; p. 115: colophon, 'THIS EDITION WAS SET IN MONOTYPE DANTE | AND PRINTED AT THE STAMPERIA VALDONEGA | VERONA • MARCH 1985 | [printer's device]'; p. 116: blank.

Running Titles: head, '*A STAND IN THE MOUNTAINS | PREFACE* [or '*FIRST*' through '*SEVENTH SCENE*']'.

Typography: text, 11/13.5 Monotype Dante; 36 lines per normal page (text); 176 (188) × 104 mm.; 20 lines = 105 mm.

Paper and Binding: leaf measures 9⁹⁄₁₆ × 6³⁄₁₆ in. (244 × 156 mm.); yWhite (Centroid 92) wove, unwatermarked paper; uncoated smooth; d. gy. G (approx. Centroid 151) linen-cloth (304) boards measure 9⅞ × 6½ in. (252 × 166 mm.); front: unstamped but contains white laid paper label, 55 × 60 mm., printed in dark grayish green, '[within a single-rule frame] Peter Taylor | A STAND | IN THE | MOUNTAINS'; spine: stamped in white, '[vert. from top to bottom] PETER TAYLOR — A STAND IN THE MOUNTAINS BEIL'; all edges trimmed, unstained; cloth head and tail bands have alternating green and white stripes; very pale yellow (no Centroid equiv.) laid endpapers, vert. chainlines 38 mm. apart; uncoated rough; laid in publisher's slipcase of very thin, light gray unprinted binder's board; issued without dust jacket.

Text Contents: first separate publication of "A Stand in the Mountains" (**C89**).

Publication: published 25 April 1986 at $24.95; 1,500 copies printed.

Locations: PT (6) STW (2).

A14 *A SUMMONS TO MEMPHIS*

First Edition (1986)

Title Page: 8⅜ × 5½ in. (214 × 140 mm.).

Collation: signatures Smyth-sewn; 112 leaves; [i–viii], [1–4] 5 [6] 7[8], etc., through [216] [recto pages are foliated and verso pages contain book title but are unfoliated, except for numbered chapter pages, which are neither foliated nor contain the title].

Contents: p. i: blank; p. ii: list of books by PT; p. iii: half title; p. iv: blank; p. v: title page; p. vi: copyright page; p. vii: dedication, '*For Eleanor, Katie and Ross | With love*'; p. viii: blank; p. 1: second half title; p. 2: blank; pp. 3–209: text; p. 210: blank; p. 211: note about the author; p. 212: note on the type; 213–216: blank.

Running Titles: head, 'A SUMMONS TO MEMPHIS | [page number in arabic numerals]'.

Typography: 11/14 Linotype Janson; 33 lines; 170 (178) × 101 mm.; 20 lines = 99 mm.

Paper and Binding: leaf measures 8⅜ × 5½ in. (214 × 140 mm.); yWhite (Centroid 92) wove, unwatermarked paper; uncoated smooth; quarter-bound in black linen-cloth (304) and very pale yellow (no Centroid equiv.) boards, 8⅝ × 5⅞ in. (220 × 151 mm.); front and spine stamped in gold; front: '[in open-face] PT'; spine: [in open-face, vert. from top to bottom] Peter Taylor A SUMMONS TO MEMPHIS | [horiz. at base, in roman] KNOPF'; back: publisher's device blindstamped at right; top and bottom edges trimmed, front edges rough cut, unstained; brown cloth head and tail bands; yWhite (Centroid 92) wove, unwatermarked endpapers; uncoated smooth.

Dust Jacket: total measurement, 8⅝ × 20¹⁵⁄₁₆ in. (220 × 530 mm.); front and back printed very pale yellow (no Centroid equiv.), with fore edge of front and spine printed in black, and top and bottom of front with l. grB (approx. Centroid 172) elongated panels; lettered in black, light greenish blue, d. Gy (Centroid 266), reddish brown (no Centroid equiv.), and pale yellow; front: '[in dark gray] A SUMMONS | [reddish brown rule] | [in dark gray; initial 'M', with vert. 'TO' and reddish brown horiz. rule below in the V of 'M'] MEMPHIS | [in black] A [reddish brown vert. rule] [in black] N O V E L | [in reddish brown] P E T E R | T A Y L O R'; spine: '[in light greenish blue; 2 lines, vert. from top to bottom, right side] P E T E R [left] T A Y L O R; [one line, pale yellow] A SUMMONS TO MEMPHIS | [horiz.; publisher's device in light greenish blue] | [rev. out in white] KNOPF'; back: '[all in black] Praise for | *The Old Forest and Other Stories* | [25 lines prin. in roman, including excerpts of reviews by Robert Towers (*New York Times Book Review*), Jonathan Yardley (*Washington Post Book World*), Anne Tyler (*USA Today*), Robb Forman Dew (Boston *Globe*), Paul Gray (*Time*)] | [in fancy type] ISBN 0–394–41062–9'; front flap: '[all in black] FTP $15.95 | [35 lines prin. in roman, about the book and PT] | *(continued on back flap)*'; back flap: *(continued from front flap)* | [4 lines in roman, conclusion of front flap material about the book] | [black-and-white photograph of PT, 106 × 85 mm.] | [right of photograph, vert. from bottom to top] J. WILLIAM BROADWAY | [below photograph] *Jacket design by Paul Gamarello, Eyetooth, Inc.* | [publisher's device in light greenish blue] | [in black] ALFRED A. KNOPF | *Publisher, New York* | 10/86 | [at right side, vert. from bottom to top] PRINTED IN U.S.A. © 1986 ALFRED A. KNOPF, INC.'

Text Contents: A Summons to Memphis. A brief excerpt appeared simultaneously with publication; see **C119**.

Publication: published 6 October 1986 at $15.95; 20,000 copies printed. There have been five additional printings, each of which is identified on the copyright page: 2d printing, 7,500 copies issued in Sept. 1986; 3d printing, 5,000 copies issued in Nov. 1986; 4th printing, 2,500 copies issued in Dec. 1986; 5th printing, 3,500 copies issued in May 1987; and 6th printing, 2,000 copies issued in July 1987.

Locations: DLC, GU, NcGU, NcU, NN, PT (3), STW (3), TxU, ViU.

Note: Bound uncorrected proof copies were sent to selected reviewers before publication: 103 leaves perfect bound in grayish blue wrapper; white wove, un-watermarked paper, printed on both sides but foliation reprod. from editor's original, 4–196 (for text); front and spine of wrapper printed in black. According to publisher's records, approx. 20 such advance proof copies were prepared. In a letter of 7 July 1987 to the compiler, Judith Jones, PT's editor at Knopf, reported plans for a Book-of-the-Month Club issue; a Quality Paperback Book Club issue; a new edition from Ballantine Books; and a British issue from Chatto & Windus.

B

Contributions to Books

[in black] T H E | [in dull red] *B e s t* | [in black] AMERICAN | SHORT STORIES | 1942 | [fancy rule] | *and The Yearbook of the American Short Story* | [rule] | *Edited by* | MARTHA FOLEY | [black rule broken at center by publisher's device in dull red] | HOUGHTON MIFFLIN [base of dull red publisher's device] COMPANY • BOSTON | [in semi-Gothic type] The Riverside Press Cambridge

Copyright Page: 'COPYRIGHT, 1942, BY HOUGHTON MIFFLIN COMPANY'.

Binding and Dust Jacket: dull reddish pink cloth boards measure 8⅛ × 5½ in. (206 × 140 mm.); stamped in blue, front and spine. Yellowish white, wove, unwatermarked endpapers; top and bottom edges trimmed, fore edges untrimmed. White dust jacket printed in red, light blue, pink, and pale gray.

Contains: first book appearance of "The Fancy Woman" (**C46**), on pp. 311–42.

Publication: published 10 September 1942 at $2.75; 9,000 copies printed.

B2 *A VANDERBILT MISCELLANY* (1944)

[in open-face type] A Vanderbilt Miscellany | 1919–1944 | [illustration] | [in roman] Decorated by Marion Junkin | (The Department of Fine Arts) | [in open-face type] Edited by Richmond Croom Beatty | [in roman] (The Department of English) | NASHVILLE • VANDERBILT UNIVERSITY PRESS • 1944

Copyright Page: 'Copyright, 1944 | By | THE VANDERBILT UNIVERSITY'.

Binding and Dust Jacket: light brown cloth boards measure 9⁵⁄₁₆ × 6⅛ in. (236 × 155 mm.); stamped in gold, front and spine. Grayish tan wove, unwatermarked endpapers; all edges trimmed. Orange pictorial dust jacket printed in black.

Contains: first and only appearance of story, "Attendant Evils," pp. 144–50.

Publication: published in March 1944 at $3.50; 750 copies printed.

B3 *THE BEST AMERICAN SHORT STORIES 1945* (1945)

[in black] T H E | [in dull red] *B e s t* | [in black] AMERICAN | SHORT STORIES | 1945 | [fancy rule] | *and The Yearbook of the American Short*

Story | [rule] | *Edited by* | MARTHA FOLEY | *With decorations by* | ANGNA ENTERS | [left of publisher's device] 19 | [rule] | HOUGH-TON MIFFLIN [right of publisher's device] 45 | [rule] | COMPANY • BOSTON | [in semi-Gothic] The Riverside Press Cambridge

Copyright Page: 'COPYRIGHT, 1945, BY HOUGHTON MIFFLIN COMPANY'.

Binding and Dust Jacket: grayish tan cloth boards measure 7⅞ × 5¼ in. (200 × 133 mm.); stamped in blue, front and spine. Yellowish white wove, unwatermarked endpapers; all edges trimmed. White pictorial dust jacket printed in red, white, blue, yellow, and black.

Contains: first book appearance of "Rain in the Heart" (**C49**), on pp. 282–303.

Publication: published 27 November 1945 at $3.00; 9,000 copies printed.

B4 *THE BEST AMERICAN SHORT STORIES 1946*   (1946)

[in black] T H E | [in red] *B e s t* | [in black] AMERICAN | SHORT STORIES | 1946 | [fancy rule] | *and The Yearbook of the American Short Story* | [rule] | *Edited by* | MARTHA FOLEY | [left of publisher's device] 19 | [rule] | HOUGHTON MIFFLIN [right of publisher's device] 46 | [rule] | COMPANY • BOSTON | [in semi-Gothic] The Riverside Press Cambridge

Copyright Page: 'COPYRIGHT, 1946, BY HOUGHTON MIFFLIN COMPANY'.

Binding and Dust Jacket: grayish tan cloth boards measure 8¼ × 5⅝ in. (210 × 142 mm.); stamped in blue, front and spine. Deep tan wove, un-watermarked endpapers; all edges trimmed. White dust jacket printed in brownish gray, brown, blue, and light green.

Contains: first book appearance of "The Scout Master" (**C50**), on pp. 425–63.

Publication: published 26 November 1946 at $3.00; 9,000 copies printed.

B5 *A SOUTHERN VANGUARD*   (1947)

A Southern Vanguard | THE JOHN PEALE BISHOP | MEMORIAL VOLUME | *Edited by* ALLEN TATE | PRENTICE-HALL, INC. | *New York*

Copyright Page: 'Copyright, *1947, by* | PRENTICE-HALL, INC.'.

Binding and Dust Jacket: reddish brown cloth boards measure 8⁵⁄₁₆ × 5⁵⁄₈ in. (212 × 142 mm.); stamped in dark green, front and spine. Light gray wove, unwatermarked endpapers; all edges trimmed. White dust jacket printed in deep reddish pink, black, and white.

Contains: first book appearance of "A Long Fourth" (**C51**), on pp. 212–45.

Publication: published August 1947 at $4.50; number of copies printed unknown.

B6 *THE BEST AMERICAN SHORT STORIES 1950* (1950)

[in black] T H E | [in red] *B e s t* | [remainder in black] AMERICAN | SHORT STORIES | [fancy rule] | *and The Yearbook of the American Short Story* | [rule] | *Edited by* | M A R T H A F O L E Y | [next 3 lines broken by publisher's device] 19 [publ. device] 50 | [rule, broken by publ. device] | HOUGHTON MIFFLIN [base of publ. device] COMPANY BOS-TON | [in semi-Gothic] The Riverside Press Cambridge

Copyright Page: 'COPYRIGHT, 1950, BY HOUGHTON MIFFLIN COMPANY'.

Binding and Dust Jacket: light gray cloth boards measure 8⁵⁄₁₆ × 5⁵⁄₁₆ in. (214 × 142 mm.); front and spine stamped in blue. Yellowish white wove, unwatermarked endpapers; all edges trimmed. Printed dust jacket.

Contains: first book appearance of "A Wife of Nashville" (**C57**), pp. 407–31.

Publication: published 21 July 1950 at $3.75; 9,000 copies printed.

B7 *PRIZE STORIES OF 1950: THE O. HENRY AWARDS* (1950)

[Two-page title] [right] prize | stories | of | 1950 | [publisher's device] the | O. Henry Awards | [left] DOUBLEDAY & COMPANY, INC., GARDEN CITY, NEW YORK, 1950 [right] SELECTED AND EDITED BY HERSCHEL BRICKELL

Copyright Page: 'Copyright, 1950, by Doubleday & Company, Inc. | [. . .] | First Edition'.

Binding and Dust Jacket: black cloth boards measure 8½ × 5⁵⁄₈ in. (215 × 141 mm.); spine stamped in gold. Yellowish white wove, unwatermarked endpapers; all edges trimmed. White dust jacket printed in grayish green, yellow, grayish blue, and black.

Contains: first book appearance of "Their Losses" **(C59)**, on pp. 273–86.

Publication: published 21 September 1950 at $3.50; 9,000 copies printed.

B8 *NORTH CAROLINA AUTHORS:*
   A SELECTIVE HANDBOOK (1952)

THE UNIVERSITY OF NORTH CAROLINA | LIBRARY EXTENSION PUBLICATION | Vol. XVIII October 1952 No. 1 | [rule] | NORTH CAROLINA AUTHORS: | A SELECTIVE HANDBOOK | Prepared by a Joint Committee of the | North Carolina English Teachers Association | and the North Carolina Library Association | [publisher's device] | CHAPEL HILL | THE UNIVERSITY OF NORTH CAROLINA LIBRARY | 1952

Copyright Page: 'Copyright, 1952, by | THE UNIVERSITY OF NORTH CAROLINA LIBRARY'.

Paper and Binding: red cloth boards measure 9¼ × 6¼ in. (235 × 158 mm.); front and spine stamped in gold; cloth head and tail bands have alternating red and yellow stripes; dust jacket not seen; also issued in moderate yellowish green wrapper printed in black.

Contains: first and only appearance of "Taylor, Peter," an autobiographical statement, on p. 120.

Publication: published in October 1952 at $3.15 (cloth) and $2.00 (wrapper); number of copies unknown.

B9 *PRIZE STORIES 1959: THE O. HENRY AWARDS* (1959)

PRIZE STORIES 1959: | THE O. HENRY AWARDS | Selected and Edited by | *Paul Engle* | Assisted by | *Curt Harnack and Constance Urdang* | *Doubleday & Company, Inc. Garden City, New York, 1959*

Copyright Page: 'Copyright © 1959 by Doubleday & Company, Inc. | [. . .] | First Edition'.

Binding and Dust Jacket: light green cloth boards measure 8½ × 5⅝ in. (216 × 145 mm.); spine stamped in gold on greenish blue panels. Yellowish white wove, unwatermarked endpapers; top and bottom edges trimmed, fore edges rough trimmed. Printed dust jacket.

Contains: first book appearance of "Venus, Cupid, Folly and Time" (**C68**), on pp. 15–45.

Publication: published 5 February 1959 at $3.95; 9,000 copies printed.

Note: Taylor received First Prize.

B10 *THE BEST AMERICAN SHORT STORIES 1960*   (1960)

[in black] T H E | [in dull red] *B e s t* | [in black] AMERICAN | SHORT STORIES | 1960 | [fancy rule] | *and the Yearbook of the American Short Story* | [rule] | *Edited by* | MARTHA FOLEY and DAVID BURNETT | [publisher's device] | HOUGHTON MIFFLIN COMPANY • BOS-TON | [in semi-Gothic] The Riverside Press Cambridge | [in roman] 1960

Copyright Page: 'COPYRIGHT © 1960 BY HOUGHTON MIFFLIN COMPANY | [. . .] | FIRST PRINTING'.

Binding and Dust Jacket: grayish tan cloth boards measure 8¼ × 5½ in. (210 × 140 mm.); stamped in brown, front and spine. Yellowish white wove, unwatermarked endpapers; all edges trimmed. White dust jacket printed in yellow and dark gray.

Contains: first book appearance of "Who Was Jesse's Friend and Protec-tor?" (**C71**), on pp. 334–53.

Publication: published 21 September 1960 at $4.95; 9,500 copies printed.

B11 *PRIZE STORIES 1961: THE O. HENRY AWARDS*   (1961)

PRIZE STORIES | 1961 | THE | [in fancy type] O. | HENRY | [in roman] AWARDS | EDITED BY RICHARD POIRIER | DOUBLE-DAY & COMPANY, INC., GARDEN CITY, | NEW YORK 1961

Copyright Page: 'Copyright © 1961 by Richard Poirier | [. . .] | First Edi-tion'.

Binding and Dust Jacket: black cloth boards measure 8⁷⁄₁₆ × 5¾ in. (214 × 145 mm.); stamped in gold, front and spine. Yellowish white wove, unwatermarked endpapers; top and bottom edges trimmed, fore edges untrimmed. White dust jacket printed in black, red, white, and pale olive.

Contains: first book appearance of "Heads of Houses" (**C72**), on pp. 298–325.

Publication: published 17 March 1961 at $3.95; 9,000 copies printed.

B12 *THE BEST AMERICAN SHORT STORIES 1961* (1961)

[in black] T H E | [in dull red] *B e s t* | [in black] AMERICAN | SHORT STORIES | 1961 | [fancy rule] | *Edited by* | MARTHA FOLEY and DAVID BURNETT | [publisher's device] | HOUGHTON MIFFLIN COMPANY • BOSTON | [in semiscript] The Riverside Press Cambridge | [in roman] 1961

Copyright Page: 'COPYRIGHT © 1961 BY HOUGHTON MIFFLIN COMPANY'.

Binding and Dust Jacket: grayish tan cloth boards measure 8⁵⁄₁₆ × 5½ in. (211 × 140 mm.); stamped in brown on front and spine. Yellowish white wove, unwatermarked endpapers; all edges trimmed. White dust jacket printed in red, white, blue, and black.

Contains: first book appearance of "Miss Leonora When Last Seen" (**C74**), on pp. 340–67.

Publication: published 24 August 1961 at $5.50; 9,500 copies printed.

B13 *THE BEST AMERICAN SHORT STORIES 1963* (1963)

[in black] THE | [in dull red] *B E S T* | [in black] AMERICAN SHORT STORIES | [in dull red] 1963 | *and the Yearbook of the American Short Story* | EDITED BY | MARTHA FOLEY and DAVID BURNETT | HOUGHTON MIFFLIN COMPANY BOSTON | [in semi-Gothic] The Riverside Press Cambridge | [in roman] 1963

Copyright Page: 'FIRST PRINTING | COPYRIGHT © 1963 BY HOUGHTON MIFFLIN COMPANY | [. . .]'.

Binding and Dust Jacket: gray cloth boards measure 8¹¹⁄₁₆ × 5⅞ in. (220 × 150 mm.); stamped in dark gray and black, front and spine. Yellowish white wove, unwatermarked endpapers; all edges trimmed. White dust jacket printed in black, light grayish blue, and grayish pink.

Contains: first book appearance of "At the Drugstore" (**C78**), on pp. 325–53.

Publication: published 19 September 1963 at $5.50; 9,000 copies printed.

B14 *PRIZE STORIES 1965: THE O. HENRY AWARDS* (1965)

PRIZE STORIES 1965: | THE O. HENRY AWARDS | *Edited by Richard Poirier and William Abrahams* | WITH AN INTRODUCTION BY WILLIAM ABRAHAMS | DOUBLEDAY & COMPANY, INC., GARDEN CITY, NEW YORK | 1965

Copyright Page: '*Copyright © 1965 by Doubleday and Company, Inc.* | [. . .] | *First Edition*'.

Binding and Dust Jacket: light green cloth boards measure 8½ × 5¾ in. (215 × 146 mm.); spine stamped in black and gold. Yellowish white wove, unwatermarked endpapers; top and bottom edges trimmed, fore edges untrimmed. White dust jacket printed in olive-gold, dark bluish green, and black.

Contains: first book appearance of "There" (**C81**), on pp. 125–48.

Publication: published 2 April 1965 at $4.95; 9,000 copies printed.

B15 *RANDALL JARRELL 1914–1965*

B15a *Cloth Issue (1967)*

Randall Jarrell | [rule] | 1914–1965 | E D I T E D   B Y | Robert Lowell, Peter Taylor | & Robert Penn Warren | [publisher's device] | *Farrar, Straus & Giroux* | NEW YORK

Copyright Page: '*Copyright © 1967 by Farrar, Straus & Giroux, Inc.* | [. . .] | *First printing, 1967*'.

Binding and Dust Jacket: brown cloth boards measure 8¼ × 5⅝ in. (210 × 142 mm.); front blindstamped, spine stamped in gold. Yellow wove, unwatermarked endpapers; all edges trimmed; top edges stained light yellow or bluish green (no priority established). White pictorial dust jacket printed in black and orange.

Contains: first appearance of "Randall Jarrell," on pp. 241–52; book co-edited by PT.

Publication: published 29 August 1967 at $6.50; 6,500 copies printed.

B15b *Paper Issue (Noonday N332) (1968)*

Identical to **B15a** except for:

Title Page: '[. . .] THE NOONDAY PRESS | A DIVISION OF | [. . .]' .

Copyright Page: 'First Noonday Press printing, 1968'.

Paper Binding: wrapper 8 × 5⁷⁄₁₆ in. (203 × 138 mm.); lacks endpapers.

Publication: published 15 April 1968 at $2.45; 3,000 copies printed.

B16 *THE GREENSBORO READER*   (1968)

[two pages; left] *The University of | North Carolina Press | Chapel Hill* [right] *The Greensboro Reader | Edited by | Robert Watson | and | Gibbons Ruark*

Copyright Page: 'Copyright © 1968 by | The University of North Carolina at Greensboro'.

Binding and Dust Jacket: brown cloth boards measure 8¹¹⁄₁₆ × 5⁷⁄₈ in. (221 × 145 mm.); spine stamped in gold. Orange and brown decorated wove endpapers; all edges trimmed; yellow and red cloth head and tail bands. Orange and brown dust jacket printed in brown and pink.

Contains: first book appearance of "A Cheerful Disposition" (**C86**), on pp. 63–86.

Publication: published in September 1968 at $6.00; number of copies printed is unknown.

B17 *PRIZE STORIES 1969: THE O. HENRY AWARDS*   (1969)

Prize Stories 1969: | THE O. HENRY AWARDS | Edited and with an Introduction by | WILLIAM ABRAHAMS | Doubleday & Company, Inc. | GARDEN CITY, N. Y. 1969

Copyright Page: 'Copyright © 1969 by Doubleday & Company, Inc.'

Binding and Dust Jacket: gray cloth boards measure 8½ × 5¾ in. (215 × 145 mm.); spine stamped in pink and black. Yellowish white wove, unwatermarked endpapers printed gray on recto (front) and verso (back); all edges trimmed; white cloth head and tail bands. White dust jacket printed in gray, black, and purple.

Contains: first book appearance of "First Heat" (**C88**), on pp. 169–77.

Publication: published 25 April 1969 at $5.95; 9,500 copies printed.

B18   *THE WATER OF LIGHT*   (1976)

[in light grayish blue] THE | WATER | OF | LIGHT | [in black; rule] | *A Miscellany in Honor of* | *Brewster Ghiselin* | Edited by Henry Taylor | UNIVERSITY OF UTAH PRESS, SALT LAKE CITY

Copyright Page: 'Copyright © 1976 by the University of Utah Press.'

Binding and Dust Jacket: dark grayish brown cloth boards measure 9¹³⁄₁₆ × 7¼ in. (260 × 194 mm.); spine stamped in gold. Grayish blue wove, unwatermarked endpapers; all edges trimmed, unstained; brown cloth head and tail bands. Dull white dust jacket printed in light grayish blue and black.

Contains: first and only appearance of an untitled prose statement about Brewster Ghiselin and the Utah Writers Conference, p. 226; "The Whistler" reprinted on pp. 227–39.

Publication: published 2 March 1976 at $10.00; 1,200 copies printed.

B19   *THE BEST AMERICAN SHORT STORIES 1976*   (1976)

The Best | AMERICAN | SHORT | STORIES | 1976 | And the Yearbook of the | American Short Story | *Edited by Martha Foley* | [publisher's device] 1976 | HOUGHTON MIFFLIN COMPANY BOSTON

Copyright Page: 'Copyright © 1976 by Houghton Mifflin Company | [. . .] | C 10 9 8 7 6 5 4 3 2 1'.

Binding and Dust Jacket: tan cloth boards measure 8⅝ × 5⅞ in. (218 × 148 mm.); stamped in red and blue, front and spine. Yellowish white wove, unwatermarked endpapers; all edges trimmed; top edges stained blue; blue and white cloth head and tail bands. White dust jacket printed in light blue, dull red, and dark blue.

Contains: first book appearance of "The Hand of Emmagene" (**C105**), on pp. 314–32.

Publication: published 27 October 1976 at $10.00; 10,000 copies printed.

B20   *THE BEST AMERICAN SHORT STORIES 1978*   (1978)

The Best | AMERICAN | SHORT | STORIES | 1978 | [rule] | Selected from | U. S. and Canadian Magazines | by Ted Solotaroff | with Shannon Ravenel | *With an Introduction by Ted Solotaroff* | *Including the Yearbook of the* | *American Short Story* | [publisher's device] 1978 | Houghton Mifflin Company Boston

Copyright Page: 'Copyright © 1978 by Houghton Mifflin Company |
[. . .] | V 10 9 8 7 6 5 4 3 2 1'.

Binding and Dust Jacket: pale orange cloth boards measure 8⅝ × 5⅞ in.
(219 × 150 mm.); stamped in medium purple and black, on front and
spine. Yellowish white wove, unwatermarked endpapers; all edges
trimmed; pale orange cloth head and tail bands. White dust jacket printed
in black and yellowish green.

Contains: first book appearance of "In the Miro District" (**C112**), on pp.
98–135.

Publication: published 24 October 1978 at $10.95; 10,000 copies printed.

B21   *THE BEST AMERICAN SHORT STORIES 1980*   (1980)

The Best | AMERICAN | SHORT | STORIES | 1980 | [rule] | Selected
from | U. S. and Canadian Magazines | by Stanley Elkin | with Shannon
Ravenel | [rule] | *With an Introduction by Stanley Elkin* | INCLUDING
THE YEARBOOK OF THE | AMERICAN SHORT STORY | [pub-
lisher's device] 1980 | Houghton Mifflin Company Boston

Copyright Page: 'Copyright © 1980 by Houghton Mifflin Company |
[. . .] | V 10 9 8 7 6 5 4 3 2 1'.

Binding and Dust Jacket: tan cloth boards measure 8⅝ × 5⅞ in.
(218 × 150 mm.); stamped in deep red and black, front and spine. Yellowish white wove, unwatermarked endpapers; all edges trimmed; yellow
cloth head and tail bands. Tan dust jacket printed in deep red and black.

Contains: first book appearance of "The Old Forest" (**C114**), on pp. 356–
408.

Publication: published 20 October 1980 at $12.95; 12,000 copies printed.

B22   *THE RANDOM REVIEW 1982*   (1982)

[all within a box of single rules topped by a decorative ornament] THE |
RANDOM | REVIEW | 1982 | Edited by | Gary Fisketjon | and Jonathan
Galassi | [publisher's device] | RANDOM HOUSE • NEW YORK

Copyright Page: 'Copyright © 1982 by Random House, Inc. | [. . .] | 9 8 7
6 5 4 3 2 | First Edition'.

Binding and Dust Jacket: red quarter-cloth and tan paper boards measure
8½ × 5¾ in. (215 × 145 mm.); front blindstamped with publisher's de-

vice, spine stamped in silver. Yellowish white wove, unwatermarked end-papers; all edges trimmed; red and white cloth head and tail bands. White dust jacket printed in red, black, and tan. Also issued in paper wrapper like dust jacket.

Contains: first book appearance of "The Gift of the Prodigal" (**C118**), on pp. 234–56.

Publication: published 26 March 1982; 27,000 copies printed, of which 7,000 were issued in cloth at $14.50 and 20,000 in paper wrappers at $3.95.

B23 *EUDORA WELTY: A TRIBUTE*   (1984)

[in red] Eudora Welty: A Tribute | [in black] *13 April 1984* | [strong red rule, 102 mm.] | [in black] Cleanth Brooks | Bernard Malamud | William Maxwell | Reynolds Price | William Jay Smith | Elizabeth Spencer | Peter Taylor | Anne Tyler | Robert Penn Warren | Richard Wilbur | Printed for Stuart Wright : 1984

Copyright Page: '[. . .] | *Eudora Welty,* Copyright © 1984 by Peter Taylor | [. . .]'.

Paper and Binding: white wove paper, watermarked '[in script] Arches'; *binding 1:* full calf boards measure 9½ × 6⅛ in. (240 × 155 mm.); stamped in gold; front and back contain a frame of gold single rules, 231 × 143 mm.; spine: '[at top, three horiz. rules, 15 mm.] | [vert.] EU-DORA WELTY A TRIBUTE | [at base, three horiz. rules, 15 mm.]'; *binding 2:* quarter-leather and English Cockerell paper boards measure 9⁷⁄₁₆ × 6¼ in. (239 × 158 mm.); spine stamped in gold, '[vert.] EU-DORA WELTY [ornament] A TRIBUTE 13 APRIL 1984'; *binding 3:* flexible paper boards, 9⅜ × 6 in. (234 × 152 mm.), with French marbled-paper jacket glued to spine, with white paper label on front, printed in black, 'Eudora Welty: A Tribute'.

Contains: first and only appearance of "Eudora Welty," pp. 31–32.

Publication: published 13 April 1984 on the occasion of the 75th birthday of Eudora Welty; 75 copies printed, of which two in full calf were reserved for Welty and Wright; 23 copies in quarter leather (10 reserved for contributors); and 50 in flexible paper boards for public sale, at $50.00 each.

Note: Contributions are signed by their respective authors in all copies. Five additional copies of Taylor's contribution were issued separately in a white wire-stitched wrapper, printed in black on front, '*Eudora Welty* | PETER TAYLOR | *Reprinted from* | EUDORA WELTY: A TRIBUTE | Stuart Wright, 1984'; at the conclusion of PT's text, this notice is printed: 'THIS IS NUMBER [arabic numeral supplied in red ink] OF FIVE COPIES'.

B24 *THE FUGITIVES, THE AGRARIANS AND OTHER TWENTIETH-CENTURY SOUTHERN WRITERS* (1985)

[in black, swelled rule, 85 mm.] *The* | FUGITIVES, | *The* | AGRARIANS | *And Other* | *Twentieth-Century* | *Southern Writers* | [swelled rule, 85 mm.] | [illus. of unicorn] | CHARLOTTESVILLE | Alderman Library | UNIVERSITY OF VIRGINIA | 1985

Copyright Page: 'Individual contributions copyright © 1985 | by Ben C. Toledano, Peter Taylor, and | George Garrett.'

Paper Binding: saddle-stitched in green wrapper, 8 × 5¼ in. (203 × 134 mm.); printed in black and white.

Contains: first and only appearance of "Reminiscences," pp. 17–21.

Publication: published for distribution on the occasion of an exhibition of Fugitive and Agrarian material, at the Alderman Library, Univ. of Virginia, 28 April 1985; not for sale.

B25 *TENNESSEE: A HOMECOMING* (1985)

[two-page title; left] TENNESSEE: [right] A HOMECOMING | [left] PHOTOGRAPHERS | [24 lines in roman caps, list of photographers] [right] EDITOR | JOHN NETHERTON | ASSISTANT EDITOR | MARTHA WEESNER | ASSISTANT PICTURE EDITOR | ANN CLEMENTS BORUM | ESSAYS BY | WILMA DYKEMAN *Tennessee: Where Yesterday Walks With Tomorrow* | PETER TAYLOR *Tennessee Caravan: 1920–1940* | JOHN EGERTON *Laurel Bloomery to Gold Dust: A Tennessee Journey* | THIRD NATIONAL CORPORATION

Copyright Page: '[. . .] | Essays copyright © 1985 by the authors. | [. . .]'.

Binding and Dust Jacket: quarter-bound in deep reddish brown and black cloth boards, 12½ × 9¼ in. (322 × 246 mm.); front and spine stamped in gold. Light gray wove, unwatermarked endpapers; all edges trimmed, unstained; white cloth head and tail bands. White pictorial dust jacket printed in shades of pink and purplish pink, and black.

Contains: first and only appearance of an essay, "Tennessee Caravan: 1920–1940," pp. 59–66.

Publication: published in September 1985 at $29.95; 10,000 copies printed.

B26 *IMAGES OF THE SOUTHERN WRITER* (1985)

Images of the Southern Writer | Photographs by Mark Morrow | [publisher's device] The University of Georgia Press Athens

Copyright Page: '© 1985 by the University of Georgia Press | [. . .] | 89 88 87 86 85 5 4 3 2 1 | [. . .]'.

Binding and Dust Jacket: reddish brown cloth boards measure $8\frac{5}{8} \times 11\frac{1}{8}$ in. (229 × 291 mm.); spine stamped in black. Blackish blue wove, unwatermarked endpapers; all edges trimmed, unstained; cloth head and tail bands have alternating blue and white stripes. White pictorial dust jacket printed grayish blue and black.

Contains: first and only publication of PT's untitled comments on his family and work, p. 78.

Publication: published 19 November 1985 at $24.95; 3,000 copies printed.

C

Contributions to Periodicals

C1 "Tenth Annual Meet at Washington [and] Lee: Taylor Represents Central." *Central High Warrior* (Central High School, Memphis, Tenn.), 18 (1 Nov. 1934), 1. Unsigned article.

Note: Although Taylor is listed as a reporter for the *Central High Warrior* in the issues of 21 Sept., 5 Oct., 2 Nov., 16 Nov., and 29 Nov., and 14 Dec. 1933 and 11 Jan. 1934, he was unable to identify any given piece in these issues as his own. For the 1934 winter-spring semester he is not listed on the masthead and apparently did not serve on the newspaper staff at all. For the first semester of 1934–35, he served as assistant editor of the *Central High Warrior*, including the seven issues dated 4 Oct., 19 Oct., 1 Nov., 22 Nov., and 13 Dec. 1934 and 10 Jan. and 24 Jan. 1935. His unsigned articles and editorials listed here were identified with his assistance.

C2 "Taylor Returns from Convention: Enjoys Social Life of College." *Central High Warrior*, 18 (10 Nov. 1934), 1. Unsigned article.

C3 "News Writing Class Formed at Central." *Central High Warrior*, 19 (10 Feb. 1935), 1. Unsigned article.

Note: Taylor, as "Hillsman Taylor," served as editor of the *Central High Warrior* for the winter-spring semester of 1935, including the issues for 10 Feb., 21 Feb., 7 March, 21 March, 4 April, 17 April, and 2 May.

C4 "Editorial Comments." *Central High Warrior*, 19 (10 Feb. 1935), 2. Unsigned. Includes four titled paragraphs: "Thanks to the Ex-Editor"; "Columbus Day"; "A Queer Sense of Humor"; and "No Library!"

C5 "Editorial Comments." *Central High Warrior*, 19 (21 Feb. 1935), 2. Unsigned. Includes three titled paragraphs: "Procrastination"; "Lucky Linguists"; "Everybody's Rainy Day." The editorial page also includes an *"Editor's note"* introducing a poem by Louise Emerson, "1915–1935."

C6 "Lord Chatterfill'd's Letters to His Son." *Central High Warrior*, 19 (21 Feb. 1935), 2, 3. Unsigned humor column.

Note: This column was inspired by Lord Chesterfield's *Letters to His Son*, which Taylor had read between his junior and senior years. Taylor recollects that he originally intended to title his column "Lord Jesterfield's Letters to His Son," a play on the name of Central High's principal C. P. Jester. Also found in this particular letter is a humorous poem by Taylor, "A Lay of Ancient Rome," partly in Latin.

C7 "Two Special Warriors This Semester." *Central High Warrior*, 19 (7 March 1935), 1. Unsigned article.

C8 "Editorial Comments." *Central High Warrior*, 19 (7 March 1935), 2. Unsigned. Includes four titled paragraphs: "Chronic Objectors"; "Save and Have—"; "Quiet Please!"; and "A Real Desire for Knowledge."

C9 "Lord Chatterfill'd's Letters to His Son." *Central High Warrior*, 19 (7 March 1935), 2. Unsigned humor column.

C10 "Editorial Comments." *Central High Warrior*, 19 (21 March 1935), 2. Unsigned. Includes three titled paragraphs: "'These Shall Endure'"; "A Defense of the 'Chronic Objectors'"; "'A Boy's Will Is the Wind's Will?'".

C11 "Lord Chatterfill'd's Letters to His Son." *Central High Warrior*, 19 (21 March 1935), 2. Unsigned humor column.

C12 "Editorial Comments." *Central High Warrior*, 19 (4 April 1935), 2. Unsigned. Includes three titled paragraphs: "Floors for Feet"; "'To the Opera, James!'"; and "Thieves in Our Midst."

C13 "Lord Chatterfill'd's Letters to His Son." *Central High Warrior*, 19 (4 April 1935), 2. Unsigned humor column.

C14 "Editorial Comments." *Central High Warrior*, 19 (17 April 1935), 2. Unsigned. Includes two titled paragraphs: "'Only God Can Make a Tree'" and "Two More Issues."

C15 "Editorial Comments." *Central High Warrior*, 19 (2 May 1935), 2. Unsigned. Includes two titled paragraphs: "Unseemly Conduct" and "Let the Curtain Fall"; a third editorial paragraph, "Let We Forget—", is signed "J.K."

C16 "Lord Chatterfill'd's Letters to His Son." *Central High Warrior*, 19 (2 May 1935), 2, 4. Unsigned humor column.

Note: This column contains two poems by PT, one untitled, the other, "The Central Clock," a parody of Mother Goose.

C17 "The Party." *River* (Oxford, Miss., literary magazine), 1 (March 1937), 4–8. Story.

Note: "The Party" is Peter Taylor's first published story. *River* editor Dale Mullen wrote of Taylor, then a sophomore at Vanderbilt University, in Nashville, Tenn.: "If Peter Taylor is not wholly successful in his attempt, his work nevertheless deserves attention for the simple reason that he has attempted to express, if not for himself at least for his story's people, that search for the continuity between man and the cosmos for which Hart Crane sought and for which every sincere writer must seek if he wishes to write literature" (p. 32).

C18 "The Lady Is Civilized." *River*, 1 (April 1937), 50–54. Story.

Reprinted in *Hika* (Kenyon College, Gambier, Ohio, undergraduate literary magazine), 5 (Oct. 1938), 5–8, 22, 24.

C19 "Story of His Life Written by the Poet." *Commercial Appeal* (Memphis, Tenn.), 7 Nov. 1937, sec. IV, p. 10. Review of John Gould Fletcher, *Life Is My Song*.

C20 "'Harvest Comedy' Is Latest Frank Swinnerton Work." *Commercial Appeal*, 27 Feb. 1938, Sec. IV, p. 9. Review of Frank Swinnerton, *Harvest Comedy*.

C21 "Philip Gibbs' New Novel, 'Great Argument,' Presents Picture of Britain's Political Strife." *Commercial Appeal*, 10 April 1938, Sec. IV, p. 9. Review of Philip Gibbs, *Great Argument*.

C22 "McIntyre Writes Last Word on Art of the Racketeer." *Commercial Appeal*, 31 July 1938, Sec. IV, p. 9. Review of John T. McIntyre, *Signing Off*.

C23 "The Jew in Changing American Scene Is Background of Brilliant First Novel." *Commercial Appeal*, 4 Sept. 1938, Sec. IV, p. 9. Review of Sidney Meller, *Roots in the Sky*.

C24 "Charming Mystic Quality Flows through Novel of Modern Holland." *Commercial Appeal*, 2 Oct. 1938, Sec. IV, p. 9. Review of David Cornel DeJong, *Old Haven*.

C25 "A Departure." *Hika*, 5 (Dec. 1938), 15, 23. Story.

C26 "The Bishop's Passing." *Southwestern Journal*, 18 (1939), 79. Poem.

Reprinted in *Hika*, 6 (May 1939), 8; *Commercial Appeal*, 6 Aug. 1939, Sec. IV, p. 9.

C27 "The American Legion Retires." *Kenyon Collegian* (Kenyon College, Gambier, Ohio, weekly student newspaper), 12 Jan. 1939, p. 2. Poem.

C28 "I Am Their Music: Behold Their Sitting Down, and Their Rising Up." *Hika*, 5 (Feb. 1939), 15. Poem in four numbered parts.

C29 "The Assumptions of the Grave." *Hika*, 5 (Feb. 1939), 21–22. Review of Allen Tate, *The Fathers*.

C30 "Memorable Evening." *Hika*, 5 (March 1939), 5–7, 20–21. Story.

C31 "Symposium." *Hika*, 6 (May 1939), 8. The second of "Two Poems" which appear in this number of *Hika*. The first is "The Bishop's Passing," first published in the *Southwestern Journal* (see **C26**).

C32 "Mimsy Were the Borogoves." *Hika*, 6 (June 1939), 40–41. Dream-story.

Note: Taylor is listed in this number of *Hika* as a staff writer, and his classmate Robert T. S. Lowell as an associate editor. The contributor note on page 30 states that Peter Taylor, "who is a fine short story writer, turns to a newer form of prose composition, *the dream*." The dream was in fact real and literal and concerns Percy Shelley, Dr. Johnson, and Lord Byron.

C33 "The Elopers." *Hika*, 6 (June 1939), 21. Poem.

C34 "The Furnishings of a House." *Kenyon Review*, 1 (Summer 1939), 308. Poem.

C35 "The Life Before." *Hika*, 6 (Nov. 1939), 8–11, 28–30. Story.

Note: PT was on the *Hika* editorial staff for the 1939–40 school year.

C36 "Middle Age" (later titled "Cookie"). *Hika*, 6 (Dec. 1939), 5–7, 27. Story.

As "Cookie" in *WT, ML, CS.* Reprinted in the *New Yorker*, 24 (6 Nov. 1948), 29–32.

Hika] *New Yorker*

Middle Age] MIDDLE AGE
5.1 She was too good for less human treatment] *deleted*
5.2–3 He *had* to go home for dinner these two nights a | week, for the sake of his conscience.] [*initial T*] TWO nights a week, he *had* to be | home for supper, and some weeks, when his conscience was especial-|ly uneasy, he turned up three or four times.
5.3 Tonight] ~,
5.4 beans] ~,
5.5 meat] ~,
5.6 cured fat] fat
5.9 God,] ~!
5.9 himself, "Where] himself | "That's fine. Where
5.14 My] my
5.16 overcoat] ~,

5.17   She took his coat]   It was his | lightweight "fall coat," which she had | brought down from the attic only two | weeks before. She took it

5.18 *et passim*   dining room]   ~-~

5.18   chair]   ~,

5.21   it]   ~,

5.22   which]   that

5.23   He]   It

5.27   said]   ~,

5.28   with]   ~some small

5.29–30   O, let's not," he | said with a smile]   Oh, let's not. " He smiled back

5.32   Alright]   All right

5.33–34   table | cloth]   tablecloth

5.38–39   country meat for | himself.]   side | meat.

5.39   leaned]   bent

5.40   head]   ~ over

5.47–48   brown | and buxom negress]   brown, buxom Negress

5.49   sat]   set

5.50   mistress]   mistress's plate

5.53 *et passim*   Yesuh]   Yessuh

5.53   said]   ~,

5.54   door]   doorway

5.57   He said,]   he said.

5.65   switch]   row of switches

5.66–68   it twice and her hus-|band said "Ah . . . Ah," with each increase of | light in the room.]   the second switch, and the light | overhead was increased. She pushed the | third, and the wall lights by the side-|board came on. With each increase of | [. . .] room her husband said, | "Ah . . . fine. | . . . Ah . . . fine."

5.69   least]   ~, it

5.69–71   it | was an old house with | twelve-foot ceilings]   the house was | old and high-ceilinged.

5.73   walnut, but the paper]   pine, with door fac-|ings and a narrow chair rail. The paper | above the chair rail

5.77   candle-sticks]   candlesticks

5.81   safe]   press

5.81   cutglass ware]   cut-glass-|ware

5.83   frosted glass]   ~-~

5.84   by]   from

6.1   metal]   "antiqued"

6.1   table;]   ~,

6.7   A rump roast?]   *deleted*

6.9 *et passim*   'iss]   ^~

6.9–10   blink-|ing. And]   ~, and

6.10   sat]   set

6.11   it's . . . well]   it's— Well,

6.11   cold water]   ~-~

6.15   mistress]   ~,

6.19 *et passim*   c'd 'a]   could a

6.20 *et passim*   alright]   all right
6.21   burnt]   burned
6.22   Well]   Wull
6.23   'a']   ^~^
6.24   a]   the
6.28   through]   ~,
6.28–29   'a' | *mercy*]   ^~^~!
6.30   ¶ His]   *no* ¶ [*initial H*] HIS
6.31   carved.]   ~— an | outside piece, because it was more done. | He cut several slices, until he came to | one that seemed rare enough for him-|self.
6.32   'chillun']   ^~^
6.34   That's]   Now, that's
6.34   rotten.]   ~!
6.36   week.]   ~!
6.36   goin']   going
6.38   please.]   ~, honey!
6.38   so.]   ~, and | that's all I need to know.
6.39   But they're]   They're
6.40   plate. He]   ~. | ¶~
6.42   ¶ "I]   "These beets are fine," he | said. Then, after swallowing, "I
6.42   that," he said. "They]   that! He
6.44   med.]   ~^
6.46   out.]   ~, if I | hadn't.
6.47   moment]   ~,
6.47   as he shook]   shaking
6.48   her]   ~,
6.48   rather]   even more
6.50   slightly]   somewhat
6.51   at]   of
6.51   please. She]   please, honey," she said. "She
6.52   children.]   ~ and a husband who is | far from well.
6.58   quivering]   ~,
6.59   began]   started
6.60   said]   ~,
6.64   eat]   ~ her dinner
6.70   hand]   ~,
6.72   col' on y']   cole on ya
6.74   mistress']   mistress's
6.75   "Butter't while 't's hot, now."]   "Now gwine butter't [. . .] hot."
6.84   He heard f'om]   *He* heard fom
6.84   The [*sic*]]   Then
6.86   she]   *deleted*
6.87   over it]   about | its edges
6.88   *not.*]   ~!
6.97   high ceilinged]   ~-~
6.98   'em, Cookie?"]   'em? What are you | goin' to send them youngons, Cookie?"
7.1   plate]   ~,

7.5 | but] *deleted*
7.5–6 | gray-|ed] graying
7.7 | thought," she said, "that]   thought that
7.8 | hens."]   ~," she said.
7.9 | fine," he said.] fine."
7.11–12 | and]   ~—" | "Ah . . . fine." | And
7.21 | Finally]   ~,
7.22 | and]   ~,
7.23 | full]   ~,
7.25 | No! . . .]   ~! ʌ
7.27 | call-bell]   ~ʌ~
7.29–30 | yel-|low,]   ~ʌ
7.34–35 | something like, | "Psss]   some-|what like "Psss
7.43 | what, boss-]   whut, Boss-
7.44 | And]   ~,
7.44–45 | that]   from what various people | are saying around~
7.47 | What's]   Whut's
7.53 | "She never has understood niggers."]   "She doesn't realize that they | really eat it up."
7.54 | b'ilin']   bilin'
7.54 | said]   ~,
7.58 | please. Don't]   please, honey, don't
7.61–62 | brought | the coffee in.]   brought in the coffee. | She brought it on a tray|—two cups and a kitch-|en pot.
7.63 | sat]   set
7.63 | plate]   place
7.64 | them]   ~,
7.64 | sat]   set
7.64 | table cloth]   tablecloth
7.67 | boss]   Boss
7.70 | Y' mean 'at new]   Mean 'at gal
7.72 | wife whom]   wife, who
7.73–74 | Cookie. | ¶ "Yes,"]   Cookie. Then he looked at Cookie. "Yes,"
7.74 | said, "he]   said, almost absent-|mindedly. "He
7.75 | country."]   ~. That's it—Hattie! | That's her name."
7.76–77 | "Yesuh," | "She's]   "Yessuh. She's from out on Pea Ridge." | ¶ "She's
7.78–79 | Cookie?" | ¶ "Yesuh,"]   Cookie?" | ¶ "'Cep *he* didn't get | her from Pea Ridge." | ¶ "No, Cookie?" | ¶ "She put in a year for | some ladies he know out near the sand-|banks, and—" | ¶ "She's a drinker, ain't she, Cookie?" | ¶ "Yessuh."
7.80 | laugh]   ~,
7.81 | 'uz]   ʌ~
7.82 | chu'ch]   chuch
7.84 | I']   ~ʌ
7.86 | shoved]   pushed
7.91 | her]   huh
7.91 | ter'ble]   terble

7.91–92   eny-|body an' ev'ybody]   anybody and everybody

27.1–3   ¶ "Menfo'ks' runnin' roun' at night. Doc Palm-|mer's a bach'lor-man, an' she say see'em all | 'bout his place sooner 'r later."]   ¶ "Them ladies from the sandbanks—|she say they's in an' out his place mos' | any night. Doc Palmer's a bachellorman, | sho, but Hattie say hit ain't jus' Doc | Palmer! They comes there to meet the | ladies— all sorts of menfolks, married or | not. She say she see 'em *all* 'bout his | place sooner or later.

27.6   it."]   ~," he said.

27.12   time]   ~,

27.16   y']   ya

27.17   hid her face in her napkin.]   brought her napkin up | to cover her face.

27.19–20   kitchen," she | said]   kitchen."

27.23   moment]   ~,

27.26   already . . .]   all right—

27.27   about," he said.]   about."

27.28   hear]   have heard

27.29   said]   was saying

27.30   that.]   ~!

27.31   upitiness]   uppitiness

27.37–38   in a series of pats over | her hair.]   over her hair | in [. . .] pats.

27.41–42   ¶ "She ought to be given her walking papers."]   ¶ "Now I think of it, perhaps she ought | [. . .] papers." | ¶ "I'll look into the matter."

27.42   and]   ~, as he drank it, | he

27.44   you]   *you*

27.44   some day]   someday

27.50–51   Jackson to do an oper-|ation."]   "Murphreesboro."

27.51–52   "Appen-|dectomy," he said, "County Hospital."]   "There's | a lot of red throat over | there."

27.54   aloud]   ~,

27.56–57   "She honestly | loves us all, I'm sure. She's a member]   "She's too much a member

27.57–58   family. She may have spoken out of turn tonight, | but she would never speak outside the family."]   family, and I | know she'll be full of re-|morse for speaking out of | turn like that."

27.59   at her directly and she smiled.]   directly into | her eyes, and she smiled confidently.

27.60   for]   because

27.65–66   said. | ¶ And Cookie said, "Yes'm Mizz."]   said, and [. . .] | Mizz." | ¶ He [. . .] him.

New Yorker]   *WT*

MIDDLE AGE]   COOKIE

29.33   called,]   ~:

29.51   band."]   ~." "You're much too good to me," he said, now lower-|ing his eyes to his plate.

29.54   Negress]   Negro woman
29.65–66   good to | me."]   good . . ." This time he | left the sentence unfin-
ished.
29.81   Ah]   ah
29.93   frosted-glass]   ~ ∧ ~
29.112   a]   ~ small
29.127   *mercy*]   *mércy*
29.136–37   postcards." She began to taste her food.]   post cards?" | ¶ "She [
. . .] food, taking [. . .] visible.
29.138   rotten!"]   ~ he said
29.144–45   Please, hon-|ey!]   Please don't!
29.146   busy."]   ~. Young people don't have time for letters."
29.148   plate.]   ~. | "They're young."
29.149   ¶ He]   ¶ "What's that got to do with it?" he said. "They | ought
always to have time for you." He
30.8   up]   to Nashville
30.11   "No, no,"]   "No, there's no need in my going,"
30.33   bread]   cornbread
30.36 *et passim*   fom]   from
30.46   "Sho]   "Sho-God
30.69   new,]   ~∧
30.128   a Negro]   Cookie
31.49–50   sand-|banks]   sand banks
31.66   talker.]   ~. She's full of lies.
31.67   talk]   lies
31.68   talk]   lie
31.69   town]   Thornton
31.71   talk]   lies
31.73   sandbanks]   sand banks
32.1   ya!"]   ~! But she's a liar, ain't she, | Boss-Man?"
32.13   be]   get
32.13   about."]   ~. Even Cookie knows the girl's a liar."
32.30   given her walking papers."]   sent on | her way after talking like that."
32.35   "She]   "Why, she
32.42   Murfreesboro]   Huntsboro
32.48   but]   yet
32.51–52   a mem-|ber]   one of us—too much one member

WT]   *ML*

154.17   *mércy*]   *mercy*
161.4   and]   ~,
162.24   walk | wall

ML]   CS

389.1   *no* ¶]   ¶
391.12   cut-glassware]   ~^~
392.8   Post cards]   Postcards
392.9   post cards]   Postcards
393.13   of]   on
394.5–6 young-|ons]   young'ons
397.14   and,]   ~^
398.27   wall]   walk

C37   "For the School Boys." *Hika*, 6 (Feb. 1940), 10. Poem.

C38   "A Chapter from 'The Wanderer.'" *Hika*, 6 (March 1940), 5–9, 23.

Note: The Wanderer was the title of a novel Taylor worked on during his student years at Kenyon College but never completed.

C39   "Literary Studies: The Work of H. Miller." *Commercial Appeal*, 17 March 1940, Sec. IV, p. 10. Review of Henry Miller, *The Cosmological Eye*.

Note: Although this review was published under Taylor's name, it was principally written by his Kenyon College classmate Robie Macauley.

C40   "Late in the Afternoon." *Hika*, 6 (April 1940), 20. The first of "Three Poems" by PT.

C41   "The Americans." *Hika*, 6 (April 1940), 20. The second of "Three Poems" by PT.

C42   "Modest Virgin." *Hika*, 6 (April 1940), 20. The third of "Three Poems" by PT.

C43   "Winged Chariot." *Hika*, 6 (June 1940), 5–7, 16–20. Story.

Note: This story was substantially revised and published later as "Sky Line" (**C45**).

C44 "A Spinster's Tale." *Southern Review*, 6 (Autumn 1940), 270–92. Story. *LF, CS.*

Reprinted in *Short Story Masterpieces*, ed. Robert Penn Warren and Albert Erskine (New York: Dell, 1954), pp. 484–508; *Reading Modern Short Stories*, ed. Jarvis A. Thurston (Chicago: Scott, Foresman, 1955), pp. 311–30; *Fiction, Form, and Experience: 30 Stories with Essays*, ed. William M. Jones (Boston: Heath, 1969), pp. 50–60.

Southern Review] *LF*

271.6   euphemistic appelative]   euphemism
271.12   maroon]   rose
271.21   full length]   ~-~
272.7   middy-blouse]   ~-~
272.17   still-born]   stillborn
272.22   working]   busy
272.23   dark-rimmed]   *deleted*
273.19   suggestion]   request
273.24   negro]   Negro
274.5   2]   *no section number*
274.18   clean]   fresh
274.18   needlepoint]   *deleted*
274.23 *et passim*   negro]   Negro
274.29   faint]   indistinct
274.33   with:]   ~;
275.13   3]   *no section number*
275.16   had made]   made
275.32   from]   ~ the
276.28–29   long, | swerved,]   long
277.5   until]   till
277.6   towards]   toward
277.12   I quickly]   so I
277.16–17   There wasn't a sound or a motion in the | house.]   The house was quiet and still.
278.3 *et passim*   whiskey]   whisky
278.8   rehearsed]   repeated
279.3   And soon I dropped off to sleep.]   *deleted*
279.4   4]   *no section number*
279.11   gabbling]   chattering
280.1   Mr. Speed's]   his
280.22   indistinctly]   ever so faintly
280.27   chair, my breath came short]   chair; breathless
280.28–29   the kings | and queens and castles and knights]   kings and castles
280.30   oblivion]   indifference

280.34 casually] blandly
281.4 halfgrown] half-grown
281.8 panelling] paneling
281.9 hatrack] hat rack
282.2 his] Mr. Speed's
282.3 5] *no section number*
282.9 day-dreaming] daydreaming
282.29–30 fear. | ¶ But] fear. But
283.3 *et passim* moustache] mustache
283.5 looking glass] ~-~
284.18 stair] stairs
285.9–10 uncon-|scious] not unaware
285.21 poise] ~,
286.6 the suburban park] Centennial Park
286.13 "Yes, I still like to play games."] "Games are *so* much fun."
286.18 blonde] blond
286.28 pince nez] ~-~
286.31 town] Nashville
287.29 pleated] *deleted*
288.11 6] *no section number*
289.13 oscillated] *deleted*
289.14–15 my possible com-|prehension] anything I could comprehend.
289.15 and] ~ so
289.20 contemning [*sic*]] condemning
289.26 stories. Indeed, it] stories, and it
290.33 open;] ~,
291.1 hatrack] hat rack
291.10 house-number] ~ ^ ~
291.18 stair] stairs
291.19 a] the

LF] *ML*

108.14 hearth] ~,
109.9 rooms,] ~^
110.18 boardeers'] boarder's
111.8 given] ~ to
112.16 that] *deleted*
113.15 each] *deleted*
114.9 stairway] ~,
115.27–28 It was the first incident that I had ever | actively carried off.] *deleted*
116.10 parlor] ~,
116.15 conluded [*sic*]] concluded
117.21 place] ~ on his head,

117.25–26   holding his lapels with his tremendous | hand,]   *deleted*
118.40   almost]   *deleted*
123.6   house]   ~,
129.13   has]   have

ML]   CS

165.1   *no* ¶]   ¶
165.12   alway]   always
165.14–15   tone: | ¶ "Son]   ~: "~
166.32 *et passim*   gas-logs]   ~ ∧ ~
166.33   hearth,]   ~∧
166.35   mirror-panels]   ~ ∧ ~
167.6   looking-glass]   ~ ∧ ~
167.14   way-a]   way—a
167.27   there.]   ~,
167.33   rooms, the]   ~∧ ~
168.11   had had]   had
169.12   boarder's]   boarders'
170.8   to]   *deleted*
170.9   Finally]   ~,
171.9   top coat]   topcoat
171.22   doubted]   ~ that
172.9   church]   Church
172.23   again]   ~,
172.27   each]   ~ topic
172.31   persistent,]   ~∧
173.25   stairway,]   ~∧
174.21   upon]   up on
174.23 *et passim*   whisky]   whiskey
175.6–7   said: | ¶ "Tomorrow]   ~: "~
175.14   off.]   ~. It was the first | incident that I ever actively carried off.
175.26   drinking]   ~,
176.1   parlor,]   ~∧
176.20   moves]   ~,
177.17   place on his head]   place,
177.20   turned,]   ~, holding his lapels with his tre-|mendous hand,
178.26   burnt]   burned
179.2   talking]   ~ almost
179.22   half wakeful]   ~-~
180.10   good-bye]   Goodbye
180.13   looking-glass]   ~ ∧ ~
183.6   boys]   Boys
183.21   chagrin]   ~,
183.30   house,]   ~∧

184.8   Finally my uncle]   Finally, my uncle,
184.9–10   side-|burns]   ~,
184.13   over-serious]   overserious
184.22–23   brothers: | ¶ "Young]   ~: "~
184.32–33   easiness: | ¶ "Yes]   ~: "~
185.5   old maid]   ~-~
187.19   dinner time]   dinnertime
188.29   young-]   ~^
189.20   trees,]   ~^
191.2   have]   has

C45   "Sky Line." *Southern Review*, 6 (Winter 1941), 489–507. Story. *LF*, *ML*.

Reprinted in *The House of Fiction: An Anthology of the Short Story with Commentary*, ed. Caroline Gordon and Allen Tate (New York: Scribner's, 1950), pp. 604–17.

Southern Review] *LF*

489.9   hump-backed]   humpbacked
489.18 *et passim*   nigger]   Negro
490.3 *et passim*   stair]   stairs
490.26   grey]   gray
490.32   at]   to
491.5 *et passim*   "catch"]   ^ ~ ^
491.13   pant]   pants
491.22   his eyes]   *deleted*
492.29   under side]   underside
493.13 *et passim*   desk-mate's]   deskmate's
493.14   "For Sale"]   ^ ~ ~ ^
493.15 *et passim*   Church]   church
493.16 *et passim*   desk-mate]   deskmate
493.18   scab,]   ~;
493.20   So the]   The
494.30   mouth,]   ~^
494.33 *et passim*   roof tops]   rooftops
495.13   foot stool]   footstool
495.29   the rocking]   *deleted*
496.25   school-house]   schoolhouse
497.4   court room]   courtroom
497.14   lombardy]   Lombardy
497.17   "'Hold [. . .] straight!'"]   "^~ [. . .] ~^"
498.30   streetcar]   street car

499.9–10 high-|schoolers] ~ ʌ ~
499.15 licence] license
499.28 whiskey] whisky
500.16 very] mighty
501.11 try . . .] ~. . . .
502.1 school,] ~;
502.20 grey] gray
502.28 in] *deleted*
503.8 Allright] All right
503.14 O] Oh
503.32–33 "He's sound asleep." And the voice of the little girl's mother saying:] *deleted*
504.3 tree tops] treetops
504.8 something] somewhat
504.9 blonde] brown
504.24 towards] toward
504.32 her] the
505.2 like] as
505.6 if in defiance] though to deny the possibility
505.9 care, Jim] care a snap, Jim.
505.18 They've] they've
505.18 week-end] ~ ʌ ~
505.19 longer."] ~. It's a long way up to Chicago."
505.22–23 comes | a little short] seems to catch in his chest
505.35 head,] ~;
506.16 girls] girl's eyes
506.17 browner] darker
507.7 obese figure] body
507.11 the rain] falling rain
507.16 rain drop] raindrop
507.28 hands] hand
507.29 rain drops] raindrops

LF] *ML*

84.32 neighbor] ~,
87.31 suburb,] ~;
91.24 father] ~,
92.16 *I*] I
93.7 street car] streetcar
93.22 high schoolers] ~-~
102.27 sudden,] ~ʌ

C46 "The Fancy Woman." *Southern Review*, 7 (Summer 1941), 65–92.
Story. *Lf, ML, CS.*

Reprinted in **B1**; *An Anthology of Stories from the* Southern Review, ed. Cleanth Brooks and Robert Penn Warren (Baton Rouge: Louisiana State Univ. Press, 1953), pp. 387–412; *A New Southern Harvest*, ed. Robert Penn Warren and Albert Erskine (New York: Bantam, 1957), pp. 186–209; *Modern Short Stories*, ed. Gene Baro (London: Faber, 1963), pp. 167–93; *Reading Modern Fiction: Selected Stories with Critical Aids*, ed. Winifred Lynskey, 4th ed. (New York: Scribner's, 1968), pp. 473–94; *Contemporary American Short Stories*, ed. David and Sylvia Angus (Greenwich, Conn.: Fawcett-Ballantine, 1983), pp. 59–89; *Stories from Tennessee*, ed. Linda Burton (Knoxville: Univ. of Tennessee Press, 1983), pp. 150–74.

Southern Review]   *LF*

65.1   palaver?]   ~.
65.3 *et passim*   half grown]   ~-~
65.9–10   "Not a stitch on y' have you?" she said.]   *deleted*
65.11   ear, "You like it?"]   ear.
65.12   throat, and]   throat. And
65.12–13   whispered: | ¶ "You're]   ~: "~
65.20   body, and]   body;
66.3   pumps]   ~,
66.4   heself]   herself
66.5   stalked]   marched
66.6   grabbed]   seized
66.7   the room]   her
66.18   Yet]   But
66.20   curtains.]   ~, as he had promised.
66.23   house,]   ~;
66.24   and it was all windows. But the venetian]   though it was mostly windows the Venetian
66.24–25   round, | and she]   round. She
66.26   negress]   Negress
67.5   fast]   fas'
67.10   town]   Memphis
67.14   negro]   Negro
67.21   with]   ~ any
67.22   dapple grey]   dapple-gray
67.24   slits]   chinks
67.33   to]   *deleted*
67.35   *sixty-five:*]   sixty-five:
68.1–2   *all in roman*]   *all in ital.*
68.5   noise]   sound
68.10   *sixty-five*]   sixty-five
68.12   sullenly.]   and put a pouty look on her face.
68.15   far]   well
68.30   say,]   ~^

69.17 More]   more
69.18 wild.]   ~ʌ
69.29 *et passim* stair]   stairs
70.6 drink,]   ~ʌ
70.7 saddle]   ~,
70.13 back]   ~,
71.4 pant]   pants
71.7 compassions]   ~,
71.13 girl—,]   ~ . . . ,
71.34 really]   real
71.34 and young]   and real young
72.10 *Jobe's*]   Jobe's
72.12–13 him,]   ~, for there's something wrong inside everybody,
72.20–21 wife. | ¶ All]   ~. ~
72.35 Then the]   The
73.19 a]   the
73.19 *Jobe's*]   Jobe's
74.5 listening . . .]   ~. . . .
74.6 cock fight]   cockfight
75.9 It]   it
75.10 it.)]   ~ʌ),
75.16 coming]   moving
76.2 natural colored]   ~-~
76.3 *Jobe's*]   Jobe's
76.3 *Burnstein's*]   Burnstein's
76.6 bitches]   ~,
76.16 *Jobe's*]   Jobe's
76.19 of]   from
76.26 Jackson]   ~,
76.32 me?",]   ~?"ʌ
77.19 charming,]   ~;
77.28 swore]   cursed
78.2 them,] ~.
78.11 dawn,] ~ʌ
79.4 *Louisville Lady*]   "Louisville Lady"
79.11 dollar whiskey]   ~-~
79.26–27 Billy." Then [. . .] Josie: | ¶ "George]   Billy." | ¶ Then [. . .] Josie, "George
79.32 Billy]   Roberts
80.14 What]   "~
80.15 nuts?]   ~?"
80.17 Josie cried]   cried Josie
80.27 cock fight]   cockfight
81.3 others]   other's
81.21 *Jobe's*]   Jobe's
81.23 springing]   spring
81.24 net]   ~,

81.28 models] manikins
82.15 them:] ~,
82.25 maroon and white] ~-~-~
83.31 was, "Yeah," or,] was "Yeah" or
84.2 room,] ~^
84.25 hands. Jack] ~. | ¶ ~
84.26–27 said: | ¶ "Come] ~: "~
84.27 if] If
84.29 timid] kind-a-shy
85.12 "limricks."] ^limericks.^
86.6 puny looking] ~-~
86.10 laughed,] ~.
86.21–22 *extra leading*] *normal leading*
87.3 "Thank God for small favors."] "Thank your stars you're white!" It
  was something they used to say around home when she was a kid.
87.6 laughed.] ~ and for some reason she had said, "Thank your stars
  you're white!"
87.11 table!] ~^
87.24 *this*] this
88.25 go,] ~ too,
88.32 gone!] ~.
88.35 said.] ~,
89.24 that.] ~ one.
89.35 case!] ~.
90.7 travelling] traveling
90.22 peeling potatoes] chopping onions
91.4 pleasure,] ~^
91.9 smile, and she] smile. She
91.10 again.] ~ but she couldn't take her eyes off him.
91.13 know] believe
91.13 Go away.] *deleted*
91.14 Go on out of here!"] Go away!"
91.22 bourbon] Bourbon
91.27 the gate] the white gate
91.31–32 *Louisville Lady*] "Louisville Lady"

LF] *ML*

33.15 windows] ~,
33.16 round] around
40.26 real mint] mint
41.21 difference,] ~^
42.37 Burnstein's] Bernstein's
51.11 she] She
58.10 steps] stairs
58.12 Bourbon] bourbon

ML] *CS*

134.1   *no* ¶]   ¶
136.2   windows, the Venetian]   windows the venetian
136.3   around]   round
136.27   Yeah]   yeah
137.23–24   bellowing: | ¶ "I'm]   ~: "~
138.3   jodphurs]   jodhpurs
138.6 *et passim*   whisky]   whiskey
138.23   Friend]   friend
138.25   weeping. His]   ~. | ¶ ~
138.26–27   saying: | ¶ "Boochie]   ~: "~
138.28   *girl-friends*]   ~∧~
138.29   ride." That]   ~." | ¶ ~
139.4   it]   ~,
139.8   sickly looking]   sickly-look-|ing
139.21   girl.]   ~!
139.28   arms]   ~,
139.32–33   softness: | ¶ "Now]   ~: "~
140.6–7   whispered: | ¶ "Two]   ~: "~
141.5   back]   neck
141.6   burnt]   burned
142.9   easy-goin']   ~∧~
142.22   on]   of
144.1   Amelia,]   ~∧
144.12   mint]   real ~
144.23   listening. . . .]   ~ . . .
145.10   difference]   ~,
146.27   Society]   society
146.32   Bernstein's]   Burnstein's
147.16   automobile]   automobiles
148.11   navy blue]   ~-~
149.13   him]   them
150.17   whisky]   whiskey
153.1   hard,]   ~∧
153.28   She]   she
154.15   maroon-and-white]   ~ ∧ ~ ∧ ~
156.12   She]   she
156.21   brown-and-white]   ~ ∧ ~ ∧ ~
157.3–4   [*lines centered*]]   [*lines flush left*]
157.7   He]   The boy
157.16–23   [*lines centered*]]   [*lines flush left*]
157.25–32   [*lines centered*]]   [*lines flush left*]
158.11   Gets]   Get's [*sic*]
160.19   week,]   ~.
160.32   mouth,]   ~∧

161.5–6 *normal leading*] *extra leading*
162.9 whisky] whiskey

C47 "Like the Sad Heart of Ruth" (later titled "A Walled Garden"). *New Republic*, 105 (8 Dec. 1941), 783–84. Story. As "A Walled Garden" in *HF* and *OF*.

Reprinted in *Sudden Fiction: American Short Stories*, ed. Robert Shapard and James Thomas (Salt Lake City: Gibbs M. Smith, Peregrine Smith Books, 1986), pp. 58–61.

New Republic] *HF*

"Like the Sad Heart of Ruth"] "A Walled Garden"
783.1 [*initial N*] NO, MEMPHIS IN AUTUMN] No, Memphis in Autumn
783.14 *et passim* Kate] Frances
783.18 way. You] way, you
783.21 is.] ∼ hereabouts to compare with it.
783.26 met, but my daughter now most of her friends] In her League work, no doubt. She *throws* herself | so into whatever work she undertakes. Oh? Why, of | course, I should have guessed. She simply *spent* herself | on the Chest Drive this year. [. . .] But my daughter has | most of her permanent friends
783.35 back yard—Kate's] backyard—Franny's
783.59 *et passim* Ross] Harris
783.59–63 '30, | the summer of the nationwide drought when all my flowers | died in June (*All* of them, though not one from neglect. | Young man, I worked my flowers the very day Mr. Ross | passed away.] '48 (People don't generally realize what a dreadful year that was—the worst year for perennials and | annuals, alike, since Terrible '30. Things died that year | that I didn't think would *ever* die.
783.87 months,] ∼, caring for my sick mother,
783.91 *et passim* Ellen Katherine] Frances Ann
783.39 Rye. Then at] Rye. (I wasn't to have Mother much longer, and I knew it, and | it was hard to come home to this kind of scene.) At
783.53 Ross] Harris
783.56 Ellen Katherine—that frowning little girl] Frances Ann—that scowling little creature
783.57 Kate] Frances
784.11 down—you won't believe it: she didn't come to aid me | with childish apologies, but instead she deliberately climbed] down. . . . I hope | you didn't think it too odd, my telling you all this. . . . | You won't believe it: I lay

there in the ditch and she | didn't come to aid me with childish apologies and such,

HF] *OF*

142.1   No, Memphis in autumn]   No, MEMPHIS IN AUTUMN
145.6   middy-blouse]   ~ ʌ ~
145.31   lattice work]   latticework

C48   "The School Girl." *American Prefaces*, 7 (Spring 1942), 272–76. Story.

C49   "Rain in the Heart." *Sewanee Review*, 53 (Jan.–March 1945), 23–43. Story. *LF, OF. 200 Years of Great American Short Stories*, ed. Martha Foley (Boston: Houghton Mifflin, 1975), pp. 744–59.

Sewanee Review]   *LF*

23.3 *et passim*   towards]   toward
23.23 *et passim*   streetcar]   street car
24.15–16   *all in roman*]   *all in ital.*
24.18   *all in roman*]   *all in ital.*
24.21–23   *all in roman*]   *all in ital.*
25.26   replied]   said
28.5   most mawkish]   damnedest
28.16   Jack,]   ~ʌ
28.31   shirtsleeves]   shirt sleeves
30.16   man's pair of]   pair of flat heeled
30.21   straight and not]   straight not
31.16   onct]   oncet
31.18   said]   ~,
32.32   If]   '~
32.33   bad.]   ~.'
33.14 *et passim*   negro]   Negro
33.20   negroes]   Negroes
33.31 *et passim*   paper-boys]   ~ ʌ ~
34.30   Yes. . . .]   ~ . . .
35.23–24   So where I was looking at a lot of silly clothes,]   So I went off up
    the street a way and then I come back to where I
36.25   I hate 'em]   *deleted*
36.29 *et passim*   storey]   story

38.7   busses]   buses
38.13   living-room]   ∼ ∧ ∼
38.14   table- or floor-]   ∼∧ ∼ ∼∧
38.28   endless?]   ∼.
38.31   table-cloth]   ∼ ∧ ∼
39.19   said]   and
40.9   little]   *deleted*
40.26   light that burned on her]   lights in the city below. He heard her
   switching off the two | small lamps at her
41.2   chinaberry]   china-berry
41.4–5 was dark and he could | hear her moving toward him. And the room
   being dark things]   being dark, things
41.7   tree top]   treetops
43.1   now]   *deleted*
43.6   living-room]   ∼ ∧ ∼

LF]   *OF*

70.1   drilling]   DRILLING
71.33 *et passim*   pot-belly]   potbelly
71.37   Slim?]   ∼!
73.29   pot-bellied]   potbellied
73.40   window sill]   windowsill
75.2   shirt sleeves]   ∼-∼
75.24 *et passim*   army]   Army
75.37 *et passim*   street car]   streetcar
76.15   bag-like]   baglike
76.16   flat heeled]   ∼-∼
76.26   pears]   peas
77.8   got [*sic*]]   hot
78.29   siree]   sirree
79.4   Because-they-can-boss-'em]   ∼∧∼∧∼∧∼∧∼
82.4   ridge top]   ridgetop
84.3   sad sounding]   ∼-∼
85.22   china-berry]   chinaberry
86.20–21 *September of sixty-|three*]   *December of '62*
87.14   living room]   ∼-∼

C50 "The Scout Master" (later "The Scoutmaster"). *Partisan Review*,
12 (Summer 1945), 368–92. Story. *LF, OF*.

Reprinted in **B4**.
Note: "The Scout Master" received third prize in the *Partisan Review–Dial* Contest.

"The Scout Master"]   "The Scoutmaster"
369.2 *et passim*   Bazil]   Basil
369.24   confidence]   ~.
369.25   goodnight]   good night
369.36   Whoever would have]   Who would ever
370.4 *et passim*   old fashioned]   ~-~
370.20 *et passim*   travelling suit]   suit
370.22   Troop]   troop
370.27   clasp]   embrace
370.37   Look! Look]   Look! Look! Look
370.39   myself]   I
371.9 *et passim*   goodbye]   good-bye
371.17   It'll]   "~
371.19   said,]   ~.
371.23   piece]   parting~
371.28   taxi cab]   taxicab
371.29 *et passim*   streetcar]   street car
371.32   rearview]   rear-view
371.33   two story]   ~-~
371.34   tile, or slate,]   ~∧ ~ ~∧
372.1   white gloved]   ~-~
372.3   coat suit]   suit coat
372.7   breath-taking]   breathtaking
372.19   marvellous]   marvelous
372.20   Fatherhood.).]   ~.)∧
373.2   negro red-cap]   Negro redcap
373.17   myself]   me
373.30   Often times]   Oftentimes
373.36   'Fifteen minutes have passed,']   "~ ~ ~ ~,"
374.7   blues-singers]   ~ ∧ ~
374.8   *day*]   ~ . . .
374.9   *home, sleepy*]   *home, eight o'clock sleepy*
374.13   cold-cream]   ~ ∧ ~
374.15   The]   the
374.16   In The]   in the
374.17   called,]   ~∧
374.21   old time]   ~-~
374.36   brood . . .] ~. . . .
375.1   father . . .] ~. . . .
375.4   did . . .] ~. . . .
375.17   swore]   vowed
375.27   unkind]   uncivil
375.28   in any manner]   on any occasion
375.34   elder]   eldest
375.40   Louis']   Louis's
376.10   *et passim*   negroes]   Negroes

376.14 Louis'] Louis's
376.31 sidewall] side wall
376.35 *et passim* negro] Negro
377.5 upsidedown] upside-down
377.11 *et passim* Mulberry] mulberry
377.26 scissor] scissors
377.30 "I] '~
377.32 life."] ~.'"
378.34 table cloth] tablecloth
378.9–10 all after-|noon] all-afternoon
378.22 stair] stairs
379.11 there] ~ on her teeth
379.17–18 moon | shiners] moonshiners
379.31 in the forest.] out in the woods.
379.36 Child. . . .] ~ . . .
379.37 slipped from] automatically
379.37 follow,] ~ as curious witnesses to the spectacle,
380.39 hear] overhear
381.2 *et passim* Scout Master] Scoutmaster
381.38 fourth] Fourth
382.21 socially,] ~—
383.4 string-beans] ~ ∧ ~
384.2 summerlike] summer-like
384.7 even for] for even
384.8 week-end] ~ ∧ ~
384.9 ducks for] duck to serve with the spiced-round for
384.16 just] *deleted*
385.4 I, too,] ~∧ ~∧
385.8 responsibility.] ~∧
385.12 myself] me
385.26 Jake,] ~:
385.34 men.'] ~."
385.37 Customs] customs
386.4 grey] gray
386.21 Ann] ~,
386.31 shock, and fear,] ~∧ ~ ~∧
387.3 boyfriends] boy friends
387.6 grey] gray
387.24 oil cloth] oilcloth
388.14 Oh] oh
388.19 doubt] doubting
388.34 dishevelled] disheveled
388.34 navy-blue] ~ ∧ ~
388.41 *et passim* Meeting] meeting
389.4 said] ~,
389.14 Uncle Jake would be off somewhere by himself looking out a window.
] *deleted*
389.28 what] that

389.34–35   doing, for I'd not have | known exactly how to imagine it.]   doing. I rolled over on my back | and looked up at the blank ceiling. I did not know exactly how | to imagine what they might have been doing. And I couldn't | imagine why I had been left at home this afternoon since I | was not rebuked for my failure as a chaperon. A sense of my | own ignorance overshadowed all my other dark feelings. Yet | it did seem that all my elders, who knew so much, were no | less surprised than I by Virginia Ann.

390.4   "other things"]   *other things*

390.13   things now.]   things.

390.20   sudden]   *deleted*

390.32–33   *normal leading*]   *extra leading*

390.40   stair]   stairs

391.6   Boys]   boys

391.35   it]   ~,

391.37   ones]   one's

391.38   ones]   one's

LF]   OF

3.19   Airedale]   airedale

4.17   Business Administration, Accounting, Shorthand]   business adminis- tration, accounting, shorthand

4.29   ¶ "Poor]   *no*¶

7.4 *et passim*   street car]   streetcar

7.7   rear-view]   rearview

10.10   "It's Three]   "Three

14.20   ¶ Virginia]   *no* ¶

16.17   half amused]   ~-~

17.21–22   *extra leading*]   *normal leading*

18.24–25   was: | "I]   ~: "~

18.37   Bank]   bank

19.12   grocery:]   ~,

20.16   Turnip-greens]   ~ ∧ ~

21.12   ¶ In]   *no* ¶

21.20   week end]   weekend

23.26   ¶ A] *no* ¶

24.8   utter:]   ~,

24.32   boy friends]   boyfriends

26.26   ¶ After]   *no* ¶

26.30   turban-like]   turbanlike

27.2–3   said: | ¶ "Yes]   ~, "~

28.16   Casino]   casino

29.3–4   *extra leading*]   *normal leading*

29.4   ¶ The]   *no* ¶

29.12   half way]   halfway

C51 "A Long Fourth." *Sewanee Review*, 54 (July–Sept. 1946), 396–438. Story. *LF, OF*.

Reprinted in **B5**; *The Literature of the South*, ed. Richmond C. Beatty (Chicago: Scott, Foresman, 1952), pp. 943–68, and rev. ed. (1968), pp. 914–39; *26 Contemporary American Stories* (Warsaw, Poland: Państowowe Wydawnictwo "Iskry," 1964), pp. 147–85.

Sewanee Review]   *LF*

396.28   well remembered]   ~-~
397.16   Harriet]   ~,
397.18   gravel]   ~,
397.22 *et passim*   old fashioned]   ~-~
397.22   single storey]   ~-~
397.25   walk]   ~,
398.33 *et passim*   negroes]   Negroes
399.5   a.m.]   A.M.
399.7   visit]   coming ~
399.9   into]   to
399.14   unheardof]   unheard-of
399.32   now-a-days]   nowadays
400.14   birth control]   ~-~
400.15   around]   about
401.11   in back]   in the back
401.17   rigid]   perfect
401.18   superficial]   rigid
401.22   today,]   ~;
402.6   tomatoes]   ~,
402.25   bed rooms]   bedrooms
404.9   a tremble]   ~-~
404.15 *et passim*   negro]   Negro
404.17   buff colored]   ~-~
404.21 *et passim*   negress]   Negress
405.4   self pity]   ~-~
405.18   'Cause]   'cause
406.27   tear streaked]   ~-~
406.32   negro's]   Negro's
407.27–28   singu-|larness]   singularity
408.14 *et passim*   whiskey]   whisky
409.22   fair headed]   ~-~
409.25   travelled]   traveled
410.6 *et passim*   travelling]   traveling
410.7   taste)]   ~),
410.23   family.]   ~?
411.19   said]   ~,

412.18–19   Heav-|ens']   Heaven's
414.4   Several years]   Years
414.6   Yes. . . .]   ~ . . .
414.30   significantly, "—have]   significantly—"have
415.23   Golf Club]   golf club
417.24   stove]   range ~
418.1   cocoanut]   coconut
418.15   appreciation]   ~,
418.33   playing;]   ~.
419.2   *Barbara Allen*]   "Barbara Allen"
419.8   did]   seemed to
419.10   semi-circle]   semicircle
420.19–20   Oxford Book | of Verse]   *Oxford Book of Verse*
421.14–15   *Bar-|bara Allen*]   "Barbara Allen"
423.1   little-nephew]   ~ ʌ ~
423.15   own]   *deleted*
423.29   discipline]   ~,
424.29   States]   states
424.32   responsible]   ~,
424.33   sweat-shopper]   sweatshopper
425.33   sorry]   so ~
426.9 *et passim*   week-end]   ~ ʌ ~
426.20   for Harriet to]   that Harriet should
429.8   a.m.]   A.M.
429.24   moustache]   mustache
429.33   handmirror]   hand mirror
430.5   gingerale]   ginger ale
432.2   Goodbye]   Good-bye
433.1   Heavens']   Heaven's
433.13   turned-out]   ~ ʌ ~
433.20   platonic]   Platonic
435.5   stood]   stoods [*sic*]
433.16   enquiry]   inquiry
436.23   grey]   gray
436.28   mouldy]   moldy
437.28   or]   nor

LF]   *OF*

130.1   five years]   FIVE YEARS
130.2 *et passim*   BT]   B.T.
130.26   middle-age]   ~ ʌ ~
131.1 *et passim*   coupé]   coupe
131.1   War]   war
131.2   gas-rationing]   ~ʌ~
131.14   storey]   story

131.20 complaint:] ~,
131.31 picking-up] ~ ∧ ~
132.23 ¶ Harriet] *no* ¶
132.27 three] 3
133.33–34 So she | began to think of all her blessings.] *deleted*
133.38 ¶ She] *no* ¶
135.2 picked-up] ~∧~
135.17 *et passim* week-end] weekend
136.13 Army] ~,
136.33 ¶ When] *no* ¶
137.5 a-tremble] atremble
137.2 tech] tetch
138.39 female-things] ~ ∧ ~
139.35 turn-to] ~ ∧ ~
140.27 them] ~,
141.7 ¶ People] *no* ¶
141.27 semi-public] semipublic
142.36 ¶ It] *no* ¶
143.16 *et passim* make-up] makeup
143.29 man-like] manlike
145.39 *et passim* week-end] weekend
146.4 ¶ The] *no* ¶
146.8 club] Club
147.28 ¶ After] *no* ¶
148.19 reckon] reckin
148.34–35 Harriet had | hesitated to stop beyond the door sill.] *deleted*
149.4 Ambrosia] ambrosia
149.11 ¶ Among] *no* ¶
152.9 Grandpa] grandpa
152.19 ¶ At] *no* ¶
155.23 the] and the
156.4–5 *extra leading*] *normal leading*
158.17 ¶ The] *no* ¶
159.3 ¶ Most] *no* ¶
159.16 teaching-fellow] ~ ∧ ~
160.15 ¶ The] *no* ¶
160.19–20 vague, like | [. . .] dreaded, to Harriet.] vague to Harriet, | [. . .]
   dreaded.
162.31 now. . . .] ~ . . .
163.11–12 *extra leading*] *normal leading*
164.36 Love] love
165.15 *et passim* back door] backdoor

C52 "Allegiance." *Kenyon Review*, 9 (Spring 1947), 188–200. Story. *LF,
ML, OF.*

Kenyon Review] *LF*

192.31 know. . . .] ~ . . .
195.20–21 presum-|ably] presently
195.33 would. . . .] ~ . . .
197.27 goodbye] good-bye
198.16 An [*sic*]] And

LF] *ML*

59.1 COME IN] Come in
59.4 mid air] ~-~
60.23 wrist;] ~.
61.37 enquiries] inquiries
62.6 "*quiet*"] ∧~∧
63.14 pulled-out] ~ ∧ ~
64.35 speaks] ~,
65.37 would . . .] ~. . . .
66.3 dull colored] ~-~
66.7 and] And
66.28 coal black] ~-~
68.19 tiptoe] tip-toe
69.15 tea time] ~-~
69.26 cleanswept] clean-swept
69.27 halflight] half-light

ML] *OF*

192.1 Come in] COME IN
192.3 three, four steps] three steps
192.4 mid-air] midair ·
192.8 tea,] ~∧
193.8 lamp-shade] lampshade
193.21 said . . .] ~. . . .
193.22–23 young lady-|hood] ~-~
193.30 Cousin Ellen] cousin, Ellen
193.34 absent-minded] absentminded
194.8 wrist.] ~;
195.26 take-care-of] "~ ∧ ~ ∧ ~"
196.1 *quiet*] "quiet"
196.9 Englishmen] ~),
196.17 drawing-room] ~ ∧ ~
197.8–9 to so completely quit her country as I seem to | have done. Ah, I
  know . . . I know] to know . . . I know

199.31 angel-entertained-unawares] ~ ^ ~ ^ ~
199.33 for-no-reason-at-all] ~ ^ ~ ^ ~ ^ ~ ^ ~
200.14 would. . . .] ~ . . .
200.23 them! And] them, and
201.9 coal-black] ~ ^ ~
201.17 world famous] ~-~
201.24 saying:] ~,
202.27 *et passim* tea-time] teatime
203.10 tip-toe] tiptoe
204.22 clean-swept] cleanswept
204.24 place] ~,

C53 "Casa Anna." *Harper's Bazaar*, 82 (Nov. 1948), 137, 208, 211–212, 214–218, 224. Excerpt from *A Woman of Means*, a novel in progress.

Harper's Bazaar] *WM*

CASA ANNA] *untitled*
137.2–3 in their | top bureau drawer] —Laura's in her top . . . drawer, Bess's in the secret compartment of her desk.
137.6 purse.] ~ | or sometimes under the strap of an evening gown.
137.18 something.] ~. For instance: "What do men | think of a girl who late-dates?"
137.18 what] whatever
137.19 said] answered
137.21 outright,] ~ what they meant
137.22 stepsisters] ~,
137.23 They] Laura
137.24 their] her
137.26 Island.] ~. Bess had autographed | pictures from a dozen movie stars on her wall, and | she had souvenir menus from restaurants in New | Orleans and one printed in Spanish from Mexico City.
137.26 for] became
137.28–29 dress-|ing table] vanity
137.34 But] but
137.43 funny paper] ~-~
137.47 men] ~,
137.51 elevator);] ~,
137.69 asked] ~,
137.79 into] back to
137.81 grandpapa] own | father
208.36–37 Colby, you | mean] Colby —Bill, you mean
208.40 Marietta's."] ~. Ap-|parently he thinks she's the bee's knees."
208.100 beaux] beaus

208.102   awhile]   a while
208.104 *et passim*   shirt sleeves]   shirtsleeves
211.8   sleeves]   ~,
211.16   thus]   ~,
211.22–23   board-|inghouse]   boarding house
211.36–37   lik-|ing it here]   "~ ~ ~"
211.58   died!—]   ~ . . .
211.72   Quint. . . .]   ~.
211.100   house]   ~. *new material*, 20.7–23: In [. . .] while
211.105   hall]   ~,
211.113   stairs]   ~,
211.145   boardinghouse]   boarding house
211.163   room]   ~,
212.30 *et passim*   long distance]   ~-~
212.39   eyes]   eye
212.47   cinch]   clinch
212.47–48   *normal leading*]   *extra leading*
212.102   lockers]   ~,
212.109   another]   ~,
212.127   name]   ~,
212.129   talking]   ~,
214.5   Sunday-school]   School
214.11   somewhere]   ~,
214.32   board]   ~,
214.39   cheeks]   ~,
214.49   We]   As we
214.49   lobby]   vestibule
214.49–50   the apart-|ment]   our boarding
214.50   and he]   he
214.52   neighbor]   roomer
214.55   apartments | rooms
214.56   our apartment]   the rooms
214.60   living-room window]   front window of his room,
214.97   diaries.]   ~. *new material*, 40.16–49.23: I [. . .] hardware."
215.148   that]   the
216.32   stranger]   ~,
216.38   hurt]   ~,
216.51   get up and go]   ~-~-~-~
216.60   class]   ~,
216.95   strangeness]   ~,
216.119   head]   ~,
217.54   leaving]   ~,
217.56   slipcovered]   slip-covered
218.90   midmorning]   mid-morning
218.93–94   *extra leading*]   *normal leading*
218.139   him]   Father

224.30   ¶ "Oh]   ¶ I blushed, and then with a sudden self-assurance I teased her, saying, "~
224.31   Suddenly]   Presently
224.40   Did—]   ~ . . .
224.43   blushing.]   ~ again.

C54   "The Death of a Kinsman." *Sewanee Review*, 57 (Winter 1949), 86–119. Play. *WT, ML, OF.*

Reprinted in *Craft and Vision: The Best Fiction from the Sewanee Review*, ed. Andrew Lytle (New York: Delacorte, 1971), pp. 332–65.

Sewanee Review]   *WT*

86.1   ¶ *It*]   *no* ¶
86.6 *et passim*   *stairwell*]   *stair well*
87.5   *oriental*]   *Oriental*
87.7 *et passim*   *negro*]   *Negro*
87.19 *et passim*   *grey*]   *gray*
87.34   *lady-like*]   *ladylike*
88.24 *et passim (all characters)*   MYRA: *(At*]   MYRA *(at*
88.24   *darkness.*]   ~;
88.25   *Still*]   *still*
88.25   *et passim (all stage directions)*   *Lida.)*]   ~):
88.39   *navy-blue*]   ~ ^ ~
90.28 *et passim*   *five-and-a-half*]   ~ ^ ~ ^ ~ ^ ~
92.14   a.m.]   A.M.
92.20   blood-relations]   ~ ^ ~
92.37   *(pronounced "ontee")*]   *(Prounounced* ontee.")
93.29   couldn't]   Couldn't
93.34 *et passim*   screwdriver]   screw driver
94.22   *had*]   ~,
94.37 *et passim (all stage directions)*   *(still*]   *(Still*
95.6   *(complete indifference)*]   *(Complete indifference.)*
96.1   *greeneyed*]   *green-eyed*
97.2   *holds-to*]   *holds*
97.8 *et passim*   Goodmorning]   Good morning
97.14   *(fearlessly, courageously)*]   *(Fearlessly, courageously.)*
97.36   *(in*]   *(In*
98.1   so . . .]   ~. . . .
99.36   Funeral Home]   funeral home
99.38   *(taken a-back)*]   *(Taken aback.)*
100.16–17   *Wade, and then descending the | ladder)*]   *Wade):*

101.1   Paris']   Paris's
102.14 *et passim*   Mama]   mama
103.6   tow-sacks]   ~ ʌ ~
103.12   backwards]   backward
104.25   *forward) (Cordially)*]   *forward; cordially):*
104.25–26   fine | looking]   ~-~
105.8 *et passim*   Hell]   hell
105.31   ¶ *The*]   *no* ¶
105.32   *table-lamp*]   *tablelamp*
106.26   side-hall]   ~ʌ~
106.30   business-like]   ~ʌ~
107.2   grown-ups]   grownups
107.7–8   any-|body]   Anybody
107.10 *et passim*   Goodbye]   Good-by
107.10   *sotto*]   *Sotto*
108.1   It]   it
108.1   *He*]   *he*
108.25   *but. . . .*]   ~ . . .
109.2   forever. . . .]   ~ . . .
109.3   Aunt]   aunt
109.5   age. . . .]   ~ . . .
109.14   Heaven]   heaven
110.1   *chair-arm*]   ~ ʌ ~
110.2   *her) (To Miss Bluemeyer)*]   *her; to Miss Bluemeyer):*
110.2   Ma'am]   ma'am
111.38   *chairback*]   *chair back*
112.24   think. . . .]   ~ . . .
112.28   thought. . . .]   ~ . . .
112.34   herself, (*In*]   ~ʌ *(in*
112.38   (*Pointing*]   (*pointing*
114.5   carpet bag]   carpetbag
115.15   half]   ~-
115.20–21   *Half whis-|pering*]   ~-~.)
116.1   *With*]   *with*
116.1   *loud,*]   ~ʌ
117.4–5   niece! nephew! father! son! daughter! cou-|sin!]   *Niece*! Nephew!
    Father! Son! Daughter! Cousin!
117.6   lunch room]   lunch-|room
117.24   kin folks]   kinfolks
118.26   good-bye | good-by

WT]   *ML*

112.8   "niggery" stocking]   stocking

WT] *OF*

Cast of Characters] CAST OF CHARACTERS
103.2   *stair well*] stairwell
107.13 Cousin-Harry-Wilson] ~ ^ ~ ^ ~
107.17 'Course] ^~
109.14–19 AUNT [. . .] dead.]   *deleted*
110.29 Poor] poor
111.29 screw driber] screwdriber
114.6   morn . . .] ~. . . .
129.30 CURTAIN]   *deleted*
131.30 *(pronounced eet)*]   *deleted*
132.2   grownups] grown-ups
132.11 *et passim*   Good-by] Good-bye
132.20 Yehsm] Yehs'm
142.3   *these-here*]   ~ ^ ~
149.23 Toodle-loo] Toodle-oo

C55   "Dudley for the Dartmouth Cup." *New Yorker*, 25 (28 May 1949), 24–28. Excerpt from *A Woman of Means* (then in progress).

New Yorker]   *WM*

DUDLEY FOR THE DARTMOUTH CUP]   *untitled*
24.1–52   [*initial D*] DURING [. . .] it.]   *revised, as* 68.1–69.15: [*script T*]
    THE [. . .] home.
24.53–56   ¶ My [. . .] Quint. But my]   My . . . Dudley.
24.58–59   grandmother—my mother's | mother]   grandmother
24.59   long Latin]   long
24.61–64   To [. . .] embarrass-|ment.]   *deleted*
24.64–65   stepsisters, who [. . .] eighteen,]   *deleted*
24.65   those]   these
24.66   letters from my grandmother]   letters,
24.69   and calling me a rebel.]   Whenever their mother overheard them she
    did not | hesitate to remind them that mine was an aristocratic | name and
    that their surname would be forever linked | with the beer that made their
    paternal grand-|father's fortune. There was never any resentment of | her
    reminder, however, for Laura and Bess said they | were too sensible to be
    ashamed of their origin. Laura | would lament, "Snubbed again by Old No-
    bility." | And they would put their hands together and har-|monize on the
    brewery's commercial theme song: | *Serve it bottled or on draught,* | *With your
    meals, before, and aft.* | *Drink it dark, or drink it light,* | *But drink your Lauterbach
    tonight.*

24.69   It]   ¶ ~
24.69   their beaux]   Bess Lauterbach's beaus
24.71   of]   at
24.71   them]   the girls
24.72–75   Cincinnatus, and one morning | soon after my second year began, when | I was leaving chapel, one of the older | boys]   Cincinnatus. Then it happened that I was passing out | of chapel one morning when this fellow
24.76   "How's Cincinnatus?"]   '~~?'
24.76–77   drew back]   withdrew
24.80–81   my | stepsister]   she
24.88   day,]   ~∧
24.90 *et passim*   Cincey]   Cincy
24.91–92   *extra leading*]   *normal leading*
24.92   [*initial N*] NEXT morning,]   ¶ Next morning
24.92–94   for the | streetcar at the corner by the | drugstore, dreading]   by the drug store
24.95   School]   *deleted*
24.97 *et passim*   drugstore]   drug store
24.115   and,]   ~∧
24.118   Special! Special! Special!]   ~ . . .~ . . .~.
24.125   to get to school]   *deleted*
24.126   card]   lines
24.127   late.]   ~ | to school.
24.134   a new boy and a] *deleted*
24.135–39   The days when I had moved | from one Southern city to another with | my father—before he was made an ex-|ecutive in the hardware company—now | seemed the best days of my life.]   I cursed whatever it was in me that had made | me want to be known.
24.141–42   street-|car, | and for a moment I forgot how | out of place used to feel in the summer | at my grandmother's farm with my | cousins, who lived there all the time. | Though I had been born there, they | were country boys and I was a city boy, | but I remembered now only that my | cousins could repeat my full name | without a smile.]   then something made me think of my Grand-|ma's farm in Tennessee and the summers I had spent | there with my cousins—cousins who could repeat | my full name without a smile. *added material,* 72.9–79.15: I [. . .] mistake.
24.152–53   It was | my]   And it was just
24.153   should be]   was
24.154   our]   in my
24.156   of our room]   *deleted*
24.158–59   headmas-|ter before]   headmaster. Presently
24.160–61   over," he said. "Just | go]   over. Go
24.162 et passim   session]   Session
24.163–64   sir." | ¶ The]   ~." ~
24.167   got]   gotten
24.169   me. "J-just]   ~: | ¶ "~-~
24.170   son. What's—wh-what's]   ~. . . . | ~ . . .~-~

24.173–77 new | son—A-a-anna Dudley, that is?" the | headmaster asked me. Lauterbach was | the name of my stepmother's first hus-|band.] boy . . . ? A-a-anna Dudley, that is?"

24.178–79 an-|swered,] ~∧

24.179 repetition] succession

24.181 his] the

25.4 said again] repeated

25.8 stepmother] m-mother

25.17 leaped] leapt

25.29 me,] ~∧

25.33 Yet I] I

25.35 a second] the first moment

25.37–38 What was important | was that] For this was my grand realization of my sum-|mer's dream. In a sense

25.44 And suddenly] Suddenly

25.50–52 She was my mother, | and after that day—that moment—|surely nothing could ever alter that fact.] And just as | it is not necessary to re-member to breathe in the midst | of a foot race, from that day forward mere thoughts | about her would become too tedious for me to bother | with.

25.56 boys] ~,

25.63 boldness, and added,] boldness.

25.65 then,] ~∧

25.75 times,] ~∧

25.76 haircut—two] hair-cut . . . two

25.78 reëntered] re-entered

25.79 room,] ~∧

26.2 down.] ~. *added material, 83.1–108.6:* ¶ When [. . .] school.

26.3–7 [*initial A*] AFTER that day, everything at | school seemed different; every-|thing seemed very much more impor-|tant. The student body at Country Day | School was] ¶ At school all of the student body were

26.8 That year,] This year

26.17–18 —by the | master in charge—] (~~~~~)

26.21 went on] progressed

26.26 season,] ~∧

26.28–29 Though | I was careful not to make fouls myself,] *deleted*

26.35 game,] ~:

26.37 huddle,] ~∧

26.39 Sometimes,] ~∧

26.41 and] ~ as I

26.41 made,] ~∧

26.45–46 somewhere—in Mem-|phis, or in Nashville—] somewhere,

26.46 had] would have

26.49 myself,] ~:

26.50–52 And I would | wonder what these were to | me—] What are these strangers | to me?

26.53 had gone] went

26.54 "R's"] *r's*

26.56   grade,]   ~^
26.57   to;]   ~,
26.58   boys,]   ~^
26.59–60   Am-|herst]   Dartmouth
26.60   Princeton,]   ~^
26.61   had been]   were
26.67   Atta boy]   ~-~
26.68   Cup!"]   ~!"?
26.69   care,]   ~^
26.69   I could]   could
26.70   myself—I had cared more]   myself. More
26.71–72   my step-|mother]   Mother
26.74   the house with her, and]   her house,
26.75   I had missed the Special—]   she had said, | "*Tout est fini*" and had lit
    the cigarette and since I had | ceased to marvel at our mutual dependence,
26.76   more, until now,]   ~^ ~ ~^
26.78–80   life I had lived with my step-|mother and the life I had lived among
    the | Red and Whites at Country Day.]   two spheres of my existence.
26.81   only]   simply
26.83–86   I | even wanted to win the Dartmouth | Cup, a prize awarded to the
    "best all-|round boy in the Middle School."]   *deleted*
26.86–87   So | when a]   And so the
26.87   passed]   would pass
26.88   then went away, this]   away, and this
26.90   basketball]   *deleted*
26.91   ball—]   ~,
26.93   [*initial D*] DURING]   ¶ During
26.93–94   Feb-|ruary,]   ~^
26.97   everybody]   everyone
26.100   week,]   ~^
26.101   basketball]   ball
26.103   that]   ~ I heard
26.103   was called]   called,
26.107   shots.]   ~!
26.113   shots, but]   shots. But
26.117 *et passim*   Cincey]   Cincy
26.118   It]   And it
26.118   then]   ~ that
26.120   Our]   The
26.122   guileless]   innocent
26.123   My]   ~ first
26.124   innocence,]   ~;
26.126   famous]   *deleted*
26.132   popularity—]   ~,
26.134   Cup.]   ~ for the best-all-round-boy in | the Middle School.
26.135   consider,]   ~:
26.137   Yet]   And yet

26.141 words—]   ~:
26.143 or]   ~,
26.144 game?,"]   ~?"
27.1   Originally,]   ~ʌ
27.4–5 Ten-|nessee speech gave me a]   it gave me an
27.9–10 accent," from the reeyull | Deep South."]   accent."
27.10 while,]   ~ʌ
27.13 the]   *deleted*
27.14 folk]   a so-called | Southern ~
27.15–16 I thought of St. Louis as a com-|pletely Northern place, and there]   There
27.18 as]   when
27.19–21 "My Old Kentucky | Home" or about "Old Virginny," the | state where I was born."]   the old Kentucky home or about old | Virginny the-state-where-I-was-born.
27.22 Tennessee,]   ~ʌ
27.25–30 farm, and I remembered | the old times, when I was a motherless | boy whose only vestige of a permanent | home was the farm where my mother | had grown up and where I had spent | the first ten summers of my life.]   farm and the old times.
27.33 away]   ~,
27.37 a]   some
27.40 room,]   ~ʌ
27.41–42 af-|fectations,]   ~ rather indifferently;
27.44 whether]   if
27.45 exist]   ~,
27.45 exist and whether]   exist, if there
27.54 besides]   ~,
27.55 me. Usually,]   ~. | ¶ ~ʌ
27.57–58 thought. | ¶ One]   thought. But one
27.61 through]   across
27.66 race, but]   race. But
27.67 they]   it
27.72 boy,]   ~ʌ
27.73 that, though]   ~ʌ (~
27.74 why.]   ~).
27.75–110 failures on the farm . . . happy.]   *completely revised as* 113.14–114.4: failure and [. . .] sleepy.
27.112–14 things, and after a few | days I had put them out of my head com-|pletely.]   things. Within a few days I had completely put [. . .] head.
27.114 Yet thereafter]   Yet
27.114 the]   The
27.115 always]   ~ afterward
27.121 [*initial I*]   I DID]   ¶ But I did
27.122 things, though.]   things.
27.125 playground]   playgrounds
27.128 while,]   ~ʌ

27.132   knew myself]   ~, ~,

27.135–28.22   ¶ I [. . .] good.]   *deleted*

28.23   night that year I]   night, I

28.25   February,]   ~∧

28.26–27   seven | merit badges—for metalwork]   eight Merit Badges: metal work

28.29   wood-turning]   woodturning

28.30   Music Club]   music club

28.33   Upper School]   senior

28.35   "art"]   Art

28.39   series,]   ~∧

28.42–43   "Tom Swift and | His Motorcycle,"]   *Tom Swift and His Motorcycle,*

28.45–46   was Tom | Swift and His Airship,"]   were *Tom Swift and his Air-|ship,*

28.48   also]   *deleted*

28.49   *Confidante*]   ~,

28.52–53   ap-|proached, in May]   approached in February

28.62   Day,]   ~∧

28.63–64   "the best | all-round boy"]   ~ ~-~-~-~ ~

28.64–65   school. | ¶ My]   ~. ~

28.67   aisle of the chapel]   aisle

28.67–68   plat-|form,]   ~∧

28.69   head,]   ~∧

28.71   aware,]   ~∧

28.72   her,]   ~∧

28.73   annoyance,]   ~∧

28.73   resentment,]   ~∧

28.74–75   felt that she was a stranger | and an intruder.]   wished she was not there, that she | were at home in Portland Place, that she had left me | to receive the Dartmouth Cup alone.

28.81   there,]   here

28.87–88   in-|truder—]   ~,

28.90   moved]   about

28.91–92   All at once, I looked away from her | and raised]   I raised

28.94   in to]   into

28.94   hurried]   ~ with my cup

28.95   seat,]   place

28.95   last]   very ~

28.96   exercises,]   ~∧

28.100   my classwork]   the classwork

28.101–2   afterward. | ¶ By]   ~. ~

28.102   day,]   ~∧

28.104   we were]   the street-|car was

28.105   quiet]   completely ~

28.106–7   stop, | at the corner | by the drugstore; then, suddenly,]   stop. Then all of a | sudden

28.110   alone.]   ~ and was not connected with anything else that had ever | happened to me.

28.116–18   The door flew | open, and I sprang out into the early | twilight.
] *deleted*

28.119–20   ¶ As I ran past the drugstore and up | the street to the short cut
through]   *no* ¶ As I ran up the street past the drug store and into

28.122   applauding]   pretending to applaud, and

28.123   me, and]   me. And

28.127–36   Though I was taking | the short cut through the alley, I felt that | I
would never *really* get home—that | by my new strength I was freed from |
the old necessity to call some definite | house my home, or to name some
region | as the place as from, or to say that | one person or another was mother
or | grandmother or father to me. And | I kept thinking how]   *deleted*

28.136–38   hadn't ever real-|ized before]   hadn't realized

28.139   happiness and]   happiness or

C56   "Porte-Cochère" (later "Porte-Cochere"). *New Yorker*, 25 (16 July
1949), 21–24. Story. *WF, OF.*

Reprinted in *The Survival Years,* ed. Jack Salzman (New York: Pegasus, 1969),
pp. 302–9.

New Yorker]   *WT*

PORTE-COCHÈRE]   PORTE-COCHERE

21.2   birthday,]   ~.

21.3–4   Clifford from Dallas, Ben Jun-|ior from Cincinatti.]   Clifford came
all the way from Dallas. Ben Junior came only from Cincinatti.

21.6 *et passim*   weekend]   week end

21.8   Ben,]   ~ who was

21.13–17   all, Clifford the real | man amongst us. There were cer-|tain things
Clifford could understand. | Clifford was lawyer and knew some | history,
knew]   all. "Clifford's the real man amongst | them," he said to himself,
hating to say it but needing | to say it. There was no way knowing what went
on in the | heads of the other children, but there was certain | things Clifford
did know and understand. Clifford, | being a lawyer, knew something about
history—about | Tennessee history he knew, for instance,

21.19   Overton.]   ~ and could debate with you the question of whether or |
not Andy Jackson had played the part of the coward | when he and Chucky
Jack met in the wilderness that | time.

21.20–21   They | were all]   All of his grown-up children were

21.23 *et passim*   cochère]   cochere

21.24   pagoda]   ~ stuck out

21.25   was]   ~ directly

21.27–28   and | the boys called the drive-under]   called it the drive-under
and the children used to | call it the portcullis

21.34   focussed]   focused

21.55 It] Now it
21.56 now,] *deleted*
21.95 quality,] ~—strange
21.96 rarely closed them | seldom drew the draperies
21.105–6 Aunt | Nelson. She] his great-aunt Nell | Partee. Aunt Nell
21.114 *et passim* Nelson] Nell
21.116 Nelson's] Nell's shackly
21.123 barber shop] barbershop
21.127 presently] *deleted*
21.132–34 But he longed to have Cliff | come and talk to him about whatever | he would. Did] But did
21.151 Old Ben] the old man
21.165 half covering] ~-~
21.183 doorjamb] door jamb
21.188 Old Ben] his father
22.12 having?"] ~ in Texas?"
22.28 began,] ~:
22.30 travelled] traveled
22.36 moment,] ~:
22.40–41 Is someone holding you, Clif-|ford?" Old Ben] He

22.93 we] *we*
22.103 dark] darker
22.111 speech,] ~∧
22.120 house—"] ~. . . . You still are!"
23.69 half full] ~-~
24.2 plowline] plow line
24.10 plowlines] plow lines
24.19 own] ~ bearded
24.21–22 turned about | and the] and made a quick military turn. | The
24.23 three] ~ sharp
24.23 back.] ~ . . .
24.27 woollen] woolen
24.46 were] would be
24.48 were] would be
24.50 were] would be
24.97–98 in their wrath his children | would] his wrathful, merciless chil-dren | might
24.113 half darkness] ~-~
24.116 steps,] ~∧

WT] *OF*

PORTE COCHERE] ~-~
49.1 Clifford and Ben Junior] CLIFFORD AND BEN Jr.
49.3 *et passim* Junior] Jr.

49.4 *et passim*   week end]   weekend
50.2–3 *et passim*   porte-|cochere]   ~ ^ ~
50.23   Laura Nell's]   Nell's
51.29–30   chair | back]   chairback
54.27–28   mo-|ment:]   ~,
58.12 *et passim*   Pike]   pike
58.14   barber shop]   barbershop

C57   "A Wife of Nashville." *New Yorker*, 25 (3 Dec. 1949), 42–61. Story. *WT, ML, CS.*

Reprinted in **B6**; *An Approach to Literature*, ed. Cleanth Brooks et al., 4th ed. (New York: Appleton-Century-Crofts, 1964), pp. 263–76; *The Best of the Best American Short Stories, 1915–1950*, ed. Martha Foley (Boston: Houghton Mifflin, 1952), pp. 328–52.

New Yorker]   *WT*

42.4–5   months | that is.]   months.
42.35   go away, go away!]   go away!
42.60   Negress]   Negro girl
42.98   dishes. Before]   ~. | ¶ ~
42.124–25   *extra leading*]   *normal leading*
42.173   order]   ~,
42.175   said]   *said*
43.51   away,]   ~,
43.54 *et passim*   travelling]   traveling
43.58   women's]   women
43.61   whizzing]   *whizzing*
43.72   But without]   Without
43.72   hesitation]   ~, however,
43.75   *think*]   think
43.118 *et passim*   weekends]   week ends
44.5–6   eggs for | each of them in a different way]   the breakfast eggs differ-|ently for each one of them
44.8   pampered the boys]   was pampering his | sons
44.35   *Ma'am*]   *ma'am*
44.36   often afterward she told]   afterward she had often | to tell
44.43   had actually]   actually had
44.52   and]   ~,
44.55   tried]   had ~
44.56   perhaps]   possibly
44.62   till]   until
44.89   had reappeared]   reappeared
46.36   babies]   baby boys

46.68   right,]   ~ʌ
46.99   a divorce]   divorce
46.102 *et passim*   quarrelling]   quarreling
46.126–27   not with smiles but with | tears]   with tears instead of smiles
48.18   nothing]   little or
48.23–24   *extra leading*]   *normal leading*
48.29   her]   hers
48.33   him,]   ~;
48.35–39   other hunting | friends of his, among whom were the | very richest men in Nashville. "Among | the wealthiest in the whole South, for | that matter," said John R.]   other rich hunting friends that he had.
48.45–48   owned horses and dogs, which | he kept at his friends' stables and ken-|nels. And then his friends began to take | him]   acquired a few dogs and a horse of his own. | With his friends he began to go
48.49–51   not | deep-sea fishing in the Gulf, he was | deer-hunting in the State of Maine.]   not | deer hunting [. . .] Maine, he was deep-sea | fishing [. . .] Gulf.
48.57   automobile,]   ~ʌ
50.19–20 *et passim*   Low-|der]   Tol-|liver
52.12–13   as master of hounds | here and horse judge there!"]   with the | hound and hunt set."
52.51   Havemeyer]   Hines
54.6   Thornton,]   ~ʌ
54.42   nightwork]   night work
55.1   hands,]   ~ʌ
55.44–45   "How We Cook | in Tennessee"]   *How We Cook*]   *in Tennessee*
56.1   Parkes']   Parkes's
56.10   reconciliation]   ~,
56.17–18   attrac-|tion to rich people,]   choice of friends,
56.104   shrivelled]   shriveled
58.3   *I*]   I
58.63 *et passim*   depression]   Depression
59.5–6   were no longer rich | men.]   had suffered the same financial reverses that | John R. had.
59.6   their]   the Lovells'
59.8   a while]   awhile
59.8   they | the changes
59.33   were]   was
59.39   temporary,]   ~ʌ
59.62   woollen]   woolen
60.20   showed]   had shown
60.61–62   one | interest and only]   *deleted*
61.31   University]   university
61.47   mistake.]   ~, that the boys were getting big | enough to think about their manly dignity, and that | she would have to take that into consideration.
61.49   though]   although
61.50   feelings']   feelings

62.1   But the]   The
63.5   Ma'am]   ma'am
63.5   small,]   ~, unreal,
63.15–16   door-|jamb]   door jamb
64.18   even moved]   moved
64.34   Mother]   mother
64.45   announced to]   told
64.46   Jess]   ~ McGehee
64.62   carrying-on]   ~ ʌ ~
65.55   reflected]   demonstrated
65.56   loneliness of people]   lonesomeness that people felt
66.6   Jess's]   Jess McGehee's
66.21   Jess's]   Jess McGehee's
66.36   carefully | carefuly [*sic*]

WT]   *ML*

70.1   Jess]   ¶ ~
76.1   After]   ¶ ~
78.1   county]   country
81.26   After]   ¶ ~
85.7   praying,]   ~ʌ
87.22   Jess]   ¶ ~
93.15   When]   ¶ ~
99.20   carefuly]   carefully

ML]   *CS*

280.1   *no* ¶]   ¶
282.22   left]   ~ them
285.21 *et passim*   week ends]   weekends
291.18   inter-urban]   interurban
291.32   country]   county
292.8   times, mutual]   times and the new times,
293.33   a "certain]   "a
294.31   But,]   ~ʌ
297.18   praying]   ~,
297.24   baldheaded]   bald-headed
301.23   said]   ~ that
302.7   P.-T.A.]   P.T.A.
305.32   absent]   ~-
306.2   *as*]   as
306.9   mother]   Mother

C58 "Uncles." *New Yorker*, 25 (17 Dec. 1949), 24–28. Story.

C59 "Their Losses." *New Yorker*, 26 (11 March 1950), 24–30. Story. *WT, ML, CS.*

Reprinted in **B7**.

New Yorker]   *WT*

24.4   as it]   when it had
24.12   there]   in there with her aunt
24.13   out,]   ∼∧
24.16   saying.]   ∼. The train had | jerked to a standstill.
234.18   moment,]   ∼∧
24.21   nightcap]   cap
24.35 *et passim*   travelling]   traveling
24.44   moment,] . ∼∧
24.62   instant,]   ∼∧
24.77   "business people"]   ∧∼–∼∧
24.137   end—]   ∼:
25.21   Ma'am]   ma'am
25.29–30   laugh-|ing]   and she laughed
25.32–33   who still | stood]   was still there
26.122   desk,]   ∼∧
27.10   a'mighty]   a'might
27.81   Presently,]   ∼∧
27.90   Ma'am]   ma'am
28.6   keep]   carry
28.62   worth-while]   worthwhile
28.118 *et passim*   marvellous | marvelous
29.59   country,]   ∼—they hate the country | so,
29.60   Jew. | ∼. They dare | not.
30.95   *me*]   me
30.121   Presently,]   ∼∧
30.34–35   smoke, with a puzzled ex-|pression in her eyes and laughing
   ] smoke. There was a [. . .] eyes, and she was laughing

WT]   *ML*

3.12–13   train had | jerked to a standstill.]   train, which [. . .] stood motion-
    less.
12.13–14   pulled [. . .] but | apparently]   apparently with-|out

21.4–5 I really loved them,] *deleted*
23.8 up,] ~.

ML] *CS*

343.1 At] ¶ At
343.11–12 which [. . .] stood motionless.] had jerked to a standstill.
344.34 business-people] ~ ∧ ~
350.20–21 apparently [. . .] brush] pulled [. . .] but
351.11 brown-and-gray] ~ ∧ ~ ∧ ~
352.20 Pattys'] Patty's
355.18 young-ladyhood] ~ ∧ ~
357.18 we | I really [. . .] ~
357.26 Senators | senators
359.6 up.] ~,

C60 "What You Hear from 'Em?" *New Yorker*, 26 (10 Feb. 1951), 31–
38. Story. *WT*; *ML*; *CS*.

Reprinted in *The Anchor Book of Stories*, sel. and ed. by Randall Jarrell (Garden
City, N.Y.: Doubleday Anchor, 1958), pp. 113–30; *Stories from the* New Yorker,
1950–1960 (New York: Simon and Schuster and London: Gollancz, 1960), pp.
191–205; *Modern Short Stories: The Uses of Imagination*, ed. Arthur Mizener
(New York: Norton, 1962), pp. 594–609, rev. ed. (1967), pp. 676–91, 3d ed.
(1971), pp. 764–79, 4th ed. (1979), pp. 816–31; *The Modern Talent*, ed. John
Edward Hardy (New York: Holt, Rinehart & Winston, 1964), pp. 121–37; *The
Sense of Fiction*, ed. Robert L. Welker and Herschel Gower (Englewood Cliffs,
N.J.: Prentice-Hall, 1966), pp. 119–31; *American Short Stories*, ed. Eugene
Current-García and Walton P. Patrick, 3d ed. (Glenview, Ill.: Scott, Foresman,
1976), pp. 566–80; *Stories of the Modern South*, ed. Benjamin Forkner and Pat-
rick Samway (New York: Bantam, 1977), pp. 327–42.

New Yorker] *WT*

31.1 WHENEVER someone] Sometimes people
31.3 she didn't] but she wouldn't
31.8 she'd ask] she would ask. And, [. . .] louder:
31.14 It] ¶ It
31.15 the] Aunt Muncie's
31.16–17 For a num-|ber of years, Aunt Munsie was] She was, for | at least,
31.21 would] was willing to
31.29 Thad] ~ Tollier

31.35   that is.]   once and for all.
31.36   promised her]   actually given her | their word
31.36–38   For | ten years, she hadn't seen them to-|gether,]   She had not seen them together for ten | years,
31.63   washpot]   wash pot
31.69   wouldn't]   would never
31.95–96   look | here]   look-a-here
31.109   grass.)]   ~, and the ground packed hard in little | paths between the flower beds.
31.114 *et passim*   whiskey]   whisky
31.123 *et passim*   goodbye]   good-by
31.125–30   rail. (The [. . .] house.)]   rail. And [. . .] house.)
31.136–40   (The iron fence, | with [. . .] died.]   If the | children had not gone too far ahead, he might even | draw their attention to the iron fence which, with [. . .] died.
31.141   SUCH]   But such
32.4–5   high-but-|ton]   high button
32.7   street, the]   street, down the
32.8   step]   ~,
32.18–19   yard fences | already gone and]   *deleted*
32.38   Grasping]   Seizing
32.39   decidedly]   heavy,
32.40   pulled]   hauled
32.75   real]   particular
32.86   friends]   ~ and connections
32.130   before, and]   before. And
32.29   and Memphis and]   or in Memphis or
33.30   This]   It
33.34   fence sometimes.]   fence.
33.49   these]   those
33.69   seen,]   ~∧
33.70   of,]   ~∧
33.80   would.]   ~. Not ever.
33.120   more.]   ~. Not since we got the vote.
33.121   'most]   most
33.133   Ford-and-Lincoln]   ~ ∧ ~ ∧ ~
34.2   and, indirectly,]   ~∧ ~∧
34.69   Suddenly]   Then
34.76   Munsie. Miss]   ~. | ¶ ~
34.85   Ralph]   ~ bother to
34.92   Tollivers']   Tollivers
34.93   pulling]   to tug
34.94   wagon]   ~ on
34.102   make,]   ~;
34.103   or none]   did they? Or at least none
34.104   tell both]   tell
34.104   and]   ~ tell

34.105   and]   ~ tell
34.108   first-hand]   firsthand
34.108   But, of course,]   ~^ ~ ~^
34.111–12   much. She used to tell him | she]   much. She [. . .] that she
34.113   was]   ~ there ever anybody
34.119   wasn't]   was not
34.123   home,]   ~, where their granddaddy had owned land and
34.124–25   Will or | Thad]   they
34.126   could just]   could
34.138   matter;]   ~,
35.5   Will]   ~ Tolliver
36.10   the rainy season]   when the sheep-rains would begin
36.28   She's]   Mama's
36.34   gona]   gonna
36.37–38   throw | back her hand]   toss her | head about
36.39   out at]   all the way out to
36.41   wasn't]   was not
36.45 *et passim*   quarrelled]   quarreled
36.79   mock-orange]   ~ ^ ~
36.93   city]   town
37.25   city]   town
37.50   After]   And after
37.124–26   explosively, | "Now, g'wine! G'wine! G'wine! | G'wine widja!," and
  swinging]   at the top of her voice and | swinging
37.130   direction]   ~. "Now, g'wine! G'wine | widja!" she shouted after
  them.
38.3   steps]   porch
38.34   sense]   mind
38.62   Square,]   ~^
38.64   folks]   ~ the way | they liked her to and
38.77   up.]   ~:
38.78   say]   says
38.87   off. Aunt]   off. Then Aunt
38.93   The]   Indeed, these
38.100   never]   ~ again
38.101   yard again.]   yard.
38.114   old]   extreme ~
38.116   about]   ~ dates and
38.116   and]   even her voice lost some of the rasping quality that it | had
  always had, and in general

WT]   *ML*

28.1   But]   ¶ ~
31.23   Thornton]   ¶ ~

33.32   Leonora]   Florence
34.28   Leonora]   Florence
35.17   "Is]   ¶ ~
39.5   Lucrecie]   ¶ ~
42.6   That]   ¶ ~
44.7   Crecie]   ¶ ~
45.11   pickers]   pickets [*sic*]
46.21   That]   ¶ ~

ML]   *CS*

310.17   out]   ~,
311.23 *et passim*   whisky]   whiskey
311.25   good-by]   goodbye
312.11–12   *extra leading*]   *normal leading*
312.20 *et passim*   Square]   square
315.11   Factory Town]   factory town
316.26   They]   they
316.35 *et passim*   Florence]   Leonora
318.3   Lucille]   Miss
321.9   bood-read]   ~ ∧ ~
321.12   her that]   her
324.34   youngon]   young'on
325.25   pickets]   pickers

C61   "Two Ladies in Retirement." *New Yorker*, 27 (31 March 1951), 26–34, 36, 38, 40, 42, 44–45, 48–52. Story. *WT, OF.*

New Yorker]   *WT*

26.37   Womanlike]   Woman-like
26.40–71   ¶ Her [. . .] absurd."]   *deleted*
26.72   But]   By everyone, her [. . .] absurd." But
26.86–27.17   ¶ When [. . .] penniless.]   *deleted*
27.63–69   The [. . .] Nashville.]   *deleted*
27.74–80   The [. . .] different.   *deleted*
27.88–28.61   ¶ But [. . .] nephew.]   *deleted*
28.90 *et passim*   marvelled]   marveled
28.91   ¶ He]   *no* ¶
28.98–151   His [. . .] shirt.]   *deleted*
28.180   Tollivers']   Tollivers
30.32–33   field-|hand]   ~ ∧ ~

30.56–123   Flo [. . .] room?]   *deleted*

31.45 *et passim*   Nate]   Bert

32.88 *et passim*   cardroom]   card room

32.152–54   Some [. . .] cradle.]   *deleted*

32.179 *et passim*   quarrelled]   quarreled

33.26   state-capitol]   ~ ^ ~

34.3–4   despairing of making out the title | there,]   *deleted*

34.59 *et passim*   marvellous]   marvelous

34.81 *et passim*   débutante]   debutante

34.95–36.113   ¶ Miss [. . .] sale.]   *deleted*

36.117   Ma'am]   ma'am

38.8   different-size]   ~ ^ ~

38.27–28   *card-|room*]   ~ ^ ~

40.12–14   *all in ital.*]   *all in roman*

40.32–41   ¶ Ever [. . .] night.]   *deleted*

40.42   As]   ¶ ~

40.43–44   there was no language left for | her to use]   she | thought of the life she had left in Nashville

40.44   Nashville]   there

40.59   Queen]   queen

42.49–50   sup-|pertime]   supper time

42.54   *et passim*   Nate's]   Bert's

44.46   placemats]   place mats

44.54–45.3   The [. . .] last.]   *deleted*

45.4   frightened her, nonetheless. And]   ¶ And

44.34 *et passim*   James']   James's

48.60   lapin]   *lapin*

49.9   dark-green]   ~ ^ ~

52.37–38   table (the cheese toast just | would not get done!),]   table,

52.49   Bert.]   ~. There [. . .] important lessons.

WT]   *OF*

163.1   Some Nashville wit]   Some Nashville Wit

164.6   Woman-like]   Womanlike

169.10   old-timy]   old-time

174.5–6   Betty. | ¶ "It]   ~. "~

177.13   grownups]   grown-ups

183.12–13   expitation, sin and expiation, | but]   expiation, but

183.30–184.1   card | players]   cardplayers

184.18   *card* room]   *cardroom*

185.10   Why, *what*]   ~ ^ ~

190.5   slew-foot]   slewfoot

191.11   card room]   cardroom

193.14–16   Amy . . . shoulders.]   *deleted*

195.24 simple-minded] simpleminded
195.28 three-quarters] ～∧～

C62 "Bad Dreams." *New Yorker*, 27 (19 May 1951), 32–42. Story. *WT*, *ML*, *OF*.

New Yorker] *WT*

32.17–18 his wife, a thorough-|ly sensible and easy-going sort of woman] Mrs. James Tollier
32.23 *et passim* James'] James's
32.29–32 all | the rest of the Tollier family, which in-|cluded three] her three
32.58 *et passim* Nate] Bert
32.108 *et passim* Nate's] Bert's
32.110 preëminent] pre-eminent
32.114 didn't] did not
32.153 unsealed] unceiled
32.165–66 command-|ed] said
33.24 before,] ～ too,
33.89 had] ～ done
33.113 nursery!] ～.
35.36 puppylike] puppy-like
35.146 leftover] left-over
36.39 quarrelled] quarreled
36.61 wasn't] was not
35.105 well established] ～-～
37.56 smart,] ～∧
38.53 more] heaps～
38.57 showed it.] seemed | to have sunk back into their sockets.
38.130 shrieking] noise
38.141–42 baby except that she found no baby | there] baby—except [. . .] there,
39.14 to] on
39.34 to] on
39.38–39 com-|manded] demanded
39.42 to] on
39.49 woolly] wooly
39.66–67 Nate handed her the baby | without hesitation.] Bert let her take the baby from him.
39.83 other] ～,
39.86 gently on the back] be-|tween the shoulder blades or sometimes gently stroking | her little baby
39.118 Why, Nate] . . . Nate [*sic*]
39.119 All] ¶ ～

40.24–25 Em-|maline] his wife

40.28 He was out of the depths of it, anyway.] Or, anyway, he [...] it anyway.

40.36 help] ∼ none

40.45 he] Bert

40.46 her.] ∼. "What in hell you mean?"

40.76 The] Now the

40.81–82 underwear? | ¶ It] ∼? ∼

40.84 She] ¶ ∼

40.108 Momentarily,] *deleted*

40.115 the] such a

40.133 had] after

40.149 What] ¶ ∼

40.161 Suddenly] Now

40.170 half darkness] ∼-∼

40.171 focussed] focused

40.179 pigeonlike] pigeon-like

40.188 Somehow,] *deleted*

40.191 Baby,] ∼;

41.20 started] begun

41.21 him then] him

41.21 she] ∼ now

41.23 door now] door

41.23 what] the sort of thing

41.37 now, he had said,] *deleted*

41.52 be] go

41.97 hadn't] had not

41.97 leash] ∼,

41.112 up] from her nightmare

41.119 would] ∼ have to

41.120 would] ∼ have to

42.14–15 It seemed to go *quat-plat, quat-plat,* | *quat-plat.*] It went "quat-plat, quat-plat," like any old coun-|try rocking chair.

42.18 The fact was that] For

42.30 couldn't] could not

42.31 And on] On

42.43 privy and found] privy, to find

42.54–55 He | could think] *deleted*

42.56 tomorrow—] ∼,

42.60 And so he] He

42.64–65 *extra leading*] *normal leading*

42.70–71 silent-|ly and] *deleted*

42.74 there in] in

42.78 And if] If

42.78 wasn't] was

42.81 Yet who] Who

42.105 write about] encounter

42.109   life—]   ~, and in the most hopeless circum-|stances—
42.110   Had]   Is it pos-|sible that
42.121–22   Perhaps, | even,]   It might even be that
42.126   and]   ~ certainly not so many as
42.127   woolly]   wooly

WT]   *ML*

202.14   moment,]   ~ʌ
204.26   James's]   Jame's [*sic*]
209.19   *my*]   my
218.16   ain't]   aint' [*sic*]

ML]   *OF*

360.1   The old Negro man]   THE OLD NEGRO MAN
360.12   everybody]   everyone
362.8   moment]   ~,
364.17   moment!]   ~.
368.5   ¶ It]   *no* ¶
369.21   When Bert]   Bert
370.9   left-over]   leftover
372.12   wild-eyed]   wile-eyed
372.32–33   well-estab-|lished]   ~ ʌ ~
373.20   hard-working]   hardworking
373.25   fact,]   ~ʌ
373.35   lean-to kind]   ~-~-~
377.4   ¶ They]   *no* ¶
377.19   God damn]   Goddamn
378.8 *et passim*   wooly]   woolly
382.19   boogyman]   boogeyman
383.16   pigeon-like]   pigeonlike

C63   "The Dark Walk." *Harper's Bazaar*, 88 (March 1954), 120–22, 194–96, 200–205, 209–10, 214. Story. *WT*.

Harper's Bazaar]   *WT*

120.1   ¶ It]   1 | *no* ¶
120.2   Pike's]   Pikes
120.7   was,]   ~:

120.16   girls (still]   ~, ^~
120.17   patent leather pumps)]   ~-~ ~,
120.30–32   Sylvia's two younger children, Charley and Nora, | suffered even more from those Saturday nights in | Colorado.]   Those Saturday nights in Colorado were even more | painful to Sylvia's [. . .] children.
120.32–33   ten-|thirty]   10:30
120.39   and,]   ~^
120.40   muscular]   ~ little
120.48   snow white]   ~-~
120.50–51   low-|quarter]   ~-~,
120.54   dance.]   ~. . . . An unbelievable sight the old woman was. | And a dreadful reality she presently became for him or | her whose turn it happened to be.
120.59   Sylvia]   ~ and all Sylvia's con-|temporaries there
120.63   summer.]   ~. *additional material*, 238.13–30: She [. . .] Colorado!"
120.63   She]   ¶ But Sylvia Harrison
120.68   But after]   After
120.72   herself]   ~, of course,
120.73–75   it, but said it was all right if that's what she | wanted. He, of course, never set eyes on Mountain | Springs, and never danced a step with Miss Katy.]   it *additional material*, 239.11–30: and [. . .] me."
120.76–77   ¶ That summer in Colorado was a memorable one. | Ever after-ward]   *no* ¶ Afterward
120.77   it when]   that summer in Colo-|rado whenever
120.79   She said she had]   For more than ten years Nate's business had kept | the family almost constantly on the move, but Sylvia said she would
120.82   keyed-up]   ~^~
121.2–3   trip. The bad thing about moo-|ing, she admitted, was the]   trip—a certain
121.6   furniture]   furniture's
121.8   decide——"Somebody"]   ~— "somebody"
121.8–9   chil-|dren]   ~,
121.16   places.]   ~ they had lived.
121.17 *et passim*   Long Hill]   Cedar Springs
121.17   own]   ~ family
121.19   was]   had been
121.26   oak]   the ~
121.33   sunrise,]   ~^
121.37–38   seven-|thirty]   7:30
121.41   seven-thirty]   7:30
121.45–46   There was one long block between their house | and the town square, and as]   As
121.47   that block]   the one long block between their house and the town square
121.47   more than one]   a number
121.48   on his]   along their
121.55   that she made]   in her throat

121.58   sobbed,]   ~:
121.66   road,]   ~^
121.68   gave Sylvia's hand a tight squeeze]   pressed the back of it gently against her | cheek
121.69   before, "Then we]   before: "We
121.71   left before]   left, Cedar Springs
121.76   turning]   ~ just | then
121.81   lap]   ~,
121.82   Negro man ordering]   man reach-|ing back with his long arm to pet
121.83   to lie down in the back seat]   who was riding between the bundles in the back seat of the sedan
121.87   herself. For]   herself; for
121.93   ¶ Never] *no* ¶
121.93   Sylvia]   ~ Harri-|son
121.96   (of]   ^~
121.96 *et passim*   mid-South and mid-West]   Midsouth and Midwest
121.100   sympathy.]   ~. *additional material*, 243.17–26: On [. . .] another.
121.100   As]   And as
121.101–2, 122.1–2   even he | had but few oppor-|tunities to lend a hand or even to offer advice on | that subject.]   not even he felt free to offer | Sylvia advice on the subject of moving or even to lend | a hand or express any sympathy when the time for | packing arrived.
122.2   After he]   ¶ After Nate
122.3   move]   take
122.4   her very closest]   those in her Chicago circle of
124.10   husband]   ~,
124.11   children]   ~,
122.16   people—]   ~,
122.17 *et passim*   southern]   Southern
122.19   known in Cincinnati, in Detroit, in St. Louis.]   admired | everywhere for their geniality, their good breeding, | and simply for their attractive appearances.
122.20   Even]   Sylvia, | even
122.20   her husband's]   Nate's
122.21   Sylvia was]   was
122.22   her prettiness and her charm and even]   her unusual prettiness, her charming manner, and for
122.27   This sympathy she got seemed uncalled-for]   Such an attitude | seemed uncalled-for and absurd
122.30   shoestring.]   ~. The sight of an old | rattletrap truck piled high with bare bedsprings and | odd pieces of oak furniture could bring tears to her | eyes.
122.36   Tennessee.]   ~. *additional material*, 245.7–31, 246–47, 248.16: Most [. . .] South."
122.37   ¶ During] *extra leading, no* ¶
122.43 *et passim*   Twenties]   '20's
122.48   his way of reminding]   supposed to remind
122.50   would]   would flare up as though he were about | to

122.59   make himself scarce]   ~-~-~

122.64   old,]   ~ʌ

122.72   Chinese lacquer]   ~-~

194.2   obscured.]   ~. If she had papering or | painting done, it was in an effort to subdue obtrusive | architectural design. Long before it became fash-ion-|able, she was fond of painting doors, walls and all the | wood trim in a room the same color—a dusty green, a | flat gray, or an off white.

194.38   things.]   *additional material, 250.28–30, 251.1–5:* It [. . .] flowers."

194.51   loaded.]   ~. Sylvia, during most of the evening, re-|fused to recog-nize the presence of the boxes and bar-|rels. If anyone made reference to them she pretended | either not to hear or to be offended by the references.

194.83–84   *normal leading*]   *extra leading*

195.95–96   trip. | *extra leading*]   ~. *additional material, 252.15–254.18:* When [. . .] Memphis.

194.96   ¶ Once]   *no* ¶

194.97   year,]   ~ʌ

194.103   times,]   ~ʌ

194.106   And Nate]   Nate

194.112   tonight?]   ~.

194.116   She]   By the time she had | finished speaking she

194.128   own.]   ~. He stood with one | foot on the first step and leaned against the heavy newel | post. "People did to other people's stories more | than usual tonight," he said. "It was a good evening."

195.20   son Wallace]   ~, ~,

195.28–29   ash | tray]   ashtray

195.32   hoarse,]   ~ʌ

195.41   uncomfortable]   ~,

195.51   God knows where]   ~-~-~

195.63–64   shrugged her shoulders and | smiled indulgently.]   smiled af-fably, as she shrugged her shoulders.

195.67   say."]   ~." She wanted to humor him in his mood, but the words | would not come.

195.80   Why, it would be, he said,]   Why, he said to her, it would be

195.83   Sylvia]   ¶ ~

195.84   And]   ¶ ~

195.89   to hear the moving]   moving, to her,

195.95   suddenly]   ~,

195.102   the business world.]   business. *additional material, 258.8–15:* As [. . .] head.

195.103–4   he | said,]   she recalled his saying finally,

195.112–15   It had fright-|ened her when he said that in the | dark that night. It had frightened | her of him. But recalling]   When he said that in the dark that night it | had given Sylvia a scare, had made her afraid of | him. Recalling

195.119   marriage.]   ~, *additional material, 258.26–261.30:* but [. . .] world.

195.120   ¶ Nate]   *no* ¶

195.124   board-chairmen]   ~ ʌ ~

195.130 *et passim*   depression]   Depression

195.132   Chicago]   Athletic
195.138   Deer-|field Hotel, up in Lake Forest]   Indian Hills, up in Winnetka
195.5–6   *extra leading* | ¶ There] 2 | *no* ¶
196.21   friends]   ~ in Chi-|cago
196.23   children.]   ~. *additional material,* 263.8–264.26: Sometimes [. . .] reverses.
196.60   Easter]   ~,
196.108   said,]   ~:
196.124   wide]   ~,
196.132–33   fore-|head,]   ~∧
196.136   Presently Sylvia drew]   Under different circumstances Sylvia might | have attached significance to what Mr. Canada said and to | his glance out his office window. But as things were|—that is, he being only her landlord, she accepted the | old gentleman's words that day as mere gestures, as | marks of half-absentminded civility, and she replied by drawing
196.147–48   ¶ Only] *extra leading, no* ¶
200.14–16   well, had made the | first move from Long Hill to Mem-|phis with them, and had]   and had
200.44   Ah]   ~,
200.116   But]   ¶ ~
200.125   day.]   ~. | *additional material,* 270.18–274.7: The [. . .] ship.
200.147   daughter Nora]   ~, ~,
200.149   half-past]   ~ ∧ ~
201.8   business-like]   businesslike
201.51–52   impressive, if for | nothing more, for their great size and height]   impressive for their great size and height if for nothing | more.
201.68   mystification,]   ~:
201.123   eastern]   East
202.18–20   of seventy | years whose general manner and ap-|pearance to his age.]   whose [. . .] appearance | attested to his seventy years.
202.24   naiveté]   naïveté
202.58–59   sum-|mer]   "~
202.59   next.]   ~."
202.95   ¶ Before]   *no* ¶
202.121   disapproved,]   ~∧
202.211   overmuch]   over much
203.6   himself.]   ~. But Sylvia look into | his face and was aware that there was still something | different about him.
203.9   that.]   ~. *added material,* 283.15–285.7: When [. . .] morning."
203.115   known.]   ~ or someone that they or she | knew something about.
203.118–19   ¶ It]   *extra leading, no* ¶
203.130–31   things. | ¶ It] ~. ~
203.142   be.]   ~. *additional material,* 288.6–290.3: And, [. . .] china.
203.143   ¶ Even]   3 | *no* ¶
204.68   roses."]   roses, I think."
204.139   ¶ Sylvia]   *no* ¶
204.144   hall]   ~,

205.22 Then it oc-|curred to her]   Deciding against that, her next impulse was

205.58 Leander]   ~ Thompson

205.65 loading,]   ~^

205.66 knew in fact]   ~, ~ ~,

C64   "A Sentimental Journey" (later titled "1939"). *New Yorker*, 31 (12 March 1955), 33–40, 42, 44, 46, 48–50, 52, 54, 56, 58, 60–61. Story. As "1939" in *HF* and *CS*.

New Yorker]   *HF*

A SENTIMENTAL JOURNEY]   1939

Note: PT rearranged 33.1–130: 33.72–91 in the *New Yorker* correspond to ¶2 on pp. 207–8 in *HF*; 11.92–130 correspond to full ¶s on pp. 208–10 (through 1.37) in *HF*.

33.1–5 [*initial F*] FIFTEEN years ago, in 1939, Jim | Prewitt and I drove to New York | City to spend our Thanksgiving | holiday. Jim and I were then in our senior year at Kenyon College.]   Twenty years ago, in 1939, I was in my senior year | at Kenyon College. I was restless, and wasn't sure I wanted | to stay on and finish college. My roommate at Kenyon | was Jim Prewitt. Jim was restless, too. That fall, he and I | drove [. . .] holiday. Probably both of us felt restless and uneasy for the | same reasons that everyone else did in 1939, or for just the | same reasons that college seniors always do, but we im-|agined our reasons to be highly individual and beyond the | understanding of the other students.

33.5–8 There | at Kenyon, which is located in the little | village of Gambier, Ohio, he and I had | for two years]   For two years, Jim and I had

33.27 lived]   were to live

33.30 lived]   to live

33.35 the appearance of]   *deleted*

33.42 in our third year at Ken-|yon,]   *deleted*

33.43–44 from Douglass | House]   *deleted*

33.47 family.]   ~, and our | only awareness was of that plan.

33.72 in the]   on Wednesday

33.73 the village of Gambier]   the little Ohio village that gives Kenyon | its post office address

33.74 afternoon]   four | o'clock

33.75 up]   in the Gambier post office,

33.76 Mine]   My check

33.78 there]   to | New York

33.88 Douglass]   our room in ~

33.97 as]   while

33.116–17   about the two glorious girls. Or at least | I don't think they did.]
  our incentive, and they couldn't | be expected to understand.

33.118–19   Altogether, the boys who lived in | Douglass House,]   The other
  boys at Douglass House didn't know our in-|centive, and when we said good-
  bye to them there on the | front steps I really felt sorry for them. | Altogether,
  they

33.120–21   Yet they were not | studiedly so, I think.]   *deleted*

33.125   Rollins.]   ~ or almost any other college nowadays.

34.17   [*initial T*] THE]   ¶ The

34.44   department-store]   ~ ∧ ~

34.99   get]   go

35.37–40   two | small grocery stores, the barbershop, the filling station, and
  the bakery]   Dickey Doolittle's filling station, Jim Lynch's | barber shop,
  Jim Hayes' grocery store, Tom Wilson's | Home Market, and Mrs. Titus'
  lunchroom and bakery (the | Kokosing Restaurant),

35.53–54   bar-|bershop]   barbershop

36.12–23   *all in roman, flush left*]   *in ital., indented*

36.84   *book titles in parentheses*]   *book titles in ital.*

36.126   [*initial J*] JIM]   ¶ Jim

38.29   [*initial T*] THE]   ¶ The

38.94   [*initial N*] NANCY GIBAULT]   ¶ Nancy Gibault

38.143   [*initial I*] I HAD]   ¶ I had

39.7–8   garage-|man]   garage man

39.49   débutantes]   debutantes

40.65   some time]   sometime

40.86   [*initial A*] AFTER]   ¶ After

40.89   night club]   nightclub

42.49   [*initial T*] THE]   ¶ The

44.40   looking around]   gaping

44.50   simply *stupid*]   really *awfully* stupid

44.63   glass front]   ~-~

46.8   blond]   blonde

46.50   one another]   each other

48.36   [*initial I*] I DON'T]   ¶ I don't

49.24   ever]   ~ really

50.17   Two]   The

50.19–20   anthol-|ogies]   Anthologies

50.25   it was "*so*]   "it's *so*

50.50 *et passim*   university]   University

52.9   [*initial D*] DRIVING]   ¶ Driving

54.16   [*initial O*] ON]   ¶ On

56.3–13   *all in roman, flush left*]   *all in ital., indented*

56.18   reciting,]   ~∧

56.19–24   *all in roman, flush left*]   *all in ital., indented*

56.28–35   *all in roman, flush left*]   *all in ital., indented*

56.35   alone.]   *alone. . . .*

56.40–43 *all in roman, flush left*] *all in ital., indented*
56.51 [*initial I*] IT] ¶ It
60.1 expression] look
60.34 saying] ~:

HF] *CS*

207.1 Twenty] ¶ ~
209.15 gingerbread-work] ~ ∧ ~
210.28 Dean] dean
210.29 President] president
211.4 Creative Writing] creative writing
212.4 coffepot] coffeepot
214.32 House] house
215.20 Hayes'] Hayes's
215.21 Titus'] Titus's
216.17 Polo Field] polo field
216.21 Path] path
217.9 President] president
218.24–25 country-|people] ~ ∧ ~
219.5 east] East
219.8 P.M.] p.m.
221.17 makeup] make-up
223.7 A.M.] a.m.
228.31 theatre] theater
230.18 in,] ~∧
232.6 blonde] blond
232.12 ours. . . .] ~ . . .
236.23 Anthologies] anthologies
237.14 *et passim* University] university
239.1 bare-headed] bareheaded
240.28 reciting] ~:
241.1 *"Now*] ∧~
241.3 *tower . . ."*] ~ . . .∧
241.6 *"She*] ∧~
241.12 *alone. . . ."*] ~. . . .∧
241.16 *"She*] ∧~
241.17 *led—"*] ~—∧
244.19 Army] army
244.22 A.M.] a.m.

C65 "Tennessee Day in St. Louis" (Act 1). *Kenyon Review*, 18 (Winter 1956), 92–119. In *Tennessee Day in St. Louis*.

ACT 1] ACT ONE

91.1–21, 92.1–2 *scene descriptions and stage directions slightly reorganized but remain essentially unrevised in book version*

93.3 *et passim for character names and stage directions* [*indented*] Senator Caldwell] [*centered*] SENATOR CALDWELL

93.4 mercy. . . . . (*reappearing*)] ~ . . . (*Reappearing*)

93.7 He] Genius at work . . .~

93.14 go. . . .] ~ . . .

93.15 Everything] A five-course dinner! ~

93.15 vichyssoisse] Vichyssoise

93.19 child. . . .] ~ . . .

93.20 fit. . . .] ~ . . .

93.24 Nancy's] *Nancy's*

93.25–27 knowing old—old Southerner. The very worst kind. I strongly | suspect he brought Nancy along to make a match with Jim. Yes, I | strongly suspect that!] nonage-|narian.

93.28–31 In that case, judging from last evening, she is not | so ineffectual, Betty. Jim had said he wasn't going to take her to | that dance. But after he saw her he waited two hours for her to | get dressed. And I never did hear them come in.] Well, old octogenarian, old . . . old Southerner! Of the very worst kind! I strongly [93.26–27 *inserted*]

94.1–2 *et passim (capitalization in stage directions)* turn-|ing] *Turning*

94.5 *et passim (in stage directions)* You [. . .] (*dropping* [. . .])] [*centered*] (*Dropping*[. . .]) You

94.13 It's] It is

94.20 man!] ~.

94.24–25 (*in a whining | voice*)] *deleted*

94.33 aspirations. . . .] ~ . . .

94.4 James] James'

95.14 He's. . . .] ~—

95.15–16 not (*with great | feeling*)] not,

95.16 it's] it is

95.21 he's] he has

95.23 . . . . I] . . .~

95.23–24 impeach-|ment. . . .] ~ . . .

95.26 we're] we are

95.30 *et passim* sotto] *Sotto*

96.4 James] James'

96.7–8 old. . . . old nonogenarian! (*twisting a piece of the puzzle | violently*)] old. . . . old coot! the old covite! the old cohee! | (*She twists*[. . .].)

96.12 could hardly] couldn't

96.15 days. . . .] ~.

96.18 *They look*] (*They stand looking*

96.19 *slowly*] ~,

96.22 *James* [. . .] *others*] JAMES' [. . .] *others'*

96.24   *Bert*]   BERT,
96.24   *a new set*]   *an enormous brown-paper package which contains a set*
96.27   They're awful]   I'm certainly sure they must be
96.27–28   love | those]   *love* some new
96.29   They're]   They are
97.6   *at*]   ~ *the*
97.7   *at*]   ~ *the*
97.8   *her.*]   ~^
97.8   He's]   He is
97.10   (*an*[. . .]*voice.*]   (*In an*[. . .]*voice, hardly moving his lips when he* | *speaks*
97.10   he'll]   he will
97.11   minutes?] ~,
97.13–15   Who'll [. . .] Mind."]   JAMES | What [. . .] him? He [. . .] Mind."
97.16   that.]   ~, as far as I am concerned.
97.19   *James.* Wait, Bert. Jim,]   AUNTIE BET | [. . .] | Jim's muttering . . .
97.20   brought]   bought
97.20–21   *clubs* | *again*]   *the package.*
97.22   Don't say "what we bought,"]   What *we* bought,
97.24   birthday.]   ~, and so he bought him a set | of golf clubs
97.25–26   golf or | anything like that. You should give the clubs to Helen.
       ]   golf. Why, he's quite | funny on the subject.
97.27   Put them back, Bert.]   *Who* thinks he's funny on the subject? *You* and
       Flo Dear . . . | Don't open them, Bert. Put them back.
97.28   *clubs*]   *the package*
97.28   *doors*]   *the* ~
97.29   *closet*]   *the* ~
97.30   You forget,]   *deleted*
97.31   themselves]   for
97.32   Where]   *Where*
97.34   He's]   He has
98.5–6   Bet, (*beck-*|*oning*) there]   Bet. ([. . .]) There
98.8   *at*]   ~ *the*
98.10   *He*]   JIM
98.12   *talk*]   *confer*
98.13   *card*]   *the*
98.17   *Bet*]   BET, *downstage,*
98.17   *downstage*]   *deleted*
98.20   He]   William
98.24   *indifferently*]   *Indifferent*
98.26   too. . . .]   ~ . . .
99.4   grand]   overly
99.5   I don't mind William's leaving.]   If William is leaving us, why of course
       it's his own business.
99.17   McDougal. . . .]   ~ . . .
99.18   everybody]   us all
99.18   all]   what
99.18–19   Wil-|liam]   Brother ~

99.20   you'll]   you will
99.21   meal. . . .]   ~ . . .
99.22   *table*.)]   ~ʌ) . . .
99.22–23   Speak of the | devil!]   What did I tell | you?
99.24   her]   *her*
99.25   I've]   I have
99.26   *card*]   *the* ~
99.30   Cameron.]   ~. You were making a race for some-|thing or other, I
    reckon.
99.30   dreamed then that]   thought then
99.32   cousin]   Cousin
100.11   girls,]   ~ʌ
100.14   platform]   ~ʌ
100.30   man. . . .]   ~ . . .
100.31   freshen-up]   ~ ʌ ~
101.3   James's]   JAMES'
101.4–5   *He stands staring*]   *He even starts to speak, but then he only*
101.11   he's]   he is
101.12   He's]   *He's*
101.20   James. . . .]   ~ . . .
101.26   old fashioned]   ~-~
101.32   admit. . . .]   ~ . . .
101.34   exactly. (*taking*]   ~. Exactly. (*Taking*
102.1   Daniel]   Daniel's
102.5   Delighted. . . .]   ~ . . .
102.10   verisimilitude.]   ~. It is as though I can really have my cake | and eat
    it too. I can enjoy all the family patterns, all the cher-|ished paraphernalia of
    my long life yet without the . . . responsi-|bility.
102.16–18   It is not primarily as a Southerner | that I am speaking, but as an
    old fashioned person.]   This may | be only an illusion, but it seems to me
    that most of what was | bad has gone out out family life in the new America.
    People now | seem free to take only whatever was good about it and to dis-
    |card the rest. The young people seem to be loved by their fami-|lies, yet it is
    not that kind of love which was heaped upon you | till you felt that you could
    not move a lift without shifting | the whole world.
102.21   May]   Yes, that so . . .~
102.23   Tennessee!. . . .]   ~! . . .
102.26   then. . . .]   ~ . . .
102.28   James. . . .]   ~ . . .
102.31   travelled]   traveled
102.34   ago]   ~,
103.1   off. . . .]   ~ . . .
103.10   *hands glass*]   *He hands his*
103.12   *to*]   ~ *the*
103.14   after]   during
103.20   of]   ~ prin-|cipally
103.22   Well, before]   Before
104.3   *down on the couch and*]   *down,*

104.5   *couch.*]   ~, *and closes his eyes.*
104.8   twenties.]   ~—in his own country way.
104.9–10   He's | a little]   In a way he is
104.10   out of]   left | over from
104.14   schooling.]   ~. It may be | he couldn't. Other boys used to call him a blockhead.
104.17   day-laborer]   ~ ∧ ~
104.20   country]   ~,
104.22   before.]   ~—that's the kind of fellow he is.
104.24   He]   ~ never | seemed to have any book sense, but he always had a lot of | pride. Anyway, he
104.28   here.]   ~. His | country accent and his rough manner seemed to act in his favor | and reassure his clients.
104.34   *man*]   ~,
105.3   *Lucy.*]   JAMES | Sh-sh! Genius resting!
105.5   *into a kind of*]   *into*
105.15   *(opening his eyes).*]   *deleted*
105.20   lunch. . . .]   ~ . . .
105.23   lunch, anyway.]   lunch!
105.24   Well! Did you ever?]   Oh, oh! It can't be.
105.27   General Washington's]   somebody's
105.29   Mother! Nobody]   ~, nobody
105.30   Cameron.]   ~. | (*Even while examining the book with* LUCY, *he has been* | *glancing at* SENATOR CASWELL.)
105.32   She's]   She is
105.33   fiancee]   fiancée
106.1   *fairly giggling*]   *Giggling*
106.4   years. . . .]   ~ . . .
106.6–7   talented. Every-|one acknowledges it.]   talented, but nobody | appreciates her. She doesn't even appreciate herself.
106.9   Lucy's]   *Lucy's*
106.10   Nancy.]   ~. He's forgotten you, Lucy.
106.12   Lanny]   ~ | (*To* NANCY)
106.12–14   I've tried her on the most | difficult modern poetry, and she breezes through it with no | trouble at all.]   And appreciates everything.
106.15–16   *Nancy explodes* [. . .] *steps.*]   LUCY | Myself [. . .] tried her [106.12–14 *inserted*]
106.21   Lanny!]   ~! | LANNY | (*Suddenly delighted, addressing the whole group*) | They were downstairs for four chapters of *The Decline and* | *Fall of the Roman Empire,* which makes it about three cen-|turies. And that's about right! | (*He is convulsed with laughter.*) | JAMES | Don't laugh at your own jokes, Lanny. | NANCY | He *is* a scream, Uncle James. Up there reading on Saturday | night. What *was* it he was reading?
106.26   *table, Nancy's arm*]   card table. NANCY *puts her arm*
106.27   It's a grand picture.]   You had better have a look. I | think maybe it's Napoleon and Josephine.
106.28–31   *Helen.* So that's who that old lady is. I must admit that Lanny | knows more than I do about art. | *Lanny.* Art, Mother? (*laughs superciliously*)

Please don't call | that picture art.] JAMES | *(With pride)* | Lanny is quite an authority on Napoleon. | LANNY | *(To* HELEN*)* | Oh, you were faking. You knew it wasn't Bonaparte. It's | Washington's farewell to his mother. | HELEN | So that's who that old lady is. I must admit that Lanny knows | more than I do about historical pictures. | LANNY | Historical, Mother? *(Laughs superciliously)* That picture | should be classed as one of the greatest mythological paintings.

106.34–107.1–2   But look. The General | is on his knees before his mother, a picture of humility. There's a lesson in that for you.]   Of course, you're right, and there is a fine lesson | in that for you. The General . . . humility.

107.9   no.]   ~. Indeed, no.

107.12   aplenty;]   ~.

107.17   art]   historical pictures

107.25   Who]   *Who*

107.26   reason]   ~,

108.13   eighty-five]   eighty-six

108.20   or [*sic*]]   of

108.25   Doesn't]   And doesn't

108.26   born]   ~,

108.28   or]   and

108.29   Grant or Forrest]   Forrest or Grant

109.3–4   Herman | Melville, Thomas Hardy, Tolstoi and Oscar Wilde] Thomas | Hardy and Tolstoi and Rudyard Kipling

109.5   Isn't that terrifying? It]   When you think of it, it

109.8   Oh,]   ~∧

109.11   am]   ~ . . .

109.12   Have you forgotten? You're *fifteen*]   You're *fif*teen. Have you forgotten?

109.14   Sh!]   ~! I said "fourteen" on purpose,

109.18   Senator's. . . .]   ~ . . .

109.21   him]   his coming here

109.21   Oh, you]   You

109.23   I've]   I have

109.26   from.]   ~ and what they were | there.

109.32   of me—]   *deleted*

110.22   *Lucy.*]   LUCY | *(Giggling)*

110.20   something.]   ~ . . .

110.25   see. . . .]   ~ . . .

110.25   *here*]   here

110.28   said: There]   said there

111.10   It's]   it's

111.21   extent. . . .]   ~ . . .

111.27   came up]   came

112.21   sight. . . .]   ~ . . .

112.26   very silly]   rather absurd

112.32   God. . . .]   ~ . . .

112.33   easy. . . .]   ~ . . .

113.2   school]   ~,

113.3   schooldays]   school days

113.11   ridiculous!]   ~! Uncle Brother couldn't even | get through high school!

113.12   Wait.]   *deleted*

113.16   do. . . .]   ~ . . .

113.23–24   No, wait, Lanny.]   I'm afraid you don't.

113.30   *fiancee*]   *fiancée*

113.33   *(quietly at first, then with feeling).*]   *deleted*

114.2   you. . . .]   ~ . . .

114.4 *et passim*   fiancee]   fiancée

114.5   they've]   they have

114.16   young. . . .]   ~—

114.22   not. . . .]   ~ . . .

114.26   life. . . .]   ~ . . .

114.31   tell. . . .]   ~ . . .

114.33   won't]   will not

114.33   William.]   ~. You become completely | irrational

115.5   him!]   ~.

115.14–15   You sent for me, Lucy? James said you wanted to | see me.]   What's all this about? James said you craved my company, | Lucy.

115.17   *rather*]   *deleted*

115.21   *watching*]   *observing*

115.23   *When*]   *Whenever*

115.25   *unnoticeable*]   *barely audible*

115.26   Why in God's name did you come here today?]   I wasn't looking for you to be here today, Lucy. What in | God's name fetched you? | *(Pause.)*

115.28–31   goodbye? | *William.* [. . .] Aren't you]   good-bye? | WILLIAM | I [. . .] isn't it so

115.32   Hell, yes]   Yes

115.32   Lucy. . . .]   ~ . . .

115.32   played]   made like the

115.33   enough. . . .]   ~ . . .

116.2   I am going alone,]   I've bought only one ticket

116.3   cruel]   crude and

116.4–5   admired my direct-|ness.]   "appreciated [. . .]."

116.7   William. . . .]   ~ . . .

116.10   matter. . . .]   make any difference . . .

116.10   matters]   makes a difference

116.14   that's why you came today. You came to]   that's what what fetched you. To

116.17   be incidental]   be . . . *in*cidental

116.18   adventure]   venture

116.19–22   There is a big | war about to explode in Europe, and whether we get into it or | not, great fortunes are going to be made in this country. I've | gotten on to a sure thing out there.]   A lot of money is | going to change hands very soon, elsewhere. Things are going | to start popping, and I've gotten on to the surest thing there is | when things start popping. I aim to get dar fustis with the | mostis money, but I've got to move fast.

116.25–26 Playing the St. Louis | business man. Content just] Messing around in St. | Louis—just

116.28 old fashioned] old-timey

117.3 William—] ~ . . .

117.5 —you] . . . ~

117.7–8 out of a | war] in some ter-|rible way

117.8 glad. . . .] ~ . . .

117.13 Why *did* you come? Why *did* you come?] Why in hell did you come?

117.14 goodbye. . . .] good-bye . . .

117.21 appearances] looks

117.23 go. . . .”] go.” . . .

117.24–25 as | though] like

117.30 as though] like

117.31 claim] drag

118.3 Hell, stop] God. Stop

118.3 that.] ~ . . .

118.4 it.] ~ . . .

118.15 possession] hold

118.18 became] got

118.25 River.] ~. *That* place! Christ, Lucy, I | dreamed one night you and I had a still out there and the rev-|enuers were after us.

118.27 bourgeois. . . .] ~ . . .

118.34 misery.”] ~.” | (*The ticking of the clock.*)

119.8–10 *William.* It [. . .] ears.] WILLIAM | What [. . .] ears. | (*The ticking of the clock.*)

C66 “The Other Times.” *New Yorker,* 33 (23 Feb. 1957), 36–40, 42, 44, 47–48, 50, 52–54, 57–58, 60, 62–64. *HF, CS.*

New Yorker] *HF*

36.1 [*initial C*] CAN] Can

36.6–7 Mero Country | Club] Chatham Golf and Country Club

36.9 *et passim* Mero] Chatham

36.15 king’s] King’s

36.22 Sunday-afternoon] ~ ∧ ~

36.29 uncle’s] Uncle’s

36.37 Yours] yours

36.51 too] as well

36.99 [*initial T*] THE] ¶ The

36.123 Usually, they] They

37.5 like everything,] to the roots of their hair

37.16 the girls] girls

37.30 must admit] will say

37.50–51   the | most wonderful]   surpassed all others
37.90   smart]   hateful
37.95   street,]   ~∧
37.95   town,]   ~∧
38.35   everything,]   ~∧
38.36   club,]   ~∧
38.80   [*initial I*] I DON'T]   ¶ I don't
39.4   watch out]   watch
40.11   [*initial N*] NOW]   ¶Now
40.78–79   tell what the expression | meant right away.]   at | once tell what the expression meant.
40.105   timy]   time
42.8   [*initial I*] I DON'T]   ¶ I don't
42.15   powder-blue]   ~ ∧ ~
42.38–39   it would have made me burst out | laughing.]   I think the effect would have seemed | irresistibly funny to me. I would have pointed it out to | Horst and Bob, and afterward there would have been | cryptic references made to it before girls like Letitia who | normally wouldn't ever have been inside such a place.
42.78–80   means we were only about | three miles from Thompsonville. And | Thompsonville]   is in Pitt County, and this meant we [. . .]. Thompsonville
42.93–94   clear blue | eyes]   clear, smooth skin and her bright green eyes—
42.117   But]   Then
42.118   And]   Then
42.128   blue]   green
44.21   [*initial W*] WELL]   ¶ Well
44.63   broken-down]   ~ ∧ ~
44.65   junk yard]   junkyard
47.34   pale-yellow]   ~ ∧ ~
47.48   milk shake]   milkshake
50.50   bull pen]   bullpen
52.11   louder,]   ~ began to | sound more in earnest, and
52.20   only]   merely
52.21   You'd]   You
52.36   blue]   green
52.37   O.K.]   OK
52.47   eager]   earnest about it
53.2   meanest]   hardest
53.24   friendliest]   most unselfish
53.26   five-dollar bills.]   crumpled-up bills. I saw that one of them was a five.
54.26   [*initial O*] ONCE]   ¶ Once
57.20   And for]   For
57.20   just]   absolutely
57.37   towheads]   tow-heads
60.6   hassel]   hassle
60.39   marvellous]   marvelous

60.31 [*initial I*] I WAS] ¶ I was
62.35–36 crossly hurrying Letitia's three little | brothers] speaking rather crossly to Letitia's [. . .] and hurrying them
62.38–40 being older than I am, | didn't grow up during the depression | and who] who
64.3 Yeah] Yea
64.33 And, of course,] And
64.44 course,] ~^
64.45 it's all right] nobody | really minds it

HF] *CS*

3.1 Can] ¶ ~
3.4 *et passim* début] debut
4.6 Uncle's] uncle's
4.22 *et passim* depression] Depression
6.5 castlelike] castle-like
7.35–8.1 Mid-|dle Western] Midwestern
8.15 this] ~,
19.11 marvellously] marvelously
23.12 Ma'am] ma'am
23.26 OK] O.K.
28.8 tow-heads] towheads
29.31 there,] ~^
35.17 course] ~,

C67 "The Unforgivable" (later titled "Promise of Rain"). *New Yorker,* 33 (25 Jan. 1958), 32–40, 43, 46, 48, 50, 53–54. Story. As "Promise of Rain" in *HF* and *OF.*

Reprinted as "A Promise of Rain" in *Literature: An Introduction,* ed. Hollis Summers (New York: McGraw-Hill, 1960), pp. 176–87; *Adventures in Modern Literature,* ed. Robert Freier (New York: Harcourt, Brace & World, 1970), pp. 231–45.

New Yorker] *HF*

THE UNFORGIVABLE] Promise of Rain
32.1 [*initial U*] UNDERSTAND] Understand
32.36 however, mind] mind, however,
32.44–45 looking | glass] ~-~
32.46–47 Some afternoons, for Hugh's own | good,] For Hugh's own good I used, some afternoons,

32.93 [*initial I*] I CAN] ¶ I can

32.104 mitts] gloves

33.26 however] though

33.38 up.] ~. Mary says he's the only person who can remind me, | nowa-days, of how hard up we were then without making | me mad. If that is so, it is because he seems to take such | innocent pleasure in remembering it. He talks about it in | a way that makes you feel he is saying, "I owe *every*thing | to that!"

33.48 plus fours] ~-~

33.55–57 I didn't mention it | or refer to it in any way, and I wouldn't | let Mary.] Naturally, I was supposed to blow up and tell him to | fasten them. But I pretended not even to notice, and I | wouldn't let Mary mention it to him.

33.60 stopped.] ~. *additional material,* 41.5–42.5: He [. . .] with.

33.79 mirror] looking glass

33.89 mirror] glass

33.91–96 For a few seconds—be-|fore permitting our eyes to meet—he | would rudely scrutinize me, precisely as | though I were a part of the inani-mate | furnishings of the room. The first time | he did it] If I had purposely planted myself in the | library doorway, that's when his eyes would light on me. | He would look at me curiously for a split second—before | he let his eyes meet mine—look at me as he did at every-|thing else in view. The first time it happened,

33.98–99 But | next time I understood] Next time, I saw

33.101 himself.] ~. *additional material,* 43.2–16: I [. . .] hall.

33.102 [*initial D*] DURING] ¶ During

33.113 *et passim* Mero] Chatham

34.5 "Greater Mero"] the "municipal area"

34.9–10 down | town] downtown

34.71–72 I] ¶ The summer Hugh was seventeen ~

35.34 one] One

35.49 section.] ~ and | didn't get too awfully run-down during the depres-sion.

36.45 in!] ~. Or that's how it seemed.

36.51 dining-room] ~ ^ ~

36.74 any] anything

36.75 [*initial I*] IT] ¶ It

37.3 I] you

37.17 glorious] gorgeous

37.63 burst out laughing] laughed aloud

38.21 Central] West

38.67 [*initial I*] IN] ¶ In

38.102 from,] ~^

39.37 [*initial B*] BUT] ¶ But

40.48–49 old-|maid] ~ ^ ~

40.60 Hugh] my son | Robert

43.33 First,] ~^

48.13 That means more] That's a promise of

48.31   KMR]   WCM
48.39   Central]   West
50.1   straight]   ~ and stiff
50.25   five]   ten
50.33   and]   ~ that
50.46   shame . . .]   ~. . . .
50.56   Right away]   At once
50.61–62   I was too | stunned.]   *deleted*
50.63   night.]   ~. I [. . .] home.
53.5–19   almost [. . .] City.]   I could see him.
53.26–27   out of sorts and | rather lost.]   not myself at all.
53.30–54.36   I [. . .] are.]   *revised as* 68.21–69.4: And [. . .] yourself.

HF]   *OF*

36.1   Understand]   UNDERSTAND
36.12   better looking]   ~-~
37.17 *et passim*   depression]   Depression
38.20   ¶ I]   *no* ¶
43.18   ¶ During]   *no* ¶
43.19   first-hand]   firsthand
43.23   night life]   nightlife
46.6   make-up]   makeup
47.2   bird house]   birdhouse
48.14   ¶ The]   *no* ¶
48.20 *et passim*   hitch-hiking]   hitchhiking
49.3   there]   it
49.7   Canal]   canal
49.8   F.D.R.]   FDR
49.12–13   We were | just stopping for some cold beer.]   *deleted*
49.24 *et passim*   jellybeans]   jelly beans
52.20   dining room]   ~-~
53.5   ¶ It]   *no* ¶
53.24–25   ¶ "Did she]   *no* ¶ "Did he
59.3   ¶ But]   *no* ¶
59.11   out,]   ~^
60.12–13   "Mr. Hairbrain's Confession: A Comedy."]   *Mr. Hairbrain's Confession: A Comedy.*
61.16   old maid]   ~-~
67.24   shame. . . .]   ~ . . .

C68   "Venus, Cupid, Folly, and Time." *Kenyon Review*, 20 (Spring 1958), 169–202. *HF, CS.*

Reprinted in **B9**; *The Best American Short Stories 1959*, ed. Martha Foley and David Burnett (Boston: Houghton Mifflin, 1959), pp. 311–39; *Fifty Modern*

Stories, ed. Thomas M. H. Blair (New York: Harper & Row, 1960), pp. 360–84; *Gallery of Modern Fiction: Stories from the Kenyon Review*, ed. Robie Macauley (New York: Salem Press, 1966), pp. 324–53; *American Short Stories since 1945*, ed. John Hollander (New York: Harper & Row, 1968), pp. 320–52; *50 Years of the American Short Story*, ed. William Abrahams (New York: Doubleday, 1970), 2:362–87; *The Southern Experience in Short Fiction*, ed. Allen F. Stein and Thomas N. Walters (Glenview, Ill.: Scott, Foresman, 1971), pp. 93–113; *Major American Short Stories*, ed. A. Walton Litz (New York: Oxford, 1975), pp. 681–705.

Kenyon Review]   HF

169.1   [*initial T*] THEIR HOUSE]   Their house
169.8   pyjama]   pajama
170.13   home grown]   ~-~
172.7 *et passim*   Mero]   Chatham
173.8   potato-chips]   ~ ∧ ~
173.24   AND YET]   ¶ And yet
174.7   and]   or
174.17   East]   east
175.23   sun-tan]   suntan
175.31   grey]   gray
176.17   aqua-marine]   aquamarine
177.80   BUT A THING]   ¶ But a thing
180.23   EVEN]   ¶ Even
181.8   looking glass]   ~-~
181.28   Dorsets]   Dorsets'
182.20   ACTUALLY]   ¶ Actually,
184.21–22   ¶ His sister would repeat the exclamation, "For the sake of economy!" and also the ironic "Ha ha!"]   *deleted*
184.31   ball room]   ballroom
186.13   flower bedecked]   ~-~
186.33   NED MERIWETHER]   ¶ Ned Meriwether
190.8   suspicion]   suspicion [*sic*]
190.28   focussed]   focused
191.30   NONE OF]   ¶ None of
194.24   first]   front
194.27—28   clear | headed]   ~-~
196.19–20   Dorsets' | faces.]   Dorsets.
196.26   know."]   ~, that makes the difference."
196.30   sensed that she was talking to a little girl,]   recognized that it was a little girl she was talking to,
197.26   arrived]   assembled
198.12   MISS LOUISA]   ¶ Miss Louisa
198.32 *et passim*   War]   war
199.8 *et passim*   debut]   début

199.28 ever got its absurd name, and] got its name (She was just making conversation and | appealing to my interest in such things) and

199.29 last Spanish governor of Louisiana] Earl of Chatham and | pointed out that the city is located in Pitt County

199.30 I don't know exactly why.] "How very elegant," she said. "Why | has nobody ever told me that before?"

199.31 her] Ned's wife

201.26 memories] families

202.12 exhausted] covered

HF]   *CS*

70.1   Their]   ¶ ~

70.2–3 old | maid]   ~-~

70.8   closely]   ~,

70.9   hitched up]   ~-~

71.27   coveralls.]   ~∧ [*sic*]

72.15   mid-day]   midday

73.1   blue veined]   ~-~

74.3   east]   East

74.17   Also]   ~,

74.24   depression]   Depression

74.32   months]   ~,

75.2   side-curtains]   ~ ∧ ~

75.12   odd looking]   ~-~

75.16   side-curtains]   ~ ∧ ~

75.30   thirteen and fourteen]   ~- and ~-

76.8   mommy or daddy]   Mommy or Daddy

76.20   east]   East

77.5   generation]   ~,

77.8   round]   ~,

77.17   servants]   ~,

77.21   occasions]   ~,

78.20   mantel piece]   mantelpiece

78.21   book shelves]   book-|shelves

79.15   *The Kiss*]   "The Kiss"

79.22   *Venus, Cupid, Folly and Time*]   "Venus, Cupid, Folly and Time"

80.17   November]   ~,

80.20   out. . . .]   ~ . . .

81.1   that]   *deleted*

81.25   recess]   ~,

84.17   second best]   ~-~

84.22   looking-glass]   ~ ∧ ~

85.5   pitch-blackness]   ~ ∧ ~

85.30   palazzos and chateaux]   palazzi and châteaux

86.10 *et passim*   jello]   Jello

87.6   fortune-hunters]   ~ ∧ ~

89.3   example. . . .]   ~ . . .
89.24   dishevelled]   disheveled
90.1   The]   the
91.29   along,]   ~^
91.30   that]   ~^
92.12   later]   ~,
92.13   invitation]   ~,
92.27   last minute]   ~-~
94.29   round-up]   roundup
95.10   supicion [*sic*]]   suspicion
95.21   eyes]   ~,
95.23   again]   ~,
95.29   half suppressed]   ~-~
96.1   amber colored]   ~-~
96.32   failed]   wailed
97.21   dishevelled]   disheveled
98.14   rosin]   resin
101.8   fortunately]   unfortunately
101.16 him]   ~,
104.21 house]   ~,
104.30 cases]   ~,
106.8   début]   debut
106.30 She]   she
107.2   she]   ~,
108.6   old timers]   ~-~
108.32 western]   Western

HF]   *OF*

36.1   Understand]   UNDERSTAND
36.12   better looking]   ~-~
37.17 *et passim*   looking-glass]   ~^ ~
38.19 *et passim*   depression]   Depression
38.20   ¶ I]   *no* ¶
43.18   ¶ During]   *no* ¶
43.19   first-hand]   firsthand
43.23   night life]   nightlife
46.6   make-up]   makeup
47.2   bird house]   birdhouse
48.14   ¶ The]   *no* ¶
48.20 *et passim*   hitch-hiking]   hitchhiking
49.3   there]   it
49.7   Canal]   canal
49.8   F.D.R.]   FDR
49.12–13   We were | just stopping for some cold beer.]   *deleted*
49.24 *et passim*   jellybeans]   jelly beans
52.20   dining room]   ~-~

53.5 ¶ It] *no* ¶
59.3 ¶ But] *no* ¶
59.11 out,] ~∧
60.12–13 "Mr. Hairbrain's Confession: A Comedy."] *Mr. Hairbrain's Con-*
fession: A Comedy.
61.16 old maid] ~-~
67.24 shame. . . .] ~ . . .

C69 "A Pair of Bright-Blue Eyes" (later titled "*Je Suis Perdu*"). *New Yorker*, 34 (7 June 1958), 33–38. Story. *HF, CS.*

New Yorker] HF

A PAIR OF BRIGHT BLUE EYES] *Je Suis Perdu*
33.4–14 The Paris apartment [. . .] shave. On] It was [. . .] And on
33.18 stakes] ~ in Paris
33.20 day] ~.
33.22 laughter.] ~. | [. . .] *They* were in the dining room just sitting down to | breakfast. *He* had eaten when he got up with the baby | an hour before, and was now in the *salle de bain* pre-|paring to shave.
33.103 *The*] *This morning the*
33.103–4 Months | back] ¶ Months back
33.128 suède] suede
33.149–53 At first [. . .] him. But] Their [. . .] one, but
33.178 half past] ~-~
34.2 Métro] Metro
34.90 had been] was
34.121 [*initial W*] WITH] ¶ With
34.123 Clark] he
35.26 Clark] he
35.36–37 Clark ex-|claimed.] the baby's daddy now heard him-|self saying.
35.38–39 eyes—how he rolls | them," said his wife] eyes," said the mother. "Watch how he rolls | them."
35.40 is] *is*
35.40–41 Clark | said. "How really remarkable."] "How really remarkable!" | He glanced joyfully at his wife.
35.42–43 said his | wife.] she said
35.45 direction."] ~." | ¶ "It's [. . .] break!"
35.46 And having] And presently the baby, having
35.47 turns, the baby did presently begin] turns to the right, did begin
35.51 now.] ~ and exchanging intermittent glances in order to share | the moment fully.
35.77 *Je regrette*] Je regrette
35.82 Clark,] the father with unusual se-|verity in his voice,

35.85   nothings]   nothing
35.86–36.12   ¶ *"Je regrette.* [. . .] face and]   *revised, and with new material,*
   257.7–258.26: ¶ But [. . .] he
36.26   Marie.]   ~. "Accidents will happen."
36.28   Clark]   he
36.44   Clark saw that his]   His
36.45   their]   the
37.18   until . . .]   ~. . . .
37.126   twenty eyes]   ~-~
38.6   could . . .]   ~. . . .
38.64   crowd,]   ~! She was moving toward | him,

HF]   *CS*

248.8   It]   it
250.11   razor]   ~,
250.23   hard-working]   hardworking
250.27   Boulevard]   boulevard
251.3 *et psssim*   Rue]   rue
251.28   Metro]   Métro
253.2   Doctor]   doctor
253.4   Doctor]   doctor
254.6   University]   university
254.7   Paris. . . .]   ~ . . .
256.16   Je regrette]   *Je regrette*
257.8   Je regrette. Je regrette.]   *Je regrette. Je regrette.*
257.18 *et passim*   theatre]   theater
257.25   mélee]   melee
257.31   mackinaw]   ~,
258.3 *et passim*   perdue]   *perdu*
261.1 *et passim*   Palace]   palace
261.26   fellow-American]   ~ ^ ~
262.9   until. . . .]   ~ . . .
262.15   gloom. . . .]   ~ . . .
264.11   twenty-eyes]   ~ ^ ~
264.17   could. . . .]   ~ . . .
265.18   by. . . .]   ~ . . .
267.1   apartment. . . .]   ~ . . .

C70   "Cousins, Family Love, Family Life, All That" (later titled "The Little Cousins"). *New Yorker*, 35 (25 April 1959), 38–44. Story. In *HF, OF* as "The Little Cousins."

New Yorker]   *HF*

"Cousins, Family Love, Family Life, All That"]   "The Little Cousins"
38.1–3   [*initial C*] CHILDREN were not cordially | invited to the Veiled Prophet's | Ball.]   To the annual Veiled Prophet's Ball children were not | cordially invited.
38.13–14   I | have no idea]   There is no telling
38.17   V. P.]   Veiled Prophet's
38.19   Statler]   ~ Hotel
38.56   at" with]   at"—disadvantage, that is,
38.63 *et passim*   Munroe]   Calhoun
38.72   V. P.]   *deleted*
38.102   second,]   ~∧
38.156   failings,]   ~—failings that
38.158   other,]   ~—
39.1   deal, I'm afraid;]   ~;
39.23–24   so very]   so
39.49   her]   but ~
39.50   St. Louis family]   family in the city
39.57   half sister]   ~-~
40.25   low sick]   "~ ~"
40.55–56   spurn awhile—|left there for her to ignore until]   ignore
40.67   first-hand]   firsthand
40.82   our own]   our
40.122   [*initial W*] WE]   ¶ We
40.123   V.P.]   Veiled Prophet's
40.129   going to be]   to be
40.129 *et passim*   débutantes]   debutantes
41.23   silly]   stupid
41.56   even the]   the
41.70   [*initial T*] THE]   ¶ The
41.143   patent-leather]   ~ ∧ ~
42.90   [*initial O*] ONLY]   ¶ Only
42.115   focussed]   focused
42.133   tasselled]   tasseled
43.48   Court]   court
43.49   year . . .]   ~. . . .
44.7   [*initial V*] VERY]   ¶ Very
44.25   boots]   shoes
44.36–37   more."| And]   ~." | ¶ ~
44.122   a lamb I was]   "perfect lambs" we both | were
44.116   travelled]   traveled

HF]   *OF*

148.1   [*bold T*] To the annual]   To THE ANNUAL
149.2   grownups]   grown-ups

149.19   Browns]   Browns'
149.20   Dr.]   Dr
152.16   *I*]   I
153.25   half-sister]   ~ ʌ ~
156.25–27   Her eyes wan-|dered about the room for a moment, and then she looked | Corinna straight in the eye and said,]   *deleted*
157.2–3   *extra leading*]   *normal leading*
158.21   ¶ The]   *no* ¶
162.3   ¶ Only]   *no* ¶
163.5 *et passim*   portières]   portieres
165.5   year. . . .]   ~ . . .
165.22   bejewelled]   bejeweled
165.29–30   *extra leading*]   *normal leading*

C71   "Who Was Jesse's Friend and Protector?" (later titled "A Friend and Protector"). *Kenyon Review*, 21 (Summer 1959), 395–418. In *HF, OF* as "A Friend and Protector."

Reprinted as "Who Was Jesse's Friend and Protector?" in **B10**.

Kenyon Review]   *HF*

WHO WAS JESSE'S FRIEND AND PROTECTOR?]   "A Friend and Protector"
395.1   [*initial F*] FAMILY FRIENDS]   Family friends
396.6   blood-shot]   bloodshot
396.34   high-school]   ~ ʌ ~
397.18   Chatham]   Braxton
397.30   hard working]   ~-~
398.22   him]   ~,
399.2 *et pssim*   week-end]   weekend
399.12   sprees]   ~,
400.8   spirit]   ~,
403.5   Y,]   "~,"
403.12   but]   ~,
403.21   circumstances]   ~,
405.34   the]   that
407.10 *et passim*   grey]   gray
407.10   focussed]   focused
409.8   panelled]   paneled
409.30–31   the air-conditioning unit, and even the | television set]   and even the air-conditioning unit
410.6   front]   side street
410.7   ran]   went

410.7   two at a time]   so | fast that I stumbled two or three times before I got to the | third floor
410.10   the first thing I noticed]   what I noticed first
410.11   but that]   but
411.10   mant [*sic*]]   meant
411.15   Morley]   ~,
411.20–21   At least, I said to myself, | it is *something*. And]   *deleted*
411.26   that]   of steps that I had come up | half an hour earlier—two flights ~

412.31   drug store]   drugstore
414.3   Obviously]   ~,
414.17   *his*]   ~,
414.25   do]   ~,
415.17   door]   ~,
415.24   Jesse]   ~,
415.29   Instinctively]   ~,
416.4   Presently]   ~,
416.9   before]   earlier
416.29   doctor]   ~,
417.1   office]   ~,
417.2   paperwork]   paper work
417.11   said it]   said
417.4   Uncle Andrew]   Uncle
417.28   him]   ~,
418.1   aunt]   ~,
418.2   table]   ~,
418.4   theme]   ~,

HF]   *OF*

113.1   Family friends]   FAMILY FRIENDS
114.23   fierce looking]   ~-~
115.23   any more]   anymore
116.22   hard-working]   hardworking
117.27   say:]   ~,
118.9   long-johns]   ~ ∧ ~
119.16   russian-bank]   Russian bank
119.21   Margaret:]   ~,
119.32—120.1   absence-|without-leave]   ~ ∧ ~ ∧ ~,
120.28–29   this: | ¶ "You]   ~: "~
121.17   And]   ~,
122.9   he]   He
123.20   boy-friend]   boyfriend
123.21   done-in]   ~ ∧ ~
128.3   Day?]   ~.
128.22   nose]   ~,
130.26   water cooler]   watercooler

132.9 again:] ~,
137.14 nice looking] ~-~

C72 "Heads of Houses." *New Yorker*, 25 (12 Sept. 1959), 52–87. *HF*,
CS.

Reprinted in **B11**; *How We Live: Life in Contemporary Fiction*, ed. Penney Chapin
Hills and Rust Hills (New York: Macmillan, 1968), pp. 167–89.

New Yorker] *HF*

52.1 [*initial K*] KITTY'S] Kitty's
58.30 previous] previously
60.28 [*initial H*] HENRY PARKER] Henry Parker
72.4 *et passim* quarrelled] quarreled
72.24 travel-|ing] traveling
72.34 [*initial K*] KITTY] Kitty
76.47 1926] 1928
82.39 [*initial J*] JUDGE PARKER] Judge Parker
84.40–41 good. | [*extra leading; initial W*] WHEN] good. | [*normal leading*]
  ¶ When
86.5 marvelled] marveled

HF] *OS*

268.4–5 *et passim* record-|player] ~ ^ ~
269.19 Tourist Class] tourist class
269.26 *et passim* Hotel] hotel
270.28 in. . . .] ~ . . .
271.14–15 *et passim* Uni-|versity] university
272.5–6 ground. | . . .] ~ . . .
272.27 begin. . . .] ~ . . .
273.14 *et passim* Judge] judge
276.11–12 radio. | . . .] ~ . . .
276.19 Mountain] mountain
279.2 that] who
282.2–3 Mountain. | . . .] ~ . . .
284.30 father's,] ~^
289.20 faux pas] *faux pas*
291.7 Bench] bench
293.10 dacron] Dacron
297.1 mind. . . .] ~ . . .
299.18 matter. . . .] ~ . . .
305.6 benefit. . . .] ~ . . .

C73 "Guests." *New Yorker*, 35 (3 Oct. 1959), 48–50, 52, 55–56, 58, 60, 62, 65, 67–68, 70, 72, 75–76, 78, 83–86, 89. Story. *HF, CS.*

New Yorker]   *HF*

48.1   [*initial T*] THE]   The
48.22–23   table-|cloth]   ~ ∧ ~
48.51   Nashville,]   ~;
48.66–67   made Cousin Annie final-|ly]   finally made Cousin Annie
48.88   swing,]   ~—
48.99   quick]   ~,
48.166   three-]   ~∧
48.167   four-day]   ~ ∧ ~
49.6   them,]   ~∧
49.14   twelve-years]   ~ ∧ ~
49.22–24   first morn-|ing after they had fetched the old couple, | and when their]   second day of the visit, when the old couple's
49.34   "Johnny."]   ∧~.∧
49.42   but had]   but
49.48–49   now. | ¶ On]   ~. ~
49.54   was.]   ~. Since, at the mo-|ment of the telephone call,
49.55   office, and]   ~ ∧ ~ since
49.57   there, so]   there,
49.76–80   It was his | habit of mind, as a good trial lawyer, to | think any question through and find a | positive answer to it as soon as it came | up.]   As a matter of fact, he | was trying to think the problem through right then and | there.
49.91   Then,]   ~∧
49.91   flash,]   ~∧
49.92   But]   but
50.1   [*initial I*] IT]   ¶ It
50.7   hard-top]   ~ ∧ ~
50.13   five-mile]   ~ ∧ ~
50.25   travelled]   traveled
50.33   sock,]   ~∧
50.35   Somehow,]   ~∧
50.54   man,]   ~∧
50.55   man,]   ~∧
50.58   course,]   ~∧
50.60–61   grandfather—something | that]   ~, ~ which
50.70   another,]   ~∧
50.93   long]   ~—
52.22   earlier]   *deleted*
52.46   Nashville]   ~,
52.50   city-limits]   ~ ∧ ~
52.59   factory]   ~,

55.15 "Maud Muller"] *Maud Muller*

55.16–17 reversed! | ¶ Moreover] ~! ~

55.17 he] Edmund

55.30 [*initial C*] COUSIN JOHNNY'S] ¶ Cousin Johnny's

55.49 abovestairs] above stairs

55.53 evening] ~,

56.1 had come into] came in

56.6 now:] ~;

56.33 first,] ~∧

56.25 Annie] ~,

56.25 away] ~,

56.27 questions.] ~. She spoke with enthusiasm of the sights they | had taken in that day: the Parthenon, the capital building, | old Fort Nashboro.

56.36 well-staffed] ~ ∧ ~

58.14 other] ~ country

58.17 But,] ~∧

58.40 the] The

58.58 table,] ~∧

58.59 television set] ~∧

60.1 little] ~,

60.8 marvellous] marvelous

60.11 him] for the first time

60.16 'Mr. Kincaid.'] ∧~. ~.∧

60.20 course,] ~∧

60.46 [*initial A*] AT] ¶ At

60.103 first morning] day before

60.112–13 hard | of hearing] ~-~-~

60.118 countrypeople's] country people's

62.9 room,] ~∧

62.10 as] while

62.22 Finally,] ~∧

62.39 guest-room] ~ ∧ ~

62.45 on,] ~∧

62.58–59 three-quar-|ters] ~ ∧ ~

65.8 dining-room] ~ ∧ ~

65.12 lady,] ~∧

65.14–15 *et passim* Belle | Meade] Bellemeade

65.16 room,] ~∧

65.49 lowered,] ~∧

65.51 accusingly; he] ~: He

65.58 knew] had known

67.3–5 But he was so disturbed | that he forgot to shift into third gear till | he was halfway to town.] *deleted*

67.8 before. This] before. She had always managed to involve him in her | good works among relatives—having discovered his | weakness there, she had abandoned most of her other good works—but this

67.11 her.] ~. Was it really only | a difference in degree this time?

67.13 visitors,] ~∧

67.18   anyone]   ~,
67.19   felt,]   ~∧
67.36   sat]   would be
67.42   farmland]   farm land
67.52   say?]   ~. . . .
68.13   interested]   had ~
68.16   juvenile-court]   ~ ∧ ~
68.21   débutante]   debutante
68.32   Finally,]   ~∧
68.58–59   say | "and]   ~: And
68.60   itself."]   ~.∧
68.63   please her]   be the case
70.32   would be]   was
70.72   were]   was
70.41   [*initial T*] THERE]   ¶ There
70.43   noon,]   ~∧
70.59   wonderful.]   ~, really.
72.23–24   stay. | ¶ When]   ~. ~
72.24   house,]   ~∧
72.29   even,]   ~∧
72.38–39   knee-|length]   ~ ∧ ~
72.39   high-heeled]   ~ ∧ ~
72.40   immediately]   right away
72.45   Once,]   ~∧
72.45   car,]   ~∧
72.46 *et passim*   Traveller's]   Traveler's
72.47   Rest (they]   ~—~
72.48   Rest,]   ~∧
72.49   Hermitage) once]   ~—~
72.50   said (it]   ~—~
72.52   here, and]   ~ (~
75.6   me,]   ~∧
75.8–9   mov-|ing—]   ~∧
75.10–11   'Mr. | Kinkaid']   ∧~. ~∧
75.26   talked,]   ~∧
75.39–40   absorb-|ing]   ~,
75.40   intriguing]   ~,
75.45   buttons, which]   ~ that
75.51   the old]   the
76.26   wondered]   ~ silently
76.40   heating]   heat
76.45   last-minute]   ~ ∧ ~
76.46   shoe-company]   ~ ∧ ~
78.7   a]   the
78.31   bed—or]   ~, or even
78.32   floor even]   floor
78.36   [*initial W*] WHEN]   ¶ When
78.46   and]   ~,

78.47 this] ~,
83.3 shoe-company] ~ ∧ ~
83.26 [*initial A*] AT] ¶ At
83.47 watch,] ~∧
83.58 room,] ~∧
83.61 father,] ~∧
83.64 focussed] focused
84.7 bed,] ~∧
84.14–15 bed. | ¶ He] ~. ~
84.22 sure?] ~∧
84.32 mind?] ~? He didn't know what he would do if she said, yes, she | minded. He knew only that he couldn't got back to his | own room and bed before morning. He felt that it | hadn't, after all, been the voices that waked him, and | that there *had* been a dream—the kind of dream that | could never be remembered afterward.
84.33 silly." She] ~," she
84.45 him.] ~. "You know what an evil influence you are on peo-|ple." The touch of her arm was all he had needed. Once | again he believed it was the voices that had waked him, | and remembered that he must have his wits about him to-|morrow.
84.46 [*initial A*] AT | ¶ At
84.61 makeup] make-up
84.63 her,] ~∧
85.1 open,] ~∧
85.21–22 shirt | front] shirtfront
85.36 it] the question
86.19–20 He] ¶ ~
86.22 the bed] foot of the bed
86.33 underwear,] ~∧?
86.41 house,] ~∧
86.48 body!] ~! He | had heard of cases in which grief had driven people to | such madness, and surely his present anguish was grief|—if not exactly grief for Cousin Johnny. What if he | should refuse to let them have the old man's body!
86.53 distinctly, and] distinctly. And
86.54 giving way to] indulging in
86.57 them] ~,
86.60 them,] ~∧
89.14 way?] ~. . . .
89.27 Johnny? The] ~—the

HF] *CS*

170.1 The] ¶ ~
171.1 table cloth] tablecloth
172.29 University] university

180.3   for. . . .]   ~ . . .
181.25   well staffed]   ~-~
182.23   supper. . . .]   ~ . . .
183.9   The]   the
186.11–12   hard-of-|hearing]   ~ ^ ~ ^ ~
186.29   are. . . .]   ~ . . .
187.11   guest room]   ~-~
188.4   dining room]   ~-~
189.2   He]   he
189.26   felt]   ~:
190.20   say. . . .]   ~ . . .
191.19   Finally]   ~,
194.19   knee length]   ~-~
194.20   high heeled]   ~-~
196.7   down town]   downtown
196.14   apartments. . . .]   ~ . . .
197.10   last minute]   ~-~
203.14   here. . . .]   ~ . . .
203.21   himself. . . .]   ~ . . .
203.25   really. . . .]   ~ . . .
203.26   fellow. . . .]   ~ . . .
204.12   door knob]   doorknob
205.30   way. . . .]   ~ . . .

C74 "Miss Leonora When Last Seen." *New Yorker*, 36 (19 Nov. 1960), 52–58, 60, 62, 65–66, 68, 70–72, 75–76, 78, 80, 82–84, 86, 88–90. *ML*, *CS*.

Reprinted in **B12**; *Fiction 100*, ed. J. H. Pickering (New York: Macmillan, 1974), pp. 900–915.

New Yorker]   *ML*

52.53 *et passim* travelling]   traveling
53.16   travelled]   traveled
53.51–52   trav-|eller]   traveler
55.26   here]   ~,
56.78–79   "Silas Mar-|ner"]   *Silas Marner*
56.108   live]   ~ in
62.52   the]   that
66.42–43   *extra leading*]   *normal leading*
75.48–49   *extra leading*]   *normal leading*
78.28   her]   ~,
78.35–38   And I think it is some such | attitude as that that has sustained | her through all the dull, disappointing | years since.]   *deleted*

84.23–24 *extra leading*] *normal leading*
90.4 goodbye] good-bye

ML] CS

246.1 Here] ¶ ~
246.11 *et passim* Lane] lane
247.17 When] when
249.21 well worked] ~-~
251.21 *et passim* unspoilt] unspoiled
251.33 *et passim* Bypass] bypass
252.29 passerby] passer-by
252.33 chores. . . .] ~ . . .
253.11 roller-top] roll-top
256.25 *et passim* Fairgrounds] fairgrounds
256.32 Finally] ~,
258.20 be. . . .] ~ . . .
258.21 be. . . .] ~ . . .
258.29 General's] general's
259.34 stop. . . .] ~ . . .
260.3 county. . . .] ~ . . .
260.16 spoilt] spoiled
260.18 depression] Depression
262.26 hotel-keeper] hotelkeeper
267.34 air. . . .] air | . . .
269.8 her,] ~^
269.17 gone. . . .] ~ . . .
269.32 lane] ~,
271.6 not. . . .] ~ . . .
272.6 too. . . .] ~ . . .
272.23 care. . . .] ~ . . .
273.26 years] ~,
274.11 line. . . .] ~ . . .
275.5 southern] Southern
278.14 good-bye] goodbye
278.35 air-conditioning] ~ ^ ~

C75 "Reservations: A Love Story." *New Yorker*, 37 (25 Feb. 1961), 37–42, 44, 47–48, 50, 53–54, 56, 58–60, 65–67, 70–72. Story. In *ML*, *CS* as "Reservations."

Reprinted in *Studies in the Short Story*, ed. Virgil Scott (New York: Holt, Rinehart and Winston, 1971), pp. 497–518.

New Yorker] *ML*

40.58   the]   he [*sic*]
66.6   quarrelled]   quarreled

ML]   *CS*

1.1   *no* ¶]   ¶
1.13   travelling]   traveling
2.13   bride's]   brides'
2.24–25   chatter | "Your]   ~: ~
2.35   either. . . .]   ~ . . .
41.6   either. . . .]   ~ . . .
5.7   own. . . .]   ~ . . .
5.34   understood. . . .]   ~ . . .
6.2   someday]   some day
6.15 *et passim*   Miles']   Miles's
7.3   *This*]   *this*
7.10   he [*sic*]]   the
8.9   Venetian]   venetian
9.29   three-quarters]   ~ ∧ ~
10.5   bona-fide]   ~ ∧ ~
13.24   singnalled]   signaled
15.7 *et passim*   début]   debut
15.64 *et passim*   débutantes]   debutantes
15.64   realistically]   ~,
16.14   eye brows]   eyebrows
16.14   pencilled]   penciled
16.26 *et passim*   makeup]   make-up
16.35   Finally]   ~,
19.13–14   lips. | . . .]   ~ . . .
19.22   further]   farther
20.8   Then she]   Then
25.10   Army]   army
26.20   bottle]   bottom
30.16   Finally]   ~,
3.26   focussed]   focused
31.8   hearts]   ~,

C76   "Nerves." *New Yorker*, 37 (16 Sept. 1961), 38–41. Story.

Excerpt reprinted in John Egerton, *Nashville: The Face of Two Centuries, 1780–1980* (Nashville: PlusMedia, 1979), p. 199.

C77 "An Overwhelming Question." *Encounter,* 18 (March 1962), 7–15. Story. *ML*.

Encounter] *ML*

7.40–41 (to each other and to what a lot more | than just each other)] *deleted*
8.43 centre] center
8.74 humouring] humoring
8.83 *et passim* recognised] recognized
8.97–98 realis-|ing] realizing
9.4 THE] ¶ The
9.28 realised] realized
9.32 amongst] among
9.59 [*initial H*] HE] ¶ He
10.20 amongst] among
10.22 River] river
10.47 disc] disk
10.57 [*initial S*] SHE] ¶ She
10.90 neighbourhood] neighborhood
12.10 centre] center
12.14 [*initial T*] THAT] ¶ That
12.31 *et passim* to-morrow] tomorrow
12.68 realised] realized
12.80 amongst] among
13.11 coloured] colored
13.47 idealised] idealized
13.57 amongst] among
13.69 [*initial I*] ISABEL] ¶ Isabel
14.17 [*initial T*] THE] ¶ The
14.82 programme] program

C78 "At the Drugstore." *Sewanee Review,* 70 (Autumn 1962), 528–58. *ML, CS*.

Reprinted in **B13**; *Anthology of Contemporary American Literature* (Seoul, Korea: USIS, 1971), 6:557–74.

Sewanee Review] *ML*

529.27 not] no
531.21 grey haired] gray-haired
533.3 advertizers] advertisers
534.12 rabbit's. . . .] ~ . . .

534.14   close set]   ~-~
534.19   familiar]   *familiar*
536.13   thinner]   thinning
536.20   grown up]   ~-~
537.9   half gallon]   ~-~
537.26   decor]   décor
542.11–12   black | haired]   ~-~
542.16   dark haired]   ~-~
553.29   fruit-knife]   ~ ∧ ~
556.6   leaden eyed]   ~-~

C79   "Demons" (later titled "A Strange Story"). *New Yorker*, 39 (24 Aug. 1963), 30–34, 36, 39–40. 42–43, 46, 49–51, 54–56, 59, 60–63. Story. In *ML* as "A Strange Story."

New Yorker]   *ML*

DEMONS]   "A Strange Story"
30.15   big gold]   ~, ~
30.19–21   "L.P.," which were | my own initials as well as my grand-|father's and my father's.]   LP, which were my grandfather's initials, | as they were also my father's and my own.
30.25   round.]   ~ . . .
30.31   at last | my father]   my father finally
30.35   times—]   ~,
30.36   Then, later,]   ~∧ ~∧
30.37   tone,]   ~∧
30.40   all this,]   *deleted*
30.47   Lost Dauphin was, and]   "Lost Dauphin" | was and that I
30.64   remember, they]   remember. They
30.102   west]   West
30.113   "Mm-mmm"s]   "m'mmms"
30.116   used to declare]   declared
31.6   around;]   ~,
31.13   man,]   ~∧
31.16   place,]   lot
31.20   rise, beyond which I knew]   rise beyond which
31.35   home place]   ~-~
31.56   Sunday]   ~,
31.83   I, discovered]   I, (Q.A.) discovered
31.84   quarrelled]   quarreled
32.61   hearing—]   ~,
32.70   was.]   ~!
32.73   mystics.]   ~!

32.114   know, Louis Price,]   know
32.115   Still]   A few years
32.127   that]   ~,
33.47–52   I watched his lips | as he drawled my name | threateningly: "Lou-
ou-ou | is." Then I saw him | draw back his arm, and | before]   Before
33.54   side of the head]   temple
33.78   Alice,]   *deleted*
33.93   Christmas tree]   ~-~
33.112   beyond,]   ~^
34.1   me,]   ~^
34.5–6   team-|mates]   ~ ^ ~
36.62   were]   had been
39.3–4   co-|incide,]   ~^
40.21   ouch—]   ~,
40.61   books,]   ~^
40.62   to]   in
40.64   nature]   Nature
42.2   nature]   Nature
42.28   the boy]   he
42.29   him, he]   him the boy
42.45   country]   (country town)
42.56   three-quarters]   ~ ^ ~
42.58   hid]   had hidden
42.63   glass]   glassware
43.16   "Louis, you]   "You
43.37   sweet-smelling]   ~ ^ ~
46.45   silence,]   ~^
49.8   heels. . . .]   ~ . . .
49.10   family. . . .]   ~ . . .
49.38   knee and]   ~,
50.6–7   you, | Louis Price!]   you!
50.26   her,]   ~;^
50.66   schoolbook]   school book
51.2   flyleaf]   fly leaf
51.6   frown,]   ~^
51.17   corridor]   ~,
51.18   crisscrossed]   ~-~
51.42   else—]   ~;
55.16   schoolbook]   school book
56.3   retrospect,]   ~^
56.5   still,]   ~^
56.37   But, of course, I]   But I
56.42–43   par-|ties]   parents
56.44–45   Apparent-|ly,]   ~^
56.51   but]   ~,
56.52   not]   ~,
56.63   party]   ~,

59.28   taste, Louis."]   taste."
59.30   her,]   ~.
59.36   me,]   ~∧
59.39   house coat]   housecoat
59.42   children,]   ~∧
59.45   music,]   ~∧
59.42   Obviously,]   ~∧
60.8   close,]   ~∧
60.19   Louis]   he
60.23   hope." She]   hope," she
61.3   said,]   ~ suddenly,
61.27   sticks,]   ~∧
61.30   last,]   ~∧
61.39   leaving, Louis,"]   ~,"
61.48   Louis]   Brother
62.17   But]   ~,
62.28   mystery.]   ~. I *will* not have you, or anyone, ex-|plaining them.
62.33   know]   possess the knowledge
62.35   might only]   might
62.37   and in that case]   and,[. . .]case,
62.41   are. After]   are. | ¶ After
62.60   nature]   Nature
63.4   sometimes]   ~,
63.9   all,]   ~∧
63.11   nature]   Nature

ML]   *CS*

50.1   *no* ¶]   ¶
51.28   Next]   ~,
52.11–12   business. | . . .]   ~ . . .
53.17–18   night. | . . .]   ~ . . .
54.20   family—]   ~.
54.21   family! They]   family; they
54.23   his two]   his
54.27   here]   there
54.29   They]   they
54.30   abrupt. And]   abrupt; and
55.11   disreputable looking]   ~-~
55.26   hide and seek]   ~-~-~
56.12   uncalled-for]   ~ ∧ ~
56.29   . . .]   *deleted*
56.31   . . .]   *deleted*
57.12   Finally]   ~,

58.12 school boy] schoolboy
59.6 seventy forty-five a.m.] 7:45 A.M.
59.30 paper-backs] paperbacks
60.11 décor] decor
60.15 it. . . .] ~- . . .
61.17 rosy cheeked] ~-~
62.3 week day] weekday
62.5 buses. . . .] ~ . . .
62.21 pleasant looking] pleasant-|looking
63.14 easy-going] easygoing
64.7 Boldly] ~,
64.19 It] it
64.26 rough-house] roughhouse
65.5 cokes] Cokes
65.10 Finally] ~,
65.22 cokes] Cokes
65.26 candy-bars] ~ ^ ~
65.32 fumbling. . . .] ~ . . .
66.3–4 mystery. | . . .] ~ . . .
67.7 shoulder. . . .] ~ . . .
67.8 him. . . .] ~ . . .
67.25 paper-back] paperback
68.8 rosy cheeked] rosy-|cheeked
68.10 work. . . .] ~ . . .
68.17 boys'] boy's
68.21 about. . . .] ~ . . .
68.31 focussing] focusing
70.10 coke] Coke
71.20 little-gentleman] ~ ^ ~
75.3 days. . . .] ~ . . .
76.8 morning. . . .] ~ . . .
77.21 strokes. . . .] ~ . . .
78.13 It] it
78.19 Inadvertently] ~,
78.29 still-life] ~ ^ ~
79.24 year. . . .] ~ . . .
80.3–4 boogy | man] boogyman
80.35 quarrelling] quarreling
81.18 knife] ~,

C80 "Two Pilgrims." *New Yorker*, 39 (7 Sept. 1963), 36–42. Story. *ML*, *CS*.

Reprinted in *An Approach to Literature*, ed. Brooks et al., 5th ed. (Englewood Cliffs, N.J.: Prentice-Hall, 1975), pp. 273–80.

New Yorker] *ML*

36.7 *et passim*   travelling]   traveling
36.32 *et passim*   neoclassic]   neo-classic
36.100–101   black | shingled]   ~-~
38.124   [*initial A*] A FEW]   ¶ A few
40.176   [*initial O*] ONCE]   ¶ Once
41.10   damnedest]   damndest

ML]   *CS*

328.1   *no* ¶]   ¶
330.14   a]   an
330.30   travellers]   travelers
332.24   shame-facedly]   shamefacedly
332.27   gray green]   ~-~
334.30–31   enam-|elled]   enameled
335.4   Ma'am]   ma'am
336.11   floor boards]   floorboards
338.3   burnt]   burned
338.11   Mister]   mister

C81   "There." *Kenyon Review*, 26 (Winter 1964), 144–70. *CS*.

Reprinted in **B14**; *The Best American Short Stories 1965*, ed. Martha Foley (Boston: Houghton Mifflin, 1965), pp. 345–70.

Kenyon Review]   *CS*

144.1   "LET ME TELL YOU SOMETHING ABOUT THE BUSBYS," THE OLD]   "Let me tell you
144.17 *et passim*   hometown]   home town
144.23   have. . . .]   ~ . . .
144.30   finger thumping]   ~-~
145.22   shirt. . . .]   ~ . . .
146.14   people. . . .]   ~ . . .
147.11   Continental]   conti-|nental
147.37   Port]   port
148.5   matter,]   ~,"
149.19   maids. . . .]   ~ . . .
149.25   unarmed. . . .]   ~ . . .
152.14   50]   fifty
155.22   Morris']   Morris's

156.10   is [*sic*]]   as
156.29   late-afternoon]   ~ ∧ ~
156.37   me....]   ~ ...
157.33   died....]   ~ ...
158.32   100]   a hundred
159.3   broken down]   ~-~
159.4   tradition....]   ~ ...
159.14   1.00]   one
162.66   Dawn]   dawn
163.38   cerulian]   cerulean
164.10   so....]   ~ ...
165.24   later....]   ~ ...
166.7   studio-portrait]   ~ ∧ ~
166.34   word....]   ~ ...
168.37   other....]   ~ ...
169.21   quarter-hour]   ~ ∧ ~
169.37   days....]   ~ ...
169.38   best....]   ~ ...
170.4   again....]   ~ ...

C82   "The Throughway." *Sewanee Review*, 72 (Fall 1964), 559–78.
Story. *MD*.

Sewanee Review]   *MD*

559.6 *et passim*   Irene]   Isabel
559.24   newer, fashionable developments]   newer developments
559.26 *et passim*   Irene's]   Isabel's
560.8   day,]   ~∧
560.9   his acquaintance]   the world
560.30   living room]   ~-~
561.10   mantel piece]   mantelpiece
561.19   bird cage]   ~-|~
561.20   fish bowl]   fishbowl
562.24 *et passim*   week-end]   weekend
563.5   dining room]   ~-~
563.18   cup-handle]   ~ ∧ ~
563.32   reach. It]   ~. | ¶ ~
565.7–8   *extra leading*]   *normal leading*
565.8   her. Her]   ~. | ¶ ~
565.22   some day]   someday
566.10   long dead]   ~-~
566.34   wanted]   *wanted*
570.2 *et passim*   Negroes]   Blacks

570.5   the Negroes]   them
570.15   deep]   coldly
572.3   had had to]   had to
572.29   cancelled]   canceled
573.12   remembered too]   ~, ~,
573.26   light-weight]   lightweight
576.9   chair-back]   ~ ∧ ~
578.6   travelling]   traveling
578.19   coldly, indifferently]   with | cold indifference

C83   "The End of Play." *Virginia Quarterly Review*, 41 (Spring 1965), 248–65. Story.

C84   "Tribute at Yale." *Alumni News* (Univ. of North Carolina at Greensboro), 54 (Spring 1966), 2–5. Tribute to Randall Jarrell given on the occasion of a memorial service held in the Law School Auditorium, Yale University, on 28 February 1966. Other participants included Robert Penn Warren, Robert Lowell, John Berryman, Adrienne Rich, William Meredith, John Hollander, Stanley Kunitz, and Mary Jarrell.

C85   "That Cloistered Jazz." *Michigan Quarterly Review*, 5 (Fall 1966), 237–45. Essay in special section titled "The Writer as Teacher—with Thoughts on Randall Jarrell."

A revised version of this essay appeared in **B15**.

C86   "A Cheerful Disposition." *Sewanee Review*, 75 (Spring 1967), 243–65. Story.

Reprinted in **B16**.

C87   "Mrs. Billingsby's Wine." *New Yorker*, 43 (14 Oct. 1967), 56–60. Story. *CS*.

Reprinted in *What Is the Short Story*, ed. Eugene Current-García and Walton R. Patrick (Glenview, Ill.: Scott, Foresman, 1974), 467–75.

New Yorker]   *CS*

56.1   [*initial S*] SHIRLEY BARNES]   ¶ Shirley Barnes
56.35   blue-and-white]   ~ ∧ ~ ∧ ~

57.11   Barnes']   Barnes's
57.66–67 *et passim*   ban-|nister]   banister
57.145   dentist. . . .]   ~ . . .
58.14   [*initial N*] "NOW]   ¶ "Now
58.59   antebellum]   ante-bellum
59.44 *et passim*   houseguests]   house guests
59.59   High School]   high school
59.22 *et passim*   Square]   square
60.108   again]   *deleted*

C88   "First Heat." *Shenandoah*, 19 (Winter 1968), 28–36. Story. *CS.*

Reprinted in **B17**.

Shenandoah]   *CS*

28.3   Session]   session
28.22 *et passim*   interstate]   Interstate
28.31   air]   ~,
28.33   ball, and]   ~ ∧ ~,
29.4   air)]   ~.)
29.7 *et passim*   State]   state
29.12 *et passim*   Mansion]   mansion
29.20   arm pits]   armpits
29.35   icewater]   ice water
30.13   much. . . .]   ~ . . .
31.12   shadow boxed]   ~-~
31.13   silk]   ~,
31.14   title]   ~,
31.19   it;]   ~:
31.22   too innocent looking]   ~-~-|~
32.4   eyes. . . .]   ~ . . .
32.19   it;]   ~:
32.23   morality. . . .]   ~ . . .
33.29   forty mile]   ~-~
33.30   He]   he
33.33 *et passim*   Governor's]   governor's
33.36   Finally]   ~,
34.3   replied]   ~,
34.8   Bill]   bill
34.25   Well—.]   ~—∧
34.29   there.]   ~?
34.34   know. . . .]   ~ . . .
35.15   himself. . . .]   ~ . . .
35.18   glass topped]   ~-~

35.26 forgiving. . . .] ~ . . .
36.4 door] ~,

C89 "A Stand in the Mountains." *Kenyon Review*, 30, no. 2 (1968), 169–264. Play. Published separately as **A13**.

Note: "A Stand in the Mountains" was first produced by the Barter Theatre, Abingdon, Virginia, on 25 May 1971. Taylor revised the play somewhat for this production.

Kenyon Review] **A13**

170.1 SCENE I] FIRST SCENE
170.8 THEY [. . .] FROM] [*initial T*] They [. . .] from
182.41 *et passim (dash deleted after stage directions) works)*—] ~)ʌ
182.43 to] To
183.5 subject.] ~. It's [. . .] end.
183.7–9 Such [. . .] see.] What [. . .] exag-|gerate?
183.14 *et passim (upper case to lower case in stage directions) Puts*] *puts*
183.14 *work*] *needlework*
183.22 she] *she*
183.23 you] *you*
183.25–26 treasure, [. . .] object.] treasure.
183.29 chamber] bedchamber
183.30 I [. . .] know.] (*annoyed*)
183.30 me.] ~. | ZACK You're [. . .] *laugh*
183.38 Pshah.] ~!
184.4 neither.] ~. | ZACK Talk [. . .] romance!
184.8–10 You must | [. . .] have.] *deleted*
184.8 Lucille.] ~. *added material, 25.20–30:* ZACK One's [. . .] "help."
184.18 Is in] In
184.23 God] Lord
184.23–24 It's [. . .] us.] Their [. . .] us'ns.
184.31 you] *you*
184.36 It] But it
184.37 it's] ~ done
185.7 company] ~!
185.7 him.] ~!
185.12 After [. . .] entirely] *expanded as* Yes, after [. . .] altogether
185.22 poems and such,] poems,
185.23 yore] y're
185.31 so] not so
185.32 himself] his-self
185.33 Jest] jest

185.36 (*posturing*)—] *deleted*
185.38 father?] ~? (*sternly*)
186.5 changed] ~.
186.20 *taking*] *She takes*
186.31 ways. We] ways, of [. . .] suppose we
186.31–32 spots, | I suppose.] suppose. Especially [. . .] children.
187.4 sister] Sister
187.6 set] laid
187.25 different.] ~. You [. . .] Zack
187.32 to.] ~. | Harry [. . .] do.
188.8 usual] we usually do
188.12 delayed] ~ in Louisville
188.18 with?] ~? | ZACK They've [. . .] do
188.25 once Cinderella] Once Cinderello [*sic*]
188.27 they're—] they [. . .] sisters.
189.3–4 cottage. | [. . .] then.] cottage, Will, *added material*, 31.9–16, the [. . .] then. (*He sighs.*)
190.33 cousin] Cousin
191.3 cousin] Cousin
192.23 uncle] Uncle
193.21 cousin] Cousin
194.20 on,] ~. [*sic*]
194.28 you] You
196.18 SCENE II] SECOND SCENE
196.19 ¶] *no* ¶
197.27 uncle] Uncle
204.4 mall] Mall
204.15 mountain] Mountain
204.26–27 No, [. . .] today.] *rewritten as* Me? [. . .] of?
206.1 uncle] Uncle
208.36 mountain] Mountain
211.37 uncle] Uncle
212.14 the Baroness] Georgia
212.16 *falls.*)] ~.) *material added:* (*as* [. . .] *is.*
212.17 SCENE III] THIRD SCENE
212.18 ¶] *no* ¶
216.30 *Oh, Bull*] Oh, Bull
219.38 co-operation] cooperation
221.38 cousin] Cousin
228.17 *left*)] ~.) | *additional material*, 73.28–30: LOUISA [. . .] us?
228.18 SCENE IV] FOURTH SCENE
228.19 ¶] *no* ¶
230.37 uncle] Uncle
240.35–36 is, | [. . .] walks?] is? | [. . .] know.
240.37 *throws* [. . .] *aloud.*] *continues to laugh.*
241.1–3 HARRY I [. . .] wood!] *deleted*
241.9 She'll] Mina will

242.1 SCENE V] FIFTH SCENE
242. ¶] *no* ¶
243.11 cousin] Cousin
247.31 cousin] Cousin
254.14 SCENE VI] SIXTH SCENE
254.23 uncle] Uncle
254.28 uncle] Uncle
257.3 inside ...] ~ ... | (MINA [...] *fiercely.*)
257.4 SCENE VII] SEVENTH SCENE
257.5 ¶] *no* ¶
262.15 uncle] Uncle
263.8 yet.] ~. (*going* [...] window?
264.25 LOUISA—] ~ᴧ (*During* [...] *out.*)

C90 "The Elect." *McCall's*, 95 (April 1968), 106–7, 168–69, 172. Story. *CS*.

McCall's] *CS*

107.1 no ¶] ¶
107.28 first-lady-elect] ~ ᴧ ~-~
107.65 three A.M.] 3 a.m.
168.30 [*initial W*] With] ¶ With
168.41 six A.M.] 6 a.m.
168.150 [*initial B*] But] ¶ But
168.183 [*initial P*] Presently] ¶ Presently
168.226 low] ~,
168.262 makeup] make-up
169.10 pin-stripe] pinstripe
169.80 [*initial T*] The] ¶ The
169.112 [*initial S*] She] ¶ She
169.230 [*initial W*] When] ¶ When
172.25 ghost-writer] ~ ᴧ ~
172.48 [*initial Y*] You] ¶ You
172.204–5 mill-|workers] mill workers
172.244 [*initial M*] My] ¶ My

C91 "Tom, Tell Him." *Sewanee Review*, 76 (Spring 1968), 159–86. Story.

C92 "Dean of Men." *Virginia Quarterly Review*, 45 (Spring 1969), 258–93. Story. *CS*.

Reprinted in *Stories from the Sixties*, ed. Stanley Elkin (New York: Doubleday, 1971), pp. 161–96; *The Short Story: An Introductory Anthology*, ed. Robert A. Rees and Barry Menikoff, 2d ed. (Boston: Little, Brown, 1975), pp. 359–87; *The Norton Anthology of Short Fiction*, ed. R. V. Cassill (New York: Norton, 1978), pp. 1269–93.

Virginia Quarterly Review]   *CS*

258.1   [*initial I*] I AM]   ¶ I am
258.6 *et passim*   rôle]   role
258.16   *your*]   your
259.5   more]   ~,
259.11 *et passim*   Trustees]   trustees
259.13   in]   ~,
259.14   why]   Why
259.15 *et passim*   President [. . .] College]   president [. . .] college
259.25   before]   ~,
260.1   Mid-Western]   Midwestern
260.3   ten year old]   ~-~-~-
260.4   foolishness. . . .]   ~ | . . .
260.12   college]   ~.
261.13   is]   ~,
261.15   peace.]   ~ . . .
261.22–23   cubby | hole]   cubbyhole
262.3   typescript,]   ~ʌ
262.4   top,]   ~ʌ
262.8   eye]   ~,
262.9   book case]   bookcase
262.22   half-sat, half-leaned]   ~ ʌ ~, ~ ʌ ~
262.35   literal minded]   ~-~
263.6   business man]   businessman
263.10   blonde]   blond
263.32   men]   ~,
264.5   Park]   park
264.8   old]   ~,
264.13   it]   ~,
264.14   Naturally]   ~,
264.19   fun making]   ~-~
264.24   waddled—]   ~;
264.28   good looking]   ~-~
265.24   Father,]   ~ʌ
267.12   broad brimmed]   ~-~
267.12   men,]   ~ʌ
267.33   were. . . .]   ~ . . .
268.1   years]   ~,
268.3 *et passim*   United States]   U.S.

268.22   that]   who
269.5   that,]   ~∧
269.6   race,]   ~∧
269.7 *et passim*   Senator]   senator
269.24   trust]   entrust
269.24   in]   to
269.25   or]   nor
269.30   that]   ~,
270.3   them,]   ~∧
270.12   daughters]   ~,
270.33   recreate]   re-create
270.35   double dealing]   ~-~
271.2   Campus]   campus
271.9 *et passim*   Departmental]   departmental
271.11   at which I sat staring]   that I sat staring at
271.12   Finally]   ~,
271.19   open,]   ~∧
271.34 *et passim*   Company's]   company's
271.34–35   stock | holder]   stockholder
272.5   which]   that
272.11   us]   ~,
272.21   sour puss]   sourpuss
272.25 *et passim*   Station]   station
272.35 *et passim*   Number]   No.
273.14   that]   who
273.21   Momentarily]   ~,
273.34   train,]   ~∧
274.1   Finally]   ~,
274.15   fist-fulls]   fistfuls
274.16   said]   ~,
275.5   week end]   weekend
275.10   lobby]   ~,
275.18   concourse]   ~,
275.29   whisper]   ~,
276.10   snow storms]   snowstorms
276.14   sun room]   ~-~
276.17   funnypaper]   funny paper
276.24   grey]   gray
277.3   minutes. . . .]   minutes | . . .
277.12   wearily,]   ~∧
277.18   wire]   ~,
277.27   afternoon]   ~,
278.2   long distance]   ~-~
278.28   one's self]   oneself
279.4   man. . . .]   man . . .
279.6–7   Physi-|cally]   ~,
279.7   spot,]   ~∧

279.12–13   Ancient | World]   ancient world
279.20 *et passim*   Dean of Men]   dean of men
280.5   anti-feminist]   antifeminist
280.9–10   hus-|band's]   husbands'
280.12 *et passim*   Acting President]   acting president
280.21 *et passim*   Committee]   committee
280.28–29   intelligent | looking]   ~-~
280.35   that]   ~,
281.6   house. . . .]   ~ . . .
281.33   ramshackly]   ramshackle-
282.15   had]   ~,
282.16   were]   was
283.1   threw]   had thrown
283.4   aging,]   ~∧
283.5–6   candi-|date,]   ~;
283.8   quantity,]   ~;
283.9   them]   ~,
283.22–23   in-|volvement,]   ~∧
284.4   March]   --,
284.13   so]   So
284.16   baby,]   ~∧
284.19   baby,]   ~∧
284.34   mail box]   mailbox
284.36   April]   ~,
285.1   enquiry]   inquiry
285.4   house,]   ~∧
285.10   baby. . . .]   ~ . . .
286.22   claim]   ~,
286.28   Administration Building]   adminis-|tration
286.32   Assembly Room]   assembly room
286.35   next to last]   ~-~-~
287.5   Unconsciously]   ~,
287.32   question]   ~,
288.33   weeping,]   ~∧
289.23–24   front | porch]   ~-~
290.18–19   *normal leading*]   *extra leading*
290.27   office)]   ~),
291.3   sized, Middle-Western]   sized Midwestern
291.6   sheets]   proofs
291.8   Park]   park
291.11   jungle-gym]   ~ ∧ ~
291.18   pre-dawn hours. . . .]   predawn hours . . .
291.24   over]   ~,
291.27   round]   ~,
291.31–32   mail | box]   mailbox
292.18   University Library]   university library
293.7   Academic]   academic

293.7 years] ~,
293.14 acquaintance,] ~^
293.19 two heart] ~-~

C93 "Daphne's Lover." *Sewanee Review*, 77 (Spring 1969), 225–50.
Story. *MD*.

Sewanee Review] *MD*

225.3 together, one afternoon,] ~^ ~ ~ ~^
225.13 Frank—aged thirteen.] ~.
225.26 Mah-Jong] ~-Jongg
225.29 easy-chair] ~ ^ ~
225.29–30 *Collier's* or | the *Post*.] some magazine like *Collier's*.
226.4 *Stream, Baseball,* | *World Finance*, or] *Stream*, and
226.5 or] and
227.6 mother;] ~,
227.30 was] ~,
228.6 Baby".] ~."
228.28 *et passim* depression] Depression
228.29 land,] ~^
229.12 father] Father
230.1 hall] ~,
230.17 horse,] ~^
231.26–27 *normal leading*] *extra leading*
231.34 head-over-heels] ~ ^ ~ ~ ^ ~
232.3 some day] someday
232.4 whatsoever] ~,
232.14 contemporaries,] ~^
232.15 Lacy,] ~^
232.27 life",] ~,"
234.17 minutes,] ~^
234.33 pummelling] pummeling
234.13 into] in through
235.32 *et passim* quarrelled] quarreled
238.4 dance] ~,
238.5 lips,] ~^
238.14 *girl*. She] *girl*. | ¶ Janet
238.29 letter,] ~^
239.1 Sunday night] ~-~
241.12 pair".] ~."
241.24 responsible",] ~,"
242.5 way. . . . I] ~. . . .I
242.19 granted",] ~,"
245.4 study,] ~^

245.5   desk]   ~,
245.33   cartridge-belt]   ~ ʌ ~
247.4   anyhow,]   ~ʌ
247.5   good".]   ~."
247.6   theatre]   theater
248.12   Say,]   ~ʌ
249.6   tree-trunk]   ~ ʌ ~

C94 "Neglected Books" (column). *American Scholar*, 39 (Spring 1970), 345. Includes PT's choice, with brief commentary, of Caroline Gordon's *Aleck Maury, Sportsman.*

C95 "Two Images" ("I" of "Three Ghost Plays"). *Shenandoah*, 21 (Spring 1970), 3–13. Play. *Pr.*

Shenandoah]   *Pr*

3.1   floor length]   ~-~
3.2   mantel-piece]   mantelpiece
3.5   enormous,]   ~ʌ
3.8   fireset]   fire | set
3.14   *Nicky*]   ¶ ~
3.16   arm chair]   armchair
3.19 *et passim*   [*flush left*] Nɪᴄᴋʏ.]   [*centered*] NICKY
4.32   you? . . . . . .]   ~? . . .
9.18   pigeon toed]   ~-~
9.39   He]   he
10.36   shirt-tail]   shirttail
11.23   lovelife]   love-life
11.32   *Throws*]   throws
11.32   *ghost*]   GHOST
11.33   (*Ghost leaves.*)]   ʌGHOST *leaves.*ʌ

C96 "A Father and a Son" ("II" of "Three Ghost Plays"). *Shenandoah*, 21 (Spring 1970), 13–20. Play. *Pr.*

Shenandoah]   *Pr*

13.12   *A library converted*]   *The library, in*
13.12   *fire,*]   ~ʌ

13.14   *pale and*]   *pale*

13.14   *ailing*]   ~, *though still fiercely masculine*

13.15   *open or closed at different moments*]   *open, now closed*

13.17   ill fitting]   ~-~

13.19 *et passim*   [*flush left*] SHE]   [*centered*] ~

13.23   NATHAN]   NATHAN | (*irritated*)

13.23   presence that's]   *presence* that *is*

13.23–24   If your mother her-|self should come back, her presence could not be more comfort to me.]   *deleted*

13.26–28   (*with feeling*) I told you years ago not to talk so. I don't like | it. Not even now. If it had been Mother you wished for most, | she would no doubt be here.]   You're very sweet to say that.

13.29–32   NATHAN. Of course. That was only a manner of speaking. Of | course, it is you I wanted here. I don't deny it. All through the | years I've told myself that if I trusted you it was to me and to | this house you would come—when your *time* came.]   NATHAN (*stirring in his chair*) | Sweet, hell! Why, if [. . .] [13.23–24 *inserted*] | SHE | (*gently*) | What a way to speak to me, Father. (*soothing*) But it | doesn't matter, dearest. My only wish is to make you more | comfortable. I am here to answer your needs. I am here | because you want me here. If [. . .] [13.27–28 *inserted*] | NATHAN | Of course, of course. (*roughly, shaking his head*) That | was only a manner of speaking. Of course it is you I | wanted here. Damn it, I don't deny it! I don't deny it! | SHE | Don't upset yourself, Father honey. (*She pats his head.*) | *A pause* | NATHAN | All through the years I've told myself that if I trusted you it | was to me and to my house you would come—when your | *time* came.

13.33   all.]   ~?

13.34   possibilities.]   ~. (*all the | while ministering to him*)

14.1–2   sorry fellow and never even | bringing your child to see me.]   sorry, red-headed, low-born | bastard—abandoning me and—| SHE| (*calming down*) | Father, don't. (*shaking her head and smiling*) What a | silly you are. | NATHAN | And never even bring your child go see me.

14.3   SHE.]   She | (*ministering to him*)

14.5   To Jack?]   To your child? To the son of—| SHE | Now, now. (*laughing at him*) | NATHAN | To the son of such a union!

14.6   *Hesitating*]   *hesitating*

14.6   Jack]   my son, to ~

14.8   really.]   ~. High-strung, and *so* demanding of other people, and *awfully* lovable. My Jack's a fine | young man.

14.12–13   was, a man my | age seeing his grandson for the first time.]   was.

14.14–15   gold. I wish you could be here in more than | spirit. (*She lifts her face and laughs gently.*) I]   gold. | SHE | This house will be the cloth of gold for *that* meeting. At last | to see the two of you together under one roof. Under *this* | roof! What a satisfaction it will be for me. | NATHAN | I

14.17   be.]   ~, Father. (*Her voice trembles slightly. The | tone is somewhat nervous but affectionate still.*)

14.19–20   house, his "ancestral | home" which he has never seen before,]   house and

14.21–22 palsied old grand-|father. (*laughing*)] nearly dead old grandfather
(*laughing bitterly, hatefully*) Oh, God | damn! (*slapping chair arm*) God damn!
What a picture! | SHE | (*affectionately*) | Father, you *are* awful. Now, aren't you?
| NATHAN | Awful? If you think I'm so awful, why are you here? And | most
daughters in the world wouldn't do what you did. | SHE | Do you want me to
go now? | NATHAN | No! (*desperately*) No, of course I don't. Don't leave me
| yet. | SHE | (*gently still*) | Why, I'm not threatening to leave you, Father. Not
till | Jack comes. (*A pause*)

14.29 you since] you. From

14.29–30 the man I had | warned you against repeatedly, the man—] that
red-headed sybarite, that se-|ducer, that low-born—

14.31 SHE.] SHE | (*quetly, gently*)

14.32 that.] ~, by Christ.

14.34 mine] my name

14.35 yours] your name

14.38 NATHAN.] NATHAN | (*with assurance*) |

15.1 that. How could one ever be sure?] that [. . .] I'd like to think so. Or
would | I?

15.2 You think *Jack* loves you more? | *She is silent for several moments.*] You
think— | SHE | How could one ever be sure? (*all gentleness*) | NATHAN | You
think *Jack* loved you more? | SHE *is silent for several months and still as a statue.*

15.4 Jack] *Jack*

15.4 You] *You*

15.4 father.] ~. But— | NATHAN *opens his mouth to speak but remains* | *silent
for a moment. Then, looking directly at* | *her, he speaks.*

15.5–6 During the years since you have been returning to me | like this, you
] You have not been coming to see me so faithfully during the | last month
or so, yet

15.6 *never*] never

15.6 or] and

15.8 *stands*] *now* ~

15.14 NATHAN.] NATHAN | (*irritated*) |

15.16–17 Jack. | (*She*] Jack! (*then glancing back at* | NATHAN) And my
dearest Father! Ah, my two inno-|cents! | She

15.20 *shoulder.*)] ~.

15.33 me.] ~. | *A silence.*

16.1 intent] intention

16.1 sir.] ~. | *A silence:* | [*added material, 62 lines of dialogue, 36.12–40.18*]

16.4 *laughing*] ~—

16.11 NATHAN.] NATHAN | (*slowly*) |

16.11–13 eh?— | even though your mother and father of yours would | never
let us meet so long as your mother lived?] eh?

16.14 that. But] that. | NATHAN | Even though [. . .] [16.12–13 *inserted*]
| JACK | Yes, even so. But

16.18 either.] ~. Not in my house!

16.19 you] *you*

16.20 trooper.] ~. And have often done so in *your* time.

16.23 *is*] is

16.26 you here] *you here*

16.26 *loud*] *loudly*

16.27 (*quietly*)] Well, that's a better question than how I *got* here anyway | . . . (*quietly*)

16.27 Don't] But don't

16.28 her.] ~. (*with strong emotion*)

16.29 you] *you*

16.31 red haired devil, that father of yours?] that [. . .] yours, that—red-headed

16.32 red haired] red-head

16.32 JACK.] JACK | (*again* | *with great emotion*)

16.35 hides] suddenly buries

16.35 She is free now, free of him.] JACK *rises and stands gazing at* NA-THAN. | *A silence.* | NATHAN | Well, she is free now.

16.37 But] JACK | Free? | NATHAN | Free of *him*. | JACK | Perhaps now. But

16.38 For eternity.] For eternity, for eternity. Don't you see?

16.39 No . . . . Something] No . . . Not for so long . . . And not so free today as | yesterday. And not so free yesterday as the day before. | Each day her freedom— | NATHAN | Will you try to make yourself clearer? You're not making | any kind of sense. | JACK | I thought perhaps you understood matters better than | that. I though perhaps you understood how things stand. | NATHAN | (*assertively*) | She is free now, free of him. | JACK | Something

17.9 more.] ~. That's what she's like.

17.19 since] just~

17.23 since] just~

17.26 man?] ~!

17.32 Yes] ~,

17.37 *from his face*] *deleted*

17.38 Christ] Jesus

18.5 quarrelling] quarreling

18.14 you] *you*

18.33 But] Yes, but

18.38 downtown] out on | Skinker Boulevard

19.1 miles] ~ or | more

19.11 her . . . .] ~ . . .

19.27 dead] ~,

19.28 child . . . .] ~ . . .

19.29 we?] ~.

19.35–37 Don't torture me. You must go | now and let me rest. But come again, Jack—very soon. Neither | of us can live] Don't! You lacerate me! The pain's too damned much | to bear! You must go and [. . .] | Jack. You must come again very soon. | Neither of us can | live

20.6 red headed] ~-~

20.14 tired.] ~ from Jack.

20.16 dears] darlings

20.23   Darling, You're]   My love, you're
20.30   her!]   ~.

C97   "Missing Person" ("III" of "Three Ghost Plays"). *Shenandoah,* 21 (Spring 1970), 21–35. Play. *Pr.*

Shenandoah]   *Pr*

21.23   left-rear]   ~ ∧ ~,
21.25 *et passim*   [*flush left*] V.] [*centered*] V,
22.19   today]   *deleted*
22.35 *et passim*   business man]   businessman
23.2   Goodnight]   Good night
23.29   once . . . .]   ~ . . .
24.15   (*gesturing*) All this is extremely | attractive to me.]   *deleted*
26.1   *I*]   I
26.23   when [*sic*]]   When
26.24   possibilities, lots]   possibilities. Lots
27.18   *He*]   V
27.39   all night]   ~-~
29.6–7   off, sup-|posedly]   off. Supposedly
29.9   water front]   waterfront
29.19   *She*]   (~
29.21   *heard.*]   ~.)
29.32   eleven year old]   ~-~-~
30.15   young]   younger
30.17 *et passim*   scarey]   scary
30.30   *Lights*]   *lights*
31.20   *big*]   big
31.22   *Moving*]   *moving*
32.26   &]   and
32.39   Goodnight.]   "Good night."
33.24   there . . . .]   ~ . . .
33.35   you . . . .]   ~ . . .
34.21 $50,000]   fifty thousand dollars
35.6   suppose. . . .]   ~ . . .
35.11   slight— . . .]   ~ . . .
35.14   so—.]   ~—∧
35.34   Ours. . . .]   ~ . . .

C98   "The Whistler." *Virginia Quarterly Review,* 46 (Spring 1970), 248–63. Play *Pr.*

Reprinted in **B18**.

Virginia Quarterly Review] Pr

248.1   [*initial T*] THERE]   *There*
248.19 *et passim*   [*flush left*]] EMMA]   [*centered*] ~
248.23   fire.) . . . .]   ~.) . . .
248.24   warmth . . . .]   ~ . . .
249.1   ¶ *Several*]   no¶
249.1 *et passim (characters and stage directions)*   *Emma*]   EMMA
249.2–3   *Oh,* | *God*]   Oh, God
249.3   *If only I could pay*]   [*all in roman*]
250.35   things. . . .]   ~ . . .
251.1   . . . . He's]   . . . ~
252.10   up." . . . .]   ~." . . .
252.21   shoe laces]   shoelaces
253.16   are." . . . .]   ~." . . .
253.19   said . . . .]   ~ . . .
253.21   needlework . . . .]   ~ . . .
254.6   all . . . .]   ~ . . .
254.6   *He*]   He
255.19   awhile]   a while
255.21   in a little while]   soon
255.23   *is.*]   ~∧
256.1   turtle-neck]   turtleneck
256.12   But—.]   ~—∧
256.13   know—.]   ~—∧
256.24   is—.]   ~—∧
257.21–22   mix | up]   ~-~
257.25   in . . . .]   ~ . . .
258.1   *Begins*]   *begins*
259.12–13   close | cropped]   ~-~
259.15   grey]   gray
261.12–13   indeed! . . . . . | . . . . . .]   ~? . . .
262.9   court martial]   ~-~
262.11   half way]   half-|way
262.17   moment . . . .]   ~ . . .
262.19   Tommy . . . .]   ~ . . .
263.8   would . . . .]   ~ . . .

C99   "Arson" ("I" of "Three Plays"). *Sewanee Review*, 80 (Spring 1972), 215–32. Play. *Pr*.

Sewanee Review] Pr

215.2 *et passim*   *Rob*]   ROB
215.12   eyeing]   staring

215.13 *et passim*　Curious]　*curious*
215.5 *et passim*　(*Leo*]　∧LEO still
215.16　open door]　*door*
215.18 *et passim*　key-ring]　∼ ∧ ∼
215.26 *et passim*　[*flush left*] VOICE:]　[*centered*] ∼∧
216.1　scene,]　∼∧
216.4 *et passim*　Rob.)]　ROB.∧
216.8–9　ring—very | high]　∼ (*very high*)
216.15　*you*]　you
216.26　you]　*you*
217.26　hide-out]　hideout
217.26　Campus]　campus
218.26　*evening*]　*evening*
220.3　high-falutin']　highfalutin
223.10　burn. . . .]　∼ . . .
225.7　Oh]　oh
226.17　blackness. . . .]　∼ . . .
227.9　*head*. . . .]　∼ . . .
227.11　Leo. . . .]　∼ . . .
227.15　right. . . .]　∼ . . .
227.15　now. . . .]　∼ . . .
227.23　Goodnight]　Good night
227.24　me. . . .]　∼ . . .
227.30　neck;]　∼,
228.10　enough. . . .]　∼ . . .
230.3　course. . . .]　∼ . . .
231.10　son. . . .]　∼ . . .
231.11　1106]　eleven-o-six . . .
231.13　*draperies*,]　∼∧
231.14　*window sill*]　*windowsill*
231.31　myself.]　∼?

C100　"A Voice through the Door" ("II" of "Three Plays"). *Sewanee Review*, 80 (Spring 1972), 233–46. Play. *Pr*.

Sewanee Review]　*Pr*

233.1　¶ Maisie]　*no* ¶
233.4　*sitting-room*]　∼ ∧ ∼
233.6　*lamp-table*]　∼ ∧ ∼
233.28–29　Aunt | Maisie]　Maisie
234.4 *et passim*　(*More*]　(*more*
234.10 *et passim*　*spirits*]　SPIRITS
234.28–29 *et passim*　great-|nephew]　∼ ∧ ∼
238.21　always. . . .]　∼ . . .

241.7   "illness"?]   "~."
242.26 *straight-chair*]   ~ ∧ ~
242.27 wish]   wish—
243.18 money. . . .]   ~ . . .
244.12 yes. . . .]   ~ . . .
244.22 boy. . . .]   ~ . . .
245.13 *What,*]   ~∧
245.20 do—.]   ~—∧
245.28 toward. . . .]   ~ . . .

C101   "The Sweethearts" ("III" of "Three Plays"). *Sewanee Review*, 80 (Spring 1972), 247–60. Play. *Pr.*

Sewanee Review]   *Pr*

247.1   ¶*Granmom*]   *no* ¶
247.14 *et passim*   [*flush left*] LOUIS:]   [*centered*] ~∧
247.16 *et passim*   (*Indicating*]   (*indicating*
252.14 sorry. . . .]   ~ . . .
253.30 *Louis's*]   LOUIS'
254.13 JANET:] JANET | (*piously*)
255.21 *Gran*]   GRANMOM
258.10 Goodbye]   Good-bye
260.5–6   guests, the | other theater guests. They know what it's like.]   guests.
260.10 carry-on]   ~ ∧ ~
260.25 again. . . .]   ~ . . .

C102   "Literature, Sewanee, and the World." *Sewanee News*, Dec. 1972, 3–4. Excerpts from PT's Founder's Day address at the University of the South, Sewanee, Tenn.; see **A8**.

C103   "The Early Guest." *Shenandoah*, 24 (Winter 1973), 21–43. Play. Published separately as **A11**.

C104   "The Instruction of a Mistress." *New Review*, 1 (Sept. 1974), 15–20. Verse-story. *MD.*

New Review] MD

15.29   them]   ~—
15.41   so)   ~.)
15.45 *et passim (quotation marks)* 'Per] "~
15.45   *piú*]   *più*
16.1   Or better still]   ~, ~ ~,
16.47   masqerade]   masquerade
16.59   circle]   ~—
16.82–83   astonishment | As though till then she hadn't believed it.]   aston-
   ishment.
16.88   posterity]   ~.)
16.93   astonishment]   wonder
17.2   *Of*]   Of
17.6 *et passim (position of punctuation)* am',]   am,"
17.23   believe—.]   ~ . . .
17.40   hare-brained]   harebrained
17.77   me]   ~,
17.89   bcautiful]   ~,
17.102   anything.]   ~∧
18.3   self deceiving]   ~-~
18.4   self deflating]   ~-~
18.45   of all]   ~
18.100   memorised]   memorized
18.110   The]   the
18.115   destroyed)]   ~.)
19.6   loved]   ~,
19.54   then.]   ~∧
20.10   some day]   someday
20.21   I, myself,]   ~∧ ~∧
20.75   Refectory]   refectory
20.103   decent looking]   ~-~
20.114   well spoken]   ~-~

C105   The Hand of Emmagene." *Shenandoah,* 26 (Winter 1975), 25–43.
Verse-story. *MD.*

Reprinted in **B19**; *Understanding Fiction,* ed. Cleanth Brooks and Robert Penn
Warren, 3d ed. (Englewood Cliffs, N.J.: Prentice-Hall, 1979), pp. 270–85, with
a discussion on pp. 285–86; *Shenandoah,* 35, nos. 2–3 (1984), 368–86; *Home-
wards: A Book of Tennessee Writers,* ed. Douglas Paschall (Knoxville: Univ. of
Tennessee Press, 1986), pp. 34–51.

25.1   highschool,]   high school_∧

25.5   secretariel]   secretarial

25.6 *et passim*   highschool]   high school

25.12   nightspots]   night spots

25.15   beginning,]   ~∧

25.20   Hortonsburg,]   ~∧

25.27   can of course]   ~, ~ ~,

25.32   her]   ~,

26.6   We]   we

26.21   cooking,]   ~∧

26.22   arrived.]   ~∧

26.28   hours,]   ~∧

27.6   did]   *did*

28.16   kin of course]   ~, ~ ~,

28.18   hard bitten]   ~-~

28.19   Presyterians]   Presbyterians

28.21   best.")]   ~").

28.24   travelled]   traveled

29.14   in.]   ~∧

29.36   maids']   maid's

30.12   it of course]   ~, ~ ~,

30.36   in,]   ~.

31.18   of]   Of

31.33   Hospital]   hospital

32.31   boys.—]   ~....

32.33   necks,] ~∧

32.39   have]   Have

33.9   happens.]   ~?

33.33   offence]   offense

34.14   Emmagene.]   ~?

34.15   Well]   well

34.18   earnest]   ~,

35.4   no body]   nobody

36.12   Hortonsburg,]   ~∧

36.5   said]   ~.

36.18   dining room]   ~-~

36.36   living room]   ~-~

37.17   to,]   ~—

37.25   table]   ~,

37.30   her]   ~,

38.13   George"]   ~,"

38.28   staying]   ~,

38.31   you]   ~,

39.15   word,]   ~∧

39.24   night gown]   nightgown
39.27   make-up]   ~-~,
39.35   needle work]   needlework
40.29   white]   ~,
40.37   kitchen.]   ~^
41.3   behind]   ~,
41.32   other, to]   other | To
42.8   bannister]   banister
42.18   house.]   ~,
42.19   Hospital] hospital
42.20   She]   Though she
42.20   of course,]   *deleted*
42.21   But everybody]   It is probably true, | That if anything at all could have
saved her | It was his quiet thinking that would have done it. | Anyhow, every-
body
42.22   well—]   ~.
42.24   Station]   station
42.26   boy, really,]   ~^ ~^
42.28   Emmagene of course]   ~·, ~· ~·,

C106   "Three Heroines." *Virginia Quarterly Review*, 51 (Spring 1975),
269–81. Verse-story. *MD*.

Reprinted in the *New Review*, 2 (March 1976), 11–15; *The Treasury of American
Short Stories*, ed. Nancy Sullivan (Garden City, N.Y.: Doubleday, 1981), pp.
465–76.

Virginia Quarterly Review]   *MD*

269.1   [*initial D*] DRESSED]   ¶ Dressed
269.16 *et passim*   Lula Mae]   Willie Mae
270.4   black-tie]   ~ ^ ~
270.8 *et passim*   silvery white]   ~-~
270.10   well bred]   ~-~
270.16   Wide brimmed]   ~-~
270.20   old,]   ~^
270.21   old, burnt umber]   ~^ ~-~
270.31   yield]   ~,
271.17   pestilence)] ~),
271.19   sycamore]   ~,
271.20   endured]   ~,
271.27 *et passim*   Lula]   Willie
271.33   it.)]   ~).

272.14 Now,] ~∧
272.18 nigger)] ~).
272.28 mad woman] madwoman
272.31 . . . . And] . . . ~
273.20 mother] Mother
275.10 deepset] deep-set
275.14 us,] ~∧
275.35 knowledge] ~,
276.14 pain] ~,
276.15 life] ~,
276.18 . . . . . but] . . .~
276.23 And] and
276.29 manage] ~,
277.1 trouble] ~,
277.16 dying,] ~∧
277.19 speak)] ~),
277.19 Father,] ~∧
277.20 too)] ~),
277.21 both,] ~∧
277.23 . . . . But] . . .~
277.30 upcountry] up-country
277.33 capitol] Capitol
277.35 passed] ~,
279.8 year] ~,
279.9 doorway,] ~∧
279.10 shirtfront.] ~,
279.27 Great Grandmother] Great-grandmother
281.9 were,] ~∧

C107 "His Other Life." *Ploughshares*, 2, no. 4 (1975), 137–39. Poem.

C108 "Peach Trees Gone Wild in the Lane." *Ploughshares*, 2, no. 4 (1975), 140. Poem.

C109 "The Megalopolitans." *Ploughshares*, 2, no. 4 (1975), 141–50. Poem.

C110 "The Captain's Son." *New Yorker*, 51 (12 Jan. 1976), 30–38, 43–44, 47–50. Story. *MD*.

New Yorker] MD

30.73 *et passim* quarrelled] quarreled
31.87 [*initial I*] IT] ¶ It
32.6 land holdings] landholdings
32.15 week day] weekday
35.73 [*initial I*] I MUST] ¶ I must
36.34 [*initial A*] AS] ¶ As
37.15 [*initial W*] WHEN] ¶ When
38.59 him] ~,
43.5 [*initial B*] BY] ¶ By
43.59–60 sec-|ond,] ~^
43.192 [*initial M*] MY] ¶ My
43.200 dinner,] ~^
47.87 revery] reverie
48.7 [*initial W*] WE] ¶ We
48.18 noon,] ~^
50.20 bannister] banister
50.24 [*initial W*] WITHIN] ¶ Within

C111 "Her Need." *Shenandoah*, 27 (Summer 1976), 3–8. Verse-story.
MD.

Shenandoah] MD

3.1 gone,] ~^
3.2 wife,] ~^
3.6–7 license, | And] ~, and
3.10 town,] ~^
3.11 Which is where] Where
3.11–12 boy | Are living their life together.] boy live.
3.19 car,] ~^
3.26 *et passim* mid-town] midtown
4.19 manager,] ~^
4.30 she, herself,] ~^ ~^
5.13 needs] need
5.18 young,] ~.
6.10 Bank] bank
7.20 car,] ~^
7.30 month.] ~. | They'd never catch her.
8.16 grown up] ~-~
8.5 thoughtfully,] ~^

C112 "In the Miro District." *New Yorker*, 52 (7 Feb. 1977), 34–42, 47–48, 50–58, 63–66. Story. *MD*.

Reprinted in **B20**; *A Modern Southern Reader*, ed. Ben Forkner and Patrick Samway (Atlanta: Peachtree Publishers, 1986), pp. 170–99.

New Yorker]   *MD*

34.23–24 *et passim*   nine-|teen-twenties]   1920s
34.27–28   ei-|ther.]   ~. (Of what the one's past life had | been or of what the other's would be like in the future.)
34.49   Nashville. It]   ~. | ¶ ~
34.56–57   I had not | known before.]   nothing else had ever done.
34.70   that]   which
34.79   dishevelled]   disheveled
34.87   hidden]   ~—
34.98   The]   Neither | the
34.99   and]   nor
34.99   were]   was
34.105   [*initial T*] TO]   ¶ To
34.115   antediluvian]   quaint
34.128   boy]   ~—
34.131–32   Mon-|key Trial]   monkey-trial
34.133   about]   ~,
34.150   Grandfather,]   ~∧
34.158   Spanish]   ~,
34.165   not of course]   ~, ~ ~,
34.166   "boring."]   *boring*.
34.173   war]   War
34.183   French]   Frenchman's
34.185   [*initial M*] MY]   ¶ My
35.37 *et passim*   night riders]   nightriders
35.38   him]   ~ then
35.50   front—]   ~∧
35.56   I]   ~,
35.58   torture]   ~,
35.64   plans,]   ~∧
35.89   And]   ... ~
36.12   District,]   ~∧
36.16   grandfathers,]   ~∧
36.18   neighborhood,]   ~∧
36.35   clay,]   ~∧
36.46   [*initial T*] THIS]   ¶ This
36.49   think,]   ~—|or *has*—
36.49   results]   ~ in Nashville
36.51   in Nashville]   there

36.53–54   formal | in their speech for any modern man,]   stiff
36.62   profane and]   ~, ~ always
36.63   country-club]   Country Club
36.71–72   grandfathers—elegant grand-|fathers]   elegant grandfathers,
36.77   grandfathers]   old~
36.78–79   approached their last | years]   reached extreme old age | either
36.83   backs). Or]   ~)^ or
36.100   Basil]   *deleted*
37.43   tomatoes, strawberries, and corn]   truck farming
37.66   [*initial I*] IT]   ¶ It
37.68   wardrobe]   ~,
37.71   me]   ~,
37.73–74   when | I was eighteen,]   *deleted*
37.75   one.]   ~^ in the front hall.
38.24   surgery]   ~,
38.60   fact,]   ~^
39.7   that,]   ~^
39.17   midair]   mid-air
39.25   have]   done
39.57   oak,]   ~—
39.93 *et passim*   smelled]   smelt
40.11 *et passim*   dressing down]   ~-~
40.16   while,]   ~^
40.21   voice—]   ~,
40.44–45   all. | ¶ "Tell]   ~. "~
40.71   off]   ~ during the raid on Memphis,
40.96   son of a]   ~-~-~-~
40.98   not]   ~, of course,
40.99–100   wanted, of | course]   wanted.
40.115   War,]   ~^
40.132   swamp,] ~^
40.133   head,] ~^
40.174–75   there." | ¶ Suddenly]   ~." ~
41.24   [*initial A*] As]   ¶ I hear myself going on and on that Sunday night. As
41.45   war]   War
41.58   rough,]   ~^
41.73   thinking—or one process;]   thinking, [. . .]process,
41.74   rhythm,]   ~^
41.86   was]   is
41.96   would]   should
41.96   tears]   ~,
41.99   beds,]   ~^
42.10   years,]   ~^
42.25   thinking]   ~,
42.29   Tonight,]   ~^
42.78   predawn]   pre-dawn
42.88   Lake."]   ~. But all the while—"

42.109–10 ef-|fect]   ~,
47.4 blue]   green
47.7 singsong]   singsongy
47.9 him]   ~—
49.10 himself]   ~—
47.17 horses,]   ~ʌ
47.20–21 bed. | And]   ~. | ¶ ~
47.33 revelling]   reveling
47.58–60 re-|sponse. | ¶ I] ~. ~
47.63 it, or]   it,
47.80 last,]   ~ʌ
47.101 mama've]   mama's
47.105 [initial I] IT]   ¶ It
47.134 backwoodsmen]   ~,
47.175 knew, of course,]   ~ʌ ~ ~ʌ
47.183 sour mash]   sourmash
48.14 stopped]   ~—
48.15 way]   ~—
48.28 thereabouts]   thereabout
48.36 digress]   ~again
48.43 As]   Actually, as
48.47 lake]   Lake
48.51 attired]   decked out
48.62 very]   *deleted*
48.72 loft),]   ~)ʌ
48.74 see]   ~ in any direction
48.79–80 bot-|tomlands]   bottom lands
48.88 porch,]   ~ʌ
48.101 lodge,]   ~ʌ
48.108 folktales]   folk tales
48.126 lake]   Lake
50.4 Apocalypse]   apoca-|lypse
50.24 case,]   ~ʌ
50.27 hours,]   ~ʌ
50.34 Louis,]   ~ʌ
50.38 Everywhere,]   ~ʌ
50.44 that]   which
50.45 up]   *deleted*
50.45 places,]   ~ʌ
50.69 recurred,]   ~ʌ
50.106 reunions]   Reunions
50.133 humility. And]   ~. | ¶ ~
51.12 Memphis]   ~,
51.13 night]   ~,
51.40 *et passim* Ward-Belmont]   ~ ʌ ~
51.44 warmly.]   ~ | and want to throw caution to the wind.
51.50 girls, of course,]   ~ʌ ~ ~ʌ

51.65   I]   As I have indicated, ∼

52.53   myself.]   ∼. At last we | might begin to understand one another and make known our | real feelings, each about the other.

52.58   me.] ∼. Already I | had begun to understand that his striking me didn't have quite | the kind of significance I had imagined.

52.64   shoulder,]   ∼∧

52.65   room,]   ∼∧

52.103   desperately:]   ∼,

52.104   And]   ∼,

52.105   And]   ∼,

52.133   out]   ∼,

53.11   cleanup]   clean-up

53.17   moment.]   ∼. I knew | that one day there was something he would have to know | about me that he couldn't forgive.

53.54   must yet be]   was yet

53.56   were, and saw]   were and that

53.60   like.]   ∼. Or [. . .] own.

53.61   [*initial I*] IN]   ¶ In

54.16   garçonnière]   garconnière

54.28–29   end | chimneys]   ∼-∼

54.40   plateau]   Plateau

54.59   girl]   ∼ with

54.59—dating]   having dates

55.50   house]   home

55.53   ended]   ∼,

55.56   Candyland]   Candy Land

55.58   ended]   ∼, | that is,

56.45   was:]   ∼,

56.69   arrived.]   ∼|—dispelled for both of us, and not just for that time but proba-|bly for all future time. (As for myself, I known that I never | again in all the years since have had any taste for taking my | pleasure with such fe-males as those Eighth Avenue-Reservoir | girls—in the casual, impersonal way that one does with such | females of any class or age.)

58.19   that I would]   which I could

58.51   toward]   about

63.6   are!]   ∼?

63.17   driveway,]   ∼∧

63.22   [*initial I*] I THOUGHT]   ¶ I thought

63.29–31   Because, according | to the account which my parents gave | me later,]   Because

63.94–97   His disenchantment and his eventual | corruption had been neces-sary to their | purposes, and I had been their means | of achieving that end.] *deleted*

63.115   know,]   ∼∧

63.119   fall,]   ∼∧

63.126   there,]   ∼ or find that he had been there,

63.135–64.1   "Annals | of Tennessee,"]   *Annals of Tennessee*

63.25   friends,]   ∼∧
64.58–59   his. | ¶ I]   ∼. ∼
64.59–60   hap-|pened,]   ∼∧
64.63   arrived]   ∼,
64.67   bed]   piece
65.1   pieces]   ∼ that arrived
65.10   brought his wife to live]   moved in
65.26   fourposter]   four-poster
65.64–65   Vicksburg and Stone's River | and Franklin and]   Vicksburg, of Stone River, Franklin,
66.28   university]   Univer-|sity of course

C113   "Robert Traill Spence Lowell." *Proceedings of the American Academy and Institute of Arts and Letters*, 2d ser., no. 28 (1978), 71–79. Commemorative tribute read by PT at the 18 May 1977 ceremonial of the American Academy and Institute of Arts and Letters.

Reprinted in *Ploughshares*, 5, no. 2 (1979), 74–81.

C114   "The Old Forest." *New Yorker*, 55 (14 May 1979), 34–48, 51, 54, 57–58, 60, 63–64, 66, 69–70, 72, 75–77, 82. Story. *OF*.

Reprinted in **B21**.

New Yorker]   *OF*

34.1   already]   ALREADY
34.24 *et passim*   débutante]   debutante
34.52 *et passim*   M.C.C.]   MCC
35.47   [*initial T*] THE]   The
35.59   Odes]   *Odes*
36.2   days,]   ∼∧
37.6–7   mind. | ¶ Thirty]   ∼. ∼
37.38   Park]   park
37.60   must]   ∼,
37.61   want]   ∼,
37.109   Pond]   pond
39.51   it]   ∼,
40.65 *et passim*   dialled]   dialed
40.126   [*initial B*] BROKEN]   Broken
42.145   half converted]   ∼-∼
42.155–56   the old order; the bad they | adopted from life]   from life

44.14   [*initial T*] THE]   The
44.15   5th]   5
44.16   cold. The]   ~, the
45.56   [*initial O*] ON]   On
47.108   nineteen-thirties]   1930's
48.124–25   grav-|elled]   graveled
48.136   teen-age]   teenage
51.113   [*initial L*] LEE ANN DEEHART]   LeeAnn Deehart
51.118   they]   *they*
54.46   double-dating]   ~ ^ ~
57.56   [*initial O*] ON]   On
57.60   and,]   ~^
58.45–46   there. | ¶ A]   ~. ~
58.108   grownup]   grown-up
58.110   week,]   ~^
60.7   is,]   ~^
70.10   in]   *deleted*
72.55   [*initial T*] THE]   The

C115   "A Commemorative Tribute to Jean Stafford." *Shenandoah*, 30, no. 3 (1979), 56–60. Text of a tribute given by PT, on 13 November 1979, at the National Academy and Institute of Arts and Letters, New York City.

Reprinted in the *Proceedings of the American Academy and Institute of Arts and Letters*, 2d ser., no. 30 (1980), 79–85; *Shenandoah*, 35, nos. 2–3 (1984), 355–59.

C116   "Acceptance by Peter Taylor." *Proceedings of the American Academy and Institute of Arts and Letters*, 2d ser., no. 29 (1979), 31–32. Text of PT's acceptance of the Gold Medal for the Short Story, 17 May 1978.

C117   "Five Miles from Home." *Ploughshares*, 5, no.2 (1979), 82–84. Poem.

Note: "Robert Trail [sic] Spence Lowell." (**C113**) is reprinted in this number on pp. 74–81.

C118   "The Gift of the Prodigal." *New Yorker*, 57 (1 June 1981), 42–52. Story. *OF*.

Reprinted in **B22**; *Prize Stories 1982: The O. Henry Awards*, ed. William Abrahams (Garden City: Doubleday, 1982), pp. 166–85.

New Yorker]   *OF*

42.1   [*initial T*] THERE'S Ricky]   THERE'S RICKY
42.8   *he*]   he
42.63   house]   ~,
42.97 *et passim*   suède]   suede
43.100   grown]   ~,
43.125   Because the]   The
44.14   [*initial W*] WELL]   Well
44.56   is,]   ~∧
47.98   [*initial T*] THERE]   There
47.111   bet on anything at home.]   *deleted*
47.112   He]   he
49.88   [*initial W*] WHEN]   When
50.81   ago,]   ~∧
52.84   years,]   ~∧
52.89   cancelled]   canceled
52.101–2   her fascination or per-|haps not explain]   *deleted*
52.108–9   about | his life,]   *deleted*

C119   "A Summons to Memphis." *Memphis*, 11 (Sept. 1986), 60–74.
Excerpt (Chapter Five) from *SM*; published simultaneously with *SM*.

D

Interviews and Published Comments

D1 Jenice Jordan, "He 'Writes for Fun,' But His Stories Sell Well." *Columbus* (Ohio) *Dispatch*, 6 Dec. 1959, "Books" sec., p. 19. Review of *HF* that includes quoted comments from a phone conversation with PT. Topics include teaching at Ohio State; writing for "fun"; and work in progress.

D2 Shelby Coffey III, "Sophisticated Fugitive." *Washington Post* (*Potomac* magazine), 24 Nov. 1968, pp. 23, 28–30. Article based on an interview that includes PT's quoted comments on the short story ("not dead"); writing for the *New Yorker*; contemporary American society; his generation of Americans; teaching at the University of Virginia; writing habits; and his desire for his "writing to have a career."

D3 "Short Stories: Their Past, Present, and Future." *Publisher's Weekly*, 198 (14 Dec. 1970), 12–15. Article based on a symposium on the "health of the short story form." PT's comments are found on pp. 13, 14.

D4 Stephen Goodwin, "An Interview with Peter Taylor." *Shenandoah*, 24 (Winter 1973), 3–20. Topics include PT's student years at Kenyon College; his early interest in writing poetry; fiction as his true medium; growing up in Tennessee; Flannery O'Connor and Eudora Welty; literary influences on his work; his writing habits; sources of his stories; contrived symbolism in his story "Reservations"; Randall Jarrell; race in the South; sex in literature; writing for the *New Yorker*; his favorite stories; *WM*; his interest in drama and verse plays; teaching; future writing plans; and his personal ambitions as a writer.

D5 "News from the University of the South." *Episcopal Churchman*, April 1975, p. 4. Article that includes PT's brief comment on the University of the South, at Sewanee, Tenn.

D6 Thomas Molyneux, "Peter." *Shenandoah*, 28 (Winter 1977), 59–61. Article based on a visit with PT and Jean Stafford; includes PT's quoted comments throughout.

D7 Louise Davis, "Just Who Was That Ward-Belmont Girl Nude in the Closet?" *Tennessean* (Nashville, Tenn.), 20 Feb. 1977, pp. 1, 4(E). Article based on an interview. Topics include Tennessee as a setting for many of PT's stories; his family; writing techniques; Memphis and Nashville; and his grandfather Manley, a Civil War veteran.

D8 Susan Wood and Robert Wilson, "Charlottesville Five—Writers on the Ridge of Fame." *Washington Post*, 7 May 1978, pp. 1, 4, 5, 8(H). Article based on interviews with five Charlottesville writers. PT's quoted comments on his life and work are on pp. 5, 8(H).

D9 Ruth Dean, "Peter Taylor: A Private World of Southern Writing." *Washington Star*, 2 Oct. 1977, pp. 1, 4(B). Article based on an interview. Topics include growing up in Tennessee; PT's literary friends, especially Robert Lowell; his children; teaching; how writers have to "protect" themselves from intrusions; writing as his life; and his interest in writing a second novel.

D10 Malcolm Jones, "Mr. Peter Taylor When Last Seen . . ." *Greensboro* (N.C.) *Daily News/Record*, 27 July 1980, p. 5(C). Article based on an interview. Topics include the family in the South; living in Charlottesville, Va.; techniques of the short story; Allen Tate, Robert Lowell, and Randall Jarrell as friends and mentors.

D11 William W. Starr, "Peter Taylor Confident with His Literary Image." *State* (Columbia, S.C.), 12 April 1981, p. 11 (B). Article based on an interview. Includes PT's comments on Robert Lowell; storytelling; Andrew Lytle and Robert Penn Warren; teaching; Randall Jarrell's encouragement of his writing; and his early interest in writing poetry.

D12 Robert Taylor, "Peter Taylor Remembers Robert Lowell." *Washington Post Book World*, 14 Nov. 1982, pp. 1, 8. Article based on an interview that includes PT's reminiscences of his friend Robert Lowell.

D13 Robert Daniel, "The Inspired Voice of Mythical Tennessee." *Kenyon College Alumni Bulletin*, 7 (Winter 1983), 19–20. Article based on an interview. Topics include PT's writing habits; his fictional topics; Tolstoy and Chekhov; verse writing; and writing in progress.

D14 Jane Kisber, "Peter Taylor Draws on His Southern Roots." *Jackson* (Tenn.) *Times*, 29 Sept. 1983, p. 1(D). Article based on an interview. Topics include Steve Ross's film version of "The Old Forest"; the importance of "family" in the South; teaching; literary friends; his admiration for Henry James, Tolstoy, Chekhov, and Proust; writing habits; his plays and poems; and the pleasure derived from the act of writing.

D15 Robert Brickhouse, "Peter Taylor: Writing, Teaching, Making Discoveries." *University of Virginia Alumni News*, 72 (Nov.–Dec. 1983),

14–16. Article based on an interview. Topics include teaching; writing habits; PT's family and growing up in the South; and storytelling.

D16 Tom Jenks, "In the Works." *Esquire*, 102 (Aug. 1984), 113–16. PT's comment on his novel *SM*, a work in progress, is found on p. 116.

D17 Don Keck Dupree, "An Interview with Peter Taylor." *Touchstone* (Nashville, Tenn.), 1 (Autumn 1984), 8, 12. Topics include Steve Ross's film version of "The Old Forest"; themes of PT's stories; and his interest in writing plays and poetry.

D18 Wendy Smith, "PW Interviews: Peter Taylor." *Publisher's Weekly*, 227 (18 Jan. 1985), 77–78. Article based on an interview. Topics include writing habits; literary friends and influences; Ian Hamilton's biography of Robert Lowell; the short story; writing fiction as a "cognitive instrument"; PT's preference for reading stories instead of novels; teaching; and creating a new audience for one's work rather than answering the demands of an audience.

D19 Caryn James, "Symbols and Themes Mature into Plots." *New York Times Book Review*, 17 Feb. 1985, p. 26. Brief article accompanying Robert Towers's review of *OF*; includes PT's comments on his early career and teachers and his future writing plans.

D20 Malcolm Jones, "Peter Taylor's Work Endures." *St. Petersburg* (Fla.) *Times*, 17 Feb. 1985, p. 7(D). Article based on an interview. Topics include the art of the short story; PT's interest in writing novels ("easier in some ways"); and work in progress.

D21 Dan Shiflett, "Rise of Southern Literature." *Washington Times*, 25 Feb. 1985, pp. 1, 2(B). Article based on an interview. Topics include Taylor's beginnings as a writer and the subjects he has chosen to write about.

D22 Michael Kernan, "Peter Taylor & the Layers of Life." *Washington Post*, 4 March 1985, pp. 1, 6(B). Article based on an interview. Topics include his Tennessee forebears; his mother as storyteller; how his stories "draw from life"; writing as a means to discovery; interest in poetry as a means of compression; "The Old Forest"; universal elements in his stories; influences on his work such as Chekhov, Joyce, and Frank O'Connor; "Porte-Cochere"; writing habits; growing up in Memphis; and writing as his life.

D23 Bill Broadway, "Meet America's Best-Known Unknown Short-Story Writer." *Atlanta Journal/Constitution*, 17 March 1985, pp. 1, 6(J). Article based on an interview. Topics include PT's disappointment at not being better known as a writer; his literary friends and influences; refurbishing old houses; and the South.

D24 Bill Broadway, "Peter Taylor's Tips for Aspiring Writers." *Atlanta Journal/Constitution*, 17 March 1985, p. 6(J). Brief article that includes PT's advice on reading works about one's own cultural environment; being oneself and not trying to imitate other writers; how young writers should first submit their stories to "little magazines" and "read Henry James."

D25 J. William Broadway, "A Conversation with Peter Taylor." *Chattahoochee Review* (DeKalb Community College, Dunwoody, Ga.), 6 (Fall 1985), 17–44, 61–75. Topics include *OF* and the film version of *OF*; the "writing Rosses" of North Carolina; PT's daughter and son as writers; getting published; his relationship with the *New Yorker*; agents and critics; characters in his fiction; *SM* (in progress); writing habits; "A Spinster's Tale," "The Fancy Woman," and other stories; influences on his writing; the South as the main setting for his work; contemporary authors he admires; "Bad Dreams"; Tennessee (especially Nashville and Memphis); politics; religion; the disintegration of the family in contemporary America; his student years at Kenyon; World War II; his plays; Henry James; his interest in the supernatural; publishing in the South; teaching; living in Gainesville, Fla., and Charlottesville; his interest in restoring old houses; travel; his teaching methods; his friendship with and the death of Randall Jarrell; Ian Hamilton's biography of Robert Lowell; Jean Stafford; John Crowe Ransom and other teachers as friends.

D26 Michael Cornwell and E. Thomas Wood. "Taking New Paths by Twilight: An Interview with Peter Taylor." *Vanderbilt Review*, 2 (Spring 1986), 107–12. Topics include his student years; John Crowe Ransom, Flannery O'Connor, and Allen Tate; Vanderbilt and the Agrarians; Robert Penn Warren; *SM*; interrelation of his characters; Tolstoy as an influence; lack of recognition of his work; role of the writer in the university; difficulties in getting published; and the future of the short story.

D27 Edwin McDowell, "At 69, Master Storyteller Wins New Recognition." *New York Times*, 7 May 1986, p. 19(C). Article based on an interview that includes PT's comments on his poet-wife; his books coming back in print; Southern background of his stories; Faulkner; difficulties in getting published; D. H. Lawrence's stories; and his close literary friendship with Tate, Lowell, and Jarrell.

D28 Edwin McDowell, "Southern Author Praised for Stories." *Lexington* (Ky.) *Herald-Ledger*, 8 May 1986, p. 5(D). Article based on an interview that includes PT's comments on the lack of an audience for short-story writers and *SM* (in progress).

D29 Robert Becker, "Peter Taylor: 'Radical' Writer of the South." *Daily Progress* (Charlottesville, Va.), 15 May 1986, pp. 1, 2(D). Article based on an interview that includes PT's quoted comments on the Tennessee background of his work; his family; Randall Jarrell and Robert Lowell; his theory that "a short story ought to do as much as a novel"; women and black characters in his stories; how he writes "to form tastes rather than to follow them"; and *SM* (in progress).

D30 Caryn James, "Some Southern Rascals." *New York Times Book Review*, 19 Oct. 1986, p. 53. Brief article based on an interview that includes PT's humorous account of meeting Gertrude Stein.

D31 Robert Becker, "UVa Professor Denounces Book Award." *Daily Progress* (Charlottesville, Va.), 18 Nov. 1986, p. 1 (B). Article based on an interview that includes PT's quoted comments on receiving the 1986 American Book Award for Fiction.

D32 Charles Trueheart, "Doctorow, Lopez Win Book Awards." *Washington Post*, 18 Nov. 1986, pp. 1, 2(D). Article about the 1986 American Book Awards that includes PT's paraphrased comments on p. 2(D).

D33 John F. Baker, "American Book Awards: Back to Their Roots." *Publisher's Weekly*, 230 (28 Nov. 1986), 15. Article that includes PT's quoted comments on receiving the 1986 American Book Award for Fiction.

D34 "People" (sec.), *Time*, 129 (20 April 1987), 80. Brief article that includes PT's quoted comments on receiving the 1987 Ritz-Hemingway Prize.

D35 Joan S. Rodgers, "The Family Was the Wellspring for His Pulitzer-Prize Novel." *Winston-Salem* (N.C.) *Journal*, 26 April 1987, pp.1, 2(C). Article based on an interview that includes PT's quoted comments on his mother as a "wonderful storyteller"; southerners as "natural storytellers"; *SM*; Jarrell, Lowell, Ransom, Tate, and other literary friends; the Ritz-Hemingway Prize; and his belief that one "writes stories because you must," because there is "a need to say something about things you've heard."

D36 George M. Myers, Jr., "Taylor, Ex-OSU Prof, Basks in Pulitzer." *Columbus* (Ohio) *Dispatch*, 26 April 1987, p. 9(F). Article based on an interview that includes PT's quoted comments on receiving the Pulitzer Prize; ideas for work in progress, including a novel; growing up in the South; his literary friendships; and Chekhov as his "great model."

D37 Donald La Badie, "Delayed Accolades Are All the Sweeter." *Commercial Appeal* (Memphis, Tenn.), 10 May 1987, p. 7(J). Article based on an interview that includes PT's quoted comments on receiving the Pulitzer Prize and the Ritz-Hemingway Award; recovering from a stroke; his novel-in-progress, tentatively titled *To the Lost State*; and the forthcoming film of *WM*.

D38 William Ruehlmann, "Discovering Peter Taylor." *Virginian Pilot* (Norfolk), 2 Aug. 1987, pp. 1–3(J). Article based on an interview that includes PT's comments on receiving the Pulitzer Prize and the Ritz-Hemingway Award; his literary friends; Hemingway and Faulkner; *SM*; his family and growing up in Tennessee; the family unit as a source for much of his work; his student years at Kenyon College; and his writing habits.

E

Blurbs

E1 Robie Macauley, *The End of Pity* (New York: McDowell, Obolensky, 1957).

"For anyone who enjoys the short story, especially anyone who has a preference for that form, the discovery of this collection will be an enormous event. Robie Macauley is certainly one of the most distinguished writers of fiction to appear in America or England in the past ten years."—Peter Taylor

E2 Christina Stead, *The Man Who Loved Children*, introduction by Randall Jarrell (New York: Holt, Rinehart and Winston, 1965).

"The remarkable fact is that though THE MAN WHO LOVED CHILDREN was not written by an American, it *must* be listed among the best American novels of this century. I always think of it as one of my favorite books—one of the few novels ever written that seems a completely satisfying work of art."—PETER TAYLOR

E3 Andrew Lytle, *Stories: Alchemy and Others* (Sewanee, Tenn.: University of the South, 1984).

"His novels and stories and essays have delighted and instructed us all."—Peter Taylor

F

Sound Recordings

TAPES

F1   Randall Jarrell Memorial Service, in the Yale Law School, 28 February 1966. Washington, D.C.: Library of Congress, 1966. T 4961b.

Contains: "Reminiscences" by PT and his reading from Jarrell's *Pictures from an Institution.*

F2   Peter Taylor and John Updike Reading and Discussing Their Fiction, Coolidge Auditorium, 13 November 1967. Washington, D.C.: Library of Congress, 1967. T 5156.

Contains: PT's reading of an early version of "The Elect."

F3   "Peter Taylor Reads 'Three Heroines' and 'Instruction of a Mistress.'" Columbia, Mo.: American Audio Prose Library (for New Letters on the Air), 1984. Issued as NL 17/64110; two cassette tapes.

DISCS

F4   "Peter Taylor Reading His Story 'Two Pilgrims.'" Boston: Fassett Recording Studio, 1971. Privately issued. Recorded 20 April 1971.

F5   "Peter Taylor Reading His Play 'Two Images.'" Boston: Fassett Recording Studios, 1971. Privately issued. Recorded 20 April 1971.

G

Translations

GERMAN

G1 *Amerikanische Erzähler von F. Scott Fitzgerald bis William Goyen*, trans. and ed. by Elisabeth Schnack (Zürich: Manesse Verlag, 1957).

Contains: "Der Feldmeister," a German translation of "The Scoutmaster," on pp. 376–428.

G2 *Der Baum mit den bitteren Feigen: Erzählungen aus dem Süden der USA*, trans. and ed. by Elisabeth Schnack (Zürich: Diogenes, 1959).

Contains: "Eine Frau aus Nashville," a German translation of "A Wife from Nashville," on pp. 235–70.

SWEDISH

G3 *Den Gamla Skogen: Och Andra Berättelser*, trans. Caj Lundgren (Stockholm: Legenda, 1986).

Contains: an abbreviated version of *OF*, including: "Den förlorande sonens gavå" ("The Gift of the Prodigal," pp. 7–28; "Den gamla skogen" ("The Old Forest"), pp. 29–91; "Löfte om regn" ("Promise of Rain"), pp. 92–120; "Mardrömmar" ("Bad Dreams"), pp. 121–48; "En vän och beskyddare" ("A Friend and Protector"), pp. 149–77; "Tro och lydnad" ("Allegiance"), pp. 178–91; "De små kusinerna" ("The Little Cousins"), pp. 192–210; "En lång fjärde juli" ("A Long Fourth"), pp. 211–52; "Regn i hjärtet" ("Rain in the Heart"), pp. 253–73; "Inkörsport" ("Porte-Cochere"), pp. 274–84; "Scoutledaren" ("The Scoutmaster"), pp. 285–316.

Note: This is the only translation given over entirely to the work of Peter Taylor.

H

Drawing

H1 *Self-Portrait: Book People Picture Themselves*, comp. and ed. by Burt Britton (New York: Random House, 1976).

Contains: self-portrait by PT on p. 15.

Index